T0339233

more than pretty boxes

more than pretty boxes

HOW THE RISE OF PROFESSIONAL ORGANIZING SHOWS US THE WAY WE WORK ISN'T WORKING

carrie m. lane

The University of Chicago Press

Chicago and London

The University of Chicago Press, Chicago 60637
The University of Chicago Press, Ltd., London
© 2024 by Carrie M. Lane
Illustrations © 2023 by Charlotte Corden
Published 2024
Printed in the United States of America

33 32 31 30 29 28 27 26 25 24   1 2 3 4 5 6 7 8 9 10

ISBN-13: 978-0-226-83277-7 (cloth)
ISBN-13: 978-0-226-83659-1 (e-book)
DOI: https://doi.org/10.7208/chicago/9780226836591.001.0001

Library of Congress Cataloging-in-Publication Data

Names: Lane, Carrie M., 1974– author.
Title: More than pretty boxes : how the rise of professional organizing
    shows us the way we work isn't working / Carrie M. Lane.
Other titles: How the rise of professional organizing shows us the way
    we work isn't working
Description: Chicago ; London : The University of Chicago Press, 2024. |
    Includes bibliographical references and index.
Identifiers: LCCN 2024016815 | ISBN 9780226832777 (cloth) |
    ISBN 9780226836591 (ebook)
Subjects: LCSH: Organizers (Persons)—United States—Social conditions. |
    Self-employed—United States—Social conditions. | Women professional
    employees—United States—Social conditions. | Orderliness. | Storage in
    the home. | Work.
Classification: LCC HD9999.O742 L36 2024 | DDC 658.3/12—dc23/eng/20240609
LC record available at https://lccn.loc.gov/2024016815

♾ This paper meets the requirements of ANSI/NISO Z39.48-1992
(Permanence of Paper).

for Fran Benson

Contents

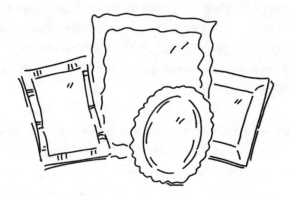

As soon as Lauren opened the door to her condo, it was clear this was going to be a fun job. A Black professional in her mid-forties, Lauren had recently left her corporate career after a health crisis and was planning to start an online business.[1] She'd hired Sara, the white fortysomething professional organizer I was assisting that day, to help clean out and organize the extra bedroom in her North Hollywood condo for use as a home office. The two had already met for an initial consultation. Sara, who'd been running a successful organizing business for more than a decade, toured the condo and they discussed what the job would entail. Although we'd never met before, Lauren greeted me with an enthusiastic hug, laughing and joking as she led us into her home.

Lauren's condo was bright and cheerfully decorated. Her furnishings were stylish and inviting—a cozy couch and upholstered armchair for TV watching, colorful throw pillows, and a corner nook with a round kitchen table and matching chairs. Lauren, who studied art history at UCLA, had hung the walls with a bold array of prints and photographs that suited her vivacious personality. Artfully arranged piles of books flanked the couch and coffee table. Crisp white curtains framed a balcony with a clear view of the mountains.

Still, it was a little tricky to get around in Lauren's condo. As we entered, we stepped gingerly around the piles of bags that filled the entryway, spilled under the legs of her table and chairs, and edged into the small kitchen nook. There were shopping bags full of new items with tags still attached; canvas tote bags packed with hangers, books, and other items; shopping bags with other shopping bags neatly folded inside them. Interspersed with these were garbage bags, stuffed full and tied at the top, waiting to be delivered to the dumpsters in the building's underground garage. The small kitchen was made even tinier by the stacks of dishes, some clean, some not, that filled the sink and spilled across the counters and bar.

Lauren invited us back to the bedroom where she wanted to begin working that day. Like many organizers, Sara likes to start "where it hurts," beginning in the space that is causing the client the most distress. For Lauren, this was her home office. As we passed by the kitchen, I was reminded why I would make a terrible organizer. As someone who can't bring herself to leave a single dish in the sink overnight, just seeing those dishes piled up made me anxious to grab some dish soap and get to work. But as Sara and many other organizers had explained to me, the organizer's job is to understand the client's priorities, even if they might be different from her own. If the dishes didn't bother Lauren, they weren't our business.

We headed down a hallway, the floor lined with picture frames, mostly empty frames with price tags still attached. They lined the left side of the hallway, stacked two to three deep and interspersed with shopping bags holding even more frames, shrinking the corridor's width by nearly a third.

The office, or the windowless room Lauren intended to use as her office, held mostly boxes—cardboard boxes, filing boxes, plastic shoe boxes, photo boxes, rolling crates with multiple drawers, boxes with smaller boxes nestled inside. We could only take a few steps into the room before the wall of boxes stopped our progress. Only later would I realize the room was not, in fact, windowless; it was just that the window on the opposite wall was completely blocked behind a tower of boxes.

Our first step, Sara explained, for Lauren's benefit and for mine (this wasn't my first assisting gig, but it was my first with Sara), would be to group like with like, bringing together items of similar type or function. Once an entire category had been assembled, Lauren would be able to see how much she had of that particular type of item, determine what to keep, and find a "home" for the kept items, somewhere they would all fit and be easy to locate as needed.

Sara started gathering office supplies. Lauren began with paperwork. My job was to take things that did not belong in the office—multi-packs of toilet paper, plastic milk crates full of unopened shampoos and body washes, case after case of Dove soap—and carry them to a more appropriate space (in this case the bathroom) where we would sort them later.

Once Lauren had assembled all of the paperwork in the room, she and Sara discussed how to start organizing it. Lauren's existing filing system—boxed hanging files arranged in clearly marked categories and subcategories—looked great, Sara said. It was just that the influx of paperwork related to her illness, job change, and new business had overwhelmed Lauren's ability to keep it all in check. Sara and I began organizing paper into general categories—personal, medical, old job, new business, taxes, etc.—and Lauren started sorting through each pile, deciding what papers could go (to be shredded and/or recycled) and which she planned to keep.

Paper is usually a slow-going part of the organizing process ("I hate paper," more than one organizer confided to me), but Sara told Lauren she was "amazing at paper!" Sara explained the rules for how long you need to keep certain documents (whether in paper or digital form): utility bills—one month; pay stubs and credit card statements—one year; medical bills and records—at least one year, longer in case of a chronic condition; tax preparation documents—three to seven years; tax returns—permanently; and so on. Documents older than these designated timeframes were to be placed in a pile to be shredded and recycled. Every piece of paper that didn't fit these clear-cut categories—and there were many, from old recipes torn from magazines to holiday cards from coworkers three jobs back—were passed to Lauren, who winnowed them down, pile after pile, bag after bag. When she came across an especially beloved item, she often exclaimed out loud, telling us what she'd unearthed before moving it to the keep pile. When she found a stack of birthday cards she'd received over the years, she hugged them to her chest, saying, "This is love, y'all!"

Within a few hours we had three garbage bags full of paper to be shredded, which Lauren would take to a local paper-shredding business over the weekend.

Since Lauren's existing filing system had been working well for her until recently, once she'd eliminated the surplus documents, everything fit neatly into two boxes. Giddy at our progress, we each donned one of the temporary butterfly tattoos Lauren had come across in the sorting process and danced a happy jig in the newly cleared-out space.

Now that we'd decided on homes for most categories (sheets in the linen closet, back-up toiletries under the bathroom sink, sentimental cards in a single decorative box on a shelf above her desk), Sara suggested we tackle the picture frames scattered throughout the entryway, living room, hallway, and office.

While the two of them gathered together all the frames already in the office, Sara sent me to bring in the frames from the rest of the condo. I started with the ones lining the hallway, careful to carry only a few at a time so as not to risk breaking the glass or scratching the frames. After a half dozen loads, I started on the bags near the door, removing frames from shopping bags and bringing them to the office, where Sara began lining them up against the wall, organized loosely by size, so Lauren could see them all at one time: tiny wrought-iron frames for snapshots; gilded gold frames suited for a museum wall; cheap plastic poster frames; modern metal frames with thin black borders; whimsical frames hand-painted with flowers or the words "girlfriends forever."

As I trudged in with load after load, I started to feel uncomfortable, embarrassed even, as if each batch of frames carried with it a silent reproach. Lauren, however, did not seem at all fazed or surprised by the assembled collection. Altogether there were more than forty frames, all empty, most with sale tags from Michaels, TJ Maxx, Target, or Aaron Brothers. Sara encouraged Lauren to choose the frames she liked best to keep and to donate the others to a charity she knew Lauren supported. Lauren, who'd been downright ruthless when eradicating paper, slowly put three small frames—one of which was broken—into the donation pile.

Sara did not directly challenge Lauren's decision to keep so many frames. Instead, she asked what Lauren intended to use the remaining frames for. Once an avid painter, Lauren had stopped making art years ago, soon after college.

Since leaving her corporate job, she'd decided to bring art back into her life and wanted to begin "creating something new every day." The empty frames, she explained, would display the paintings she had yet to paint.

Sara enthused over Lauren's plan to get back in touch with her creative side, but pointed out that Lauren's walls were already quite full; even if she covered every patch of open wall space, there would not be enough room for the dozens of frames accumulated in front of us. Looking annoyed for one of the few times that day, Lauren explained that only a few of these frames would go on her walls; the rest, once filled with her paintings and drawings, would be gifts for family and friends. Sara then suggested Lauren label each frame with a sticky note naming the intended recipient and let go of the rest.

Lauren sighed loudly, clearly frustrated. "Are you okay? Are you angry with me?" Sara asked in a playful tone. "It's okay if you're angry with me." Lauren smiled, not answering the question, and explained that while Sara's approach made sense, it would not work in this instance because the rest of the frames—homes for art not yet created—would be going to friends Lauren did not know yet, people who had yet to come into her life.

Sara seemed about to respond, then decided against it. It had been a long, productive day, and at this point we were all tired. Sara suggested we call it a day and start fresh tomorrow, when we'd return for a second four-hour organizing session. Together, we carried half a dozen garbage bags through the building's bright lobby—Lauren stopping to chat with some neighbors along the way—down to the dumpster and recycling bins in the garage. Sara took the few frames Lauren had agreed to part with out to her car, along with three large bags of items to be donated to a local teen shelter.

As we loaded the car, I asked Sara my burning question. Why did she think Lauren, who'd parted with so many items so easily, was insistent about keeping so many empty frames? Sara had a ready answer. She said the frames were an example of what Sara called "magical thinking," wherein each frame purchased brought Lauren one step closer to the ideal life she imagined for herself. The frames represented something Lauren wanted to be—an artist, a creative person, someone surrounded by friends and loved ones. Getting rid of them would mean letting go of Lauren's vision of herself and her future.

Like many other organizers I spoke with, Sara said she has to walk a fine line when it comes to confronting clients about uncomfortable or emotional issues. "I'm not a therapist," she explained. "It's hard to know what's appropriate." But if the opportunity arose when she returned the next day, Sara planned to gently suggest Lauren consider trying therapy again (the three of us had bonded earlier in the day over our positive past experiences with therapy). Sara believed working with a therapist could help Lauren address what seemed to be a recurrence of depression and some behaviors that suggested compulsive shopping and hoarding tendencies, such as keeping new purchases in shopping bags for extended times, storing items in illogical spots, such as toiletries in the office and frames in the kitchen, and acquiring so many belongings that large spaces of her home were unusable. Without therapy, Sara worried, it wouldn't matter how much Lauren donated or discarded; eventually she'd refill any space we created with new acquisitions.

This all made sense to me. I'd loved working with Lauren, and wanted to see her attain all the dreams she'd shared with us that day, about her new business, her personal relationships, and her desire to bring art and beauty back into her daily life. I was impressed by Sara's insights and skill at navigating a complicated and delicate situation, as well as her patience and compassion. Nevertheless, as I drove home along the LA freeways, I felt sad and a bit discouraged. Despite the fun we'd had that day, the female bonding, the butterfly tattoos, the amazing progress we'd made, I couldn't stop thinking of those dozens of frames lined along the wall, row after row, waiting to display art not yet created for friends not yet met.

Introduction

This book started out as a cultural critique of professional organizers, but it has expanded to include a great deal of affection and appreciation for the organizers I met and the work they do. When I began researching professional organizers, I saw them as the human equivalent of *Real Simple* magazine and the Container Store, part of a growing industry built around persuading Americans that organizing things in pretty boxes is the key to a happy life.[1] But the more time I spent with professional organizers, the more I saw I'd gotten it wrong. It's true that organizers are part of the containo-industrial complex,[2] a billion-dollar home storage and organization industry, but they are also that industry's most passionate and persuasive critics. And the work they do, which does *occasionally* involve pretty boxes, is more meaningful and culturally significant than I, and others, had imagined.[3] The rise of professional organizing has a lot to teach us, and not just about strategies for managing Americans' mountains of possessions. Studying professional organizers—the occupation's origins and rapid growth—shows us that the way Americans work today, in their jobs and in their homes, is not working, especially for women.

When the first professional organizers built this profession in the 1970s and 1980s, most of the job options available to them—as women and often as mothers—were inflexible, uninspiring, and controlled by someone else. In organizing, they found a career that had the potential to offer work that was meaningful, flexible, and self-directed. Together, they created an alternative career path, overcoming sizable obstacles in the course of establishing a female-led profession that has since spawned countless books, blogs, podcasts, and TV programs.

Of course, that growth wouldn't have been possible without expanding demand for organizers' services; that, too, has been fueled in part by problems around work. For even as new occupations have opened to women (and in part *because* they were opening to women), available jobs kept getting worse—more onerous, less secure, less fulfilling, and more all-consuming, with fewer benefits and limited opportunities for upward mobility. Despite gauzy neoliberal narratives celebrating flexibility and self-reliance, over the last half century, American households have found themselves increasingly exhausted and overwhelmed, beleaguered by competing demands around work, home, and family. In response, many have sought solutions in the form of paid support, much of it provided by women.

On the one hand, this has created an array of new jobs and occupations, such as organizing, that have the potential to provide meaningful, lucrative work, at least to those with the requisite skills, supports, and inclination. On the other, while this system of hiring women to perform the previously unpaid labor of *other* women assuages some of the pains of contemporary life, it also distracts attention from systemic problems around the way Americans are expected to work today, both in paid positions and in their unpaid labors for the household.

I began the book with Lauren's story not because it is every organizing client's story—organizing jobs vary in all sorts of ways—but because the story of Lauren and her collection of empty frames gets at the intimate, complex nature of the work organizers do to help people manage their belongings and the emotions around them. Through their work with clients, organizers offer forms of care and connection hard to come by in today's society, and that can, in their best moments, help make life more manageable, less stressful, and less isolating.

And yet, it cannot be ignored that organizers do this for money—sometimes a lot of money, sometimes not so much. This doesn't invalidate the value of what they do or the spirit in which they do it. As the therapist character in *Ted Lasso* notes when Ted, her soccer coach client, accuses her of "only listening to me 'cause you're paid to listen to me," Ted gets paid to coach and still genuinely cares about his players.[4] But the fact that such intimate connections are being offered for purchase must be understood within the cultural and historical contexts that both necessitate and enable such relationships.

This book thus works to introduce readers to the history and workings of the field of professional organizing while also using this profession as a starting point for thinking through a tangled set of questions around neoliberal work arrangements, consumerism, emotional connection, and the deeply gendered nature of both paid and unpaid work. This book is thus an inquiry and an appreciation, part portrait and part parsing. I hope it does justice to the spirit and complexity of organizers and the work they do.

• • •

When I started this project in 2012, whenever I mentioned "professional organizers" I had to clarify that I meant the kind that organize your closet or office, not the kind that organize your labor movement. More often than not, the listener had assumed I meant the latter. A decade later, I rarely need to offer such clarification. By the time I finished writing this book, organizing was everywhere.

This is thanks in part to the dozens of home organizing reality TV shows that have sprung up since the 2003 debut of *Clean House*, in which a comedian host and a cleanup-and-renovation crew helped families declutter and renovate their homes.[5] By the time Marie Kondo's Netflix organizing show, *Tidying Up with Marie Kondo* (an extension of her best-selling 2014 book *The Life-Changing Magic of Tidying Up*), debuted in 2019, the decluttering craze seemed to have reached a new level.[6] Suddenly everyone had heard of, and many had tried, Kondo's idiosyncratic folding methods, especially as Americans stuck at home during the Covid-19 lockdowns were forced to confront their mountains of stuff and reorganize their homes to accommodate tele-commuting parents and remote-schooling kids.[7] Kondo's name itself became a verb—"I Kondoed my t-shirts last night."[8] Even my husband, not a follower of organizing trends, started making jokes about things "sparking joy" (Kondo's method entails keeping only items that "spark joy"[9]).

Professional organizing has woven its way into American popular culture as well. The sitcom *The Big Bang Theory* had an episode about closet organizing; *Modern Family* had one about organizing a junk drawer and another about the family's decluttering efforts.[10] One Hallmark Channel Christmas movie featured a "frazzled widower" who falls in love with the "buttoned-up" professional organizer he hires to "get his life and his business in order."[11] Two different series of mystery books now center on professional organizers who moonlight as crime solvers.[12] I've lost count of the number of New Yorker cartoons poking fun at the organizing craze: there's the one where the baby bird looks up at the mama bird from a nest crowded with twigs, candy wrappers, straws, even an electrical cord, and says, "News flash, Mom—you're a hoarder"; the one where a woman tells her husband, "I've decided to purge our material goods, starting with your crap"; the "Zen Hoarder" meditating in a room completely bare save for *two* bonsai trees; and so on.

On the one hand, this is a positive thing; it ensures a basic level of knowledge of and interest in professional organizers. On the other hand, it means that most people who read this book will think they already know about professional organizing, while what most of them *actually* know is limited to how professional organizing has been represented in television and other media.[13] But the versions of organizers and the organizing process we see on television or read about in the news rarely align with what I heard and saw when I spoke with and worked alongside actual organizers.[14] The organizers I met are not judgmental taskmasters, nor are they tightly wound perfectionists.[15] They don't force clients to part with items, nor do they endeavor to redesign clients' homes into the pristine, perfect spaces of design magazines and furniture catalogs. In reality, the work most organizers do is more nuanced, more challenging, and, in my opinion, more valuable than the version of organizing Americans tend to see in popular culture.[16] It is also a job that must be understood within the context of the broader changes around work that have occurred over the last half century.

Contextualizing Organizing's Rise

Organizing's growth can be understood as part of a broader trend in the rise of so-called lifestyle occupations, such as personal training, life coaching, personal concierge services, and event planning, among others.[17] These fields represent a growing subset of personal care and service occupations, one of the fastest-growing occupational categories in the United States.[18] Most often, paid care workers are understood as those who provide direct or indirect care to vulnerable populations such as the very young or very old, people who are ill or unable to physically care for themselves.[19] Organizers and other "expert service workers" perform a different sort of care work for a different sort of client.[20] The services they provide may be highly valued by some people, but their work rarely means the difference between life and death. The beneficiaries of their care and expertise are also usually not technically incapable of performing this work for themselves—most people can sort their own mail, for example, even if they choose not to.[21] And yet, as I hope this book makes clear, it would be a mistake to envision all organizing clients as coddled One Percenters.

Hiring an organizer—or a personal trainer or wedding planner, for that matter—usually requires at least some disposable income; these services are not equally available to all (although they are sometimes provided pro bono). As sociologist Arlie Hochschild has argued, however, such services are no longer reserved for the elite. "Families who could afford it," she notes, "have always made use of paid services, of course; at the turn of the century, they hired servants, matchmakers, governesses, chauffeurs, wet nurses, and more."[22] Over time, however, hiring others to provide such services has become more common even among non-elites.

Those who choose to hire organizers do so for all sorts of reasons. Some organizing clients have overcrowded or messy homes, but many don't. Some are chronically disorganized, others are what organizers call "situationally disorganized" due to a major life event, such as inheriting a parent's belongings, moving to a new home, beginning or ending a marriage, retiring from a long career, or adding a new member to the family. Organizers also suggest that many Americans lack basic organizing know-how because no one ever taught them these skills, which, at least for girls, would once have been covered in home economics courses or handed down from mother to daughter. As gender-segregated and gender-stereotyped schooling fell out of fashion, and as more American women moved into paid employment, leaving fewer American households with dedicated full-time homemakers, these skills have gradually disappeared.[23] Clients' motivations for seeking organizers' help are thus as varied as the types of help they're looking for. Nevertheless, the rising demand for organizing services is undoubtedly connected to larger shifts around how Americans live and work.

In the first decade of the twenty-first century, a team of researchers spent four years documenting the homes and daily lives of middle-class families across Los Angeles. They cataloged each home's visible possessions—what they were, how they were used, and where they were placed.[24] The resulting book, *Life at Home in the Twenty-First Century*, shows families overwhelmed by their own belongings. There is a consistent "mismatch," the team found, between the number of things Americans own and the space they have to store them.[25] Most homes were "so crammed with objects that it is a challenge for household members to comfortably traverse the space."[26] Three-quarters of the households in the study could not fit their car in the garage because it was being used for storage, although they rarely accessed the items stored there.[27] Families who run out of room in the garage (or don't have a garage in the first place) often stow their surplus belongings at offsite storage units, usually for at least a year, sometimes for as long as decades.[28] There are now more self-storage facilities in the United

States than there are Starbucks, McDonalds, Dunkin' Donuts, and Pizza Hut locations *combined*.[29]

The study also found that women who perceive their homes as messy or cluttered experience increased stress levels and lower levels of marital satisfaction.[30] The same was not true for men, who were "relatively unaffected by mess," likely because women tend to be perceived—by others and by themselves—as more responsible for the home and its appearance, even in couples where both work outside the home.[31] Clutter's psychological toll is exacerbated by the time and energy it demands from households already dangerously low on both due to long work hours[32] and intensifying parenting[33] and other caregiving demands.[34] As two of the study's researchers concluded, "Dusting, cleaning, upkeep, repair, straightening, reorganization . . . Merely anticipating such work almost certainly generates anxiety and stress."[35] One survey found that the second-most-cited reason people hire organizers, behind difficulty determining what to keep or get rid of, was "to reduce stress."[36] In short, clutter costs—not only to buy it, but to store it, to maintain it, even to think about it.[37]

Some blame America's culture of consumerism for this unprecedented accumulation of goods.[38] Sociologist Juliet Schor argues that amid a growing wealth gap, status-conscious, overworked Americans seek to emulate the upscale lifestyles they see depicted on television and in advertisements.[39] Others say most of what people buy can be understood as "practical responses to contemporary living conditions," such as the decline of traditional kinship bonds and Americans' uniquely long work hours.[40] Still others point to Americans' tendency to engage in "wishful shopping," purchasing items that stand in for the activities they would like to do or the people they would like to be.[41] To part with such items is, in a sense, "to murder the version of ourselves we envision using it."[42] (Think here of Lauren and her many empty frames.)

The Covid-19 pandemic prompted its own sort of "wishful shopping," as fearful families filled their homes and garages with supplies—toilet paper, hand sanitizer, Clorox wipes. These items were arguably necessities, although perhaps not in such huge quantities as some folks believed, but they also served as talismans for those trying to keep themselves and their families safe and comfortable in uncertain and unprecedented times. More than two years after the pandemic began, organizers I spoke with said they were still helping clients figure out what to do with their enormous backstock of pandemic buys. Speaking with me in early 2022, organizer Jessica said, "I can't tell you how many houses I've gone into where the supply closet is overwhelming, you know, bursting out with so many hand sanitizers." Another organizer told me she can't count the number of times she's been asked, "What am I going to do with all this toilet paper?"

Overconsumption is not just about the people doing the purchasing, but also about the nature and durability of the items being purchased. Americans' love of shopping has been fueled at least in part by the increased availability of inexpensive goods: "The ability to acquire untold numbers of objects has expanded from the wealthy and upper middle class to families in virtually every socioeconomic bracket, including many below the poverty line."[43] Although this democratization of stuff has been associated with blurring class boundaries and increasing the power of consumers, it has also come at a high cost.[44]

The human and environmental tolls of disposable goods—from toys to clothing to electronics and beyond—have been well documented.[45] Many items are designed with the express purpose of becoming useless in a relatively short time: t-shirts that pill or lose their shape after a few washes; iPhones deliberately slowed down to encourage replacement; nonreusable batteries; ink cartridges that stop functioning before the ink in them is fully out; college textbooks that come out with new, barely changed editions every year, rendering used copies useless. This planned obsolescence leaves consumers in a double bind, needing to purchase a new version while wondering what to do with the old one—whether to keep it, where to safely dispose of it, or who else might be able to use it so it doesn't go to waste.[46]

These decisions, and the time and energy they demand, feel all the more burdensome for households already lamenting the scarcity of their time, the enormity of the responsibilities they manage on a daily basis, and how overwhelmed they feel by all of it. It is here where the rise of organizing can help us see more clearly some of the problems with the way Americans work today. As Katherine Feo Kelly writes, Americans are facing "a fundamentally postmodern problem: the anxiety around excess—in physical belongings, and also in the tempo of everyday life—reflective of the forces of late capitalism."[47] As one organizer told me, "People have always been pretty busy, but there is a perception of being so busy bordering on feeling frantic or really pressured. I think that drives a lot of people toward organizers." Households today shoulder an increasing number of responsibilities that would have been handled by someone else in the past—employers, the government, community members—or that wouldn't have existed at all.

Making sense of these responsibilities requires taking a step back to look at the broader context in which today's Americans live and work. Recent works, most notably Allison Pugh's *The Tumbleweed Society*, Marianne Cooper's *Cut Adrift*, and *Dreams of the Overworked* by Christine Beckman and Melissa Mazmanian, add new layers of complexity to discussions of overwork and overwhelm.[48] They document in moving detail how rising economic insecurity, dwindling social safety nets, and unraveling family and community ties have intensified these trends, pushing many American households to the breaking point. Families, Cooper argues, "bear the imprint of the social and economic forces that surround them."[49] Left to cobble together their own forms of security, Americans find themselves responsible for finding and keeping jobs, navigating fluctuating incomes and rising costs, and preparing themselves and their families for uncertain futures.[50] In this context, the daily demands of work and home are, if not necessarily more onerous than in the past, onerous in new ways, ways that require a combination of time, energy, knowledge, and resources that many Americans seem to lack. These new responsibilities have also come cloaked in neoliberal ideology that frames any failure to thrive in this volatile and insecure world as the natural, avoidable result of personal failings, rather than evidence of a flawed system.[51] Layered atop these new responsibilities is a palpable layer of anxiety and self-doubt, one from which even the wealthiest families are not entirely immune.[52] Families of different class backgrounds adopt different strategies for managing this anxiety, but in all sorts of families, women tend to be the ones shouldering the brunt of the "worry work" involved.

The increasingly precarious nature of Americans' jobs and finances also impacts our relationships with one another.[53] One reason the nuclear family thrived in the twentieth century—as opposed to the tightly intertwined extended kin networks of previous eras— was because shifts in the public and private sector, including social security, rising wages, and health and welfare benefits, combined to decrease Americans' reliance on extended family.[54] As those forms of support dwindled over the late twentieth century, households have been left adrift, emotionally, and often geographically, from the kin and community upon whom in previous generations they might have relied.[55] Even families who manage to cull together a tenuous support network of paid and unpaid helpers—neighbors, babysitters, grandparents—tend to downplay rather than celebrate the "scaffolding" that makes their lives work, steeped as they are in the American mythology of individualism that frames dependence as a form of weakness.[56] Into this breach step professional organizers and other expert service workers, who offer for pay the sort of assistance, empathy, and connection many Americans so desperately desire.

One longtime organizer I spoke with told me she has been surprised, over her decades working in this field, by how consistent demand for her services has remained. In the 1980s and 1990s, she said, it made sense to her that organizing was becoming so popular. "We bought so much stuff that we maybe started to need organizers then." When 9/11 hit, she said, "I thought, Carrie, for sure the business was going to go down the tube. Nope. People were so afraid at that point that they needed to now stop buying and needed to get a handle on the stuff that they have, the wills, the paperwork, the people in their lives were suddenly much more important. Stuff wasn't so important." So they hired organizers to help get rid of excess and get everything else organized in case of an emergency. "And then," she said, the recession of 2008 hit, and "I knew for sure business would go down. And it didn't. Why? Because families were now starting to merge together. People were starting to move in together. How do we manage our space? We have to leave our bigger homes?" Again, they needed the help of organizers. "It doesn't matter," she finally decided, "if we're making more money or making less, if the stocks are going up or going down, whether we have a country crisis or whether we don't." Regardless of all that's changing around us, "There's such anxiety about how we're living our life values. I believe that's why the organizing industry is doing so well and continues to do so well." As she saw it, it wasn't any one event that was bringing clients to organizers, it was the nature of modern life itself—not just the stuff Americans own, but the scarcity of their time, the enormity of the responsibilities they manage on a daily basis, and how over-whelmed they feel by all of it. Studying organizers, then, can help us understand both the sources of this sense of overwhelm and what might be done to assuage it.

Good Jobs in an Era of Bad Ones

If studying organizers can offer some insight into what's wrong with American society today, it can also illuminate some things that are right about it. In a world where unhappy workers outnumber happy ones by two to one, professional organizers love their work.[57] Not everyone who enters this field stays in it, and organizers certainly have their complaints, but for the most part the organizers I spoke with say they have the best job in the world. They describe their work as fun and meaningful. Most are self-employed, and while this has its challenges, they prefer it to the alternatives—working for someone else or not working at all. Organizers in their eighties and even nine-ties keep working with clients because, they say, they love what they do and don't want to stop doing it.[58] After more than thirty years in the field, one organizer told me, "I still love it," adding with a laugh, "most days of it. Someday I'll retire on a beach somewhere, but right now I'm having too much fun."[59]

In his book *Why We Work*, Barry Schwartz lists the features that make for satisfying work:

> Satisfied workers are engaged by their work. They lose themselves in it. Not all the time, of course, but often enough for that to be salient to them. Satisfied workers are challenged by their work. It forces them to stretch themselves—to go outside their comfort zones. These lucky people think the work they do is fun, often in the way that doing cross-word puzzles or Sudoku is fun.
>
> Why else do people work? Satisfied people do their work because they feel that they are in charge. Their workday offers them a measure of autonomy and discretion. And they use that autonomy and discretion to achieve a level of mastery of expertise.
>
> These people do their work because it's an opportunity for social engagement. They do many of their tasks as parts of teams, and even when they're working alone, there are plenty of opportunities for social interaction during work's quiet moments.
>
> Finally, these people are satisfied with their work because they find what they do meaningful. Potentially, their work makes a difference to the world. It makes other people's lives better. And it may even make other people's lives better in ways that are significant.[60]

I quote Schwartz at length because every attribute he lists, every single one, came up in my interviews with professional organizers. Organizers describe their work as a meaningful way to help others. They see organizing as a challenge, a puzzle to be solved, one they take great joy in figuring out. They like that each day is different, each job brings new challenges. They like working one-on-one with clients, getting to know people in the intimate way that organizing often entails. They like the job's flexibility, the chance to set their own hours, schedule their own vacations, and decide how they will approach each task, all things many of them were unable to do in previous jobs. The work can be hard, physically and emotionally. Clients can be difficult. Some-times jobs are so plentiful that organizers go months without a single day off, then come long stretches when they worry they'll never land another client. But for most organizers, organizing continues to be a more attractive career than the others available to them, and so they keep at it.

In her article "The Future of Work: The Rise and Fall of the Job," historian Bethany Moreton suggests that rather than lamenting the decline of the "secure, benefits-laden job," which wasn't the norm for all that long or for all that many people anyway, we should see these precarious times as an opportunity to reimagine what work *could* look like and how we might make it better.[61] How, for instance, we might create more work that matches Schwartz's description above and less work that is "monotonous, meaningless, and soul deadening."[62] I believe organizers can help us with that. Not because everyone should become an organizer—goodness knows we're not all cut out for that and, as I demonstrate later in this book, building an organizing business is more feasible for some folks than for others, due to entrenched class and racial inequalities. But whether by choice, necessity, or a bit of both, organizers have carved out a profession that provides the sort of work life they wanted but weren't finding elsewhere. In that sense, organizing is a good job in an era of bad jobs, one that can help us see more clearly the limitations and disadvantages of many of the other forms of work available to Americans today.[63]

What This Book Is Not

By this point it should be clear that this is not a book about how to get organized, although those looking for organizing tips may find some in the stories I tell. There are many excellent books on that topic available at your local library or bookstore. This is also not a book about how to become a professional organizer, although would-be organizers might find much of interest here.[64] This book is neither an exposé of the professional organizing industry nor an advertisement for it, at least not intentionally. I identify many wonderful things about professional organizers, the work they do, and its impact on clients. I also offer some critiques, most shared by organizers themselves along with a few of my own, about certain aspects of the profession. But, ultimately, this book is not about whether organizing is a good or bad thing. No phenomenon is entirely positive or negative. It's the ways in which a thing can be both good *and* bad, depending on how you look at it or whom you ask, that challenge us to think in more nuanced and constructive ways. This book is therefore an effort to use what I've learned about the organizing profession to help us all make sense of the complicated, changing nature of work and life in twenty-first-century America.

Learning about organizers' work, especially observing the actual organizing process, entailed spending time with organizing clients as well. Readers will meet many of those clients in the pages of this book, and I try to represent them and their perspectives as fully and fairly as possible. From their experiences I draw some generalizations about clients' experiences of the organizing process and the highs and lows it can entail. Ultimately, however, this book is more about organizers than clients. As I detail below, I met and interviewed many more organizers than I did clients. When I did talk with clients, I focused almost exclusively on their experience of the organizing process (why they hired an organizer, how they went about doing so, what the organizing process was like for them, how they felt afterward).

I also pay close attention to the historical context in which the organizing industry emerged, but those looking for longer histories of the concepts of minimalism, simple living, and anti-consumerism (none of which are necessarily embraced by all professional organizers) should read David Shi's excellent *The Simple Life* and Kyle Chayka's *The Longing for Less*.[65] Readers interested in how ideals of home organization and interior design have changed over time, especially with regard to storage, can turn to the many texts that explore those topics in detail.[66]

Finally, as much as I would like to count as research the hours I spent happily folding my family's clothing into KonMari-style rectangles, this is not a memoir of my own journey from clutter to order.[67] My home is certainly more organized as a result of my having done this project, in part because decluttering my cupboards was an excellent distraction on days when the writing wasn't going well. In all honesty, I was pretty organized before I began this project. And yet, although I never employed an organizer myself, sorting, discarding, and organizing my own belongings has occasionally given me insight into the experiences of organizing clients and the emotional nature of the organizing process. Sorting my son's outgrown baby clothing in preparation for a garage sale, for example, was difficult—physically painful at moments—as I let go of the material reminders of that especially wonderful phase of my life. And when I recycled a stack of unread *New Yorker* magazines that prompted feelings of guilt *every* time I looked at them, I felt both transgressive (Am I really allowed to do this?) and elated (Farewell, scolding pile of "shoulds"!). These and other experiences shaped my perspectives and conclusions and so, in the spirit of auto-ethnography, I occasionally include stories of organizing and decluttering my own home and office.[68]

Methodology

This is an ethnographic study of the professional organizing industry. Ethnography combines long-term participant observation and open-ended interviewing in an effort to understand a culture, in this case the community of professional organizers, from the perspective of its members. The strength of ethnographic research lies in its ability to understand not just what a given group of people thinks or does, but to endeavor to make sense of those unique perspectives within their broader cultural and historical context.[69]

For this study, from 2012 to 2023, I interviewed more than fifty organizers, primarily in Los Angeles and Orange County, but also in Atlanta, New York, San Francisco, St. Louis, Washington, DC, and a few smaller US cities.[70] Interviewees included four of the five founders of the National Association of Productivity and Organizing Professionals (NAPO) and founders of the National Association of Black Professional Organizers (NABPO) and #BlackGirlsWhoOrganize. The organizers I interviewed varied by age, gender, race, and years of experience, but—as in the organizing profession itself—most were white women between the ages of thirty and sixty. All owned their own businesses, and most worked full-time. At the time of our interview, more than half were married or had long-term partners and just over half had children. I also interviewed more than a dozen organizing clients, two former organizers, and a psychologist who specializes in treating people with hoarding disorders and frequently collaborates with organizers. (See the Appendix for additional details on interviews, interviewees, and other research conducted for this study.)

Over the course of my fieldwork (2012–2023), I also conducted more than 170 hours of observation at regional and national organizing meetings, classes, conferences, and events. I attended workshops on everything from the ethics of organizing to the legalities of employing contractors. I walked the red carpet at the Los Angeles Organizing Awards, where one green (environment-focused) organizer appeared in a ball gown made entirely of repurposed plastic bags. I attended hoarding task-force meetings, where organizers sat alongside social workers, public health officials, firefighters, city inspectors, and trash haulers to brainstorm solutions for extreme hoarding situations. I sat in on talks at public libraries where organizers gently informed elderly attendees that no one wants their VHS tapes or lifetime accumulation of *National Geographic* magazines. I lugged a box of irksome paperwork to an organizing boot camp, where I purged, shredded, and reorganized alongside fellow participants, each tackling her own box of pesky paraphernalia.

In what was to me the most exciting part of this project, I worked as an unpaid assistant to professional organizers in Los Angeles and Orange County.[71] During these workalongs, I cleared out attics of dusty Halloween decorations; organized a basement work space for a fashion designer; unpacked boxes for a family who'd relocated to a palatial home in the Kardashians' neighborhood; helped set up and run multiple estate sales; cleaned out the dusty pantry of a woman with a hoarding disorder; helped a preschool teacher reorganize her classroom; and assisted on a pro bono job helping a mother fleeing domestic violence settle into her new, much smaller apartment.

With the help of wonderful student assistants, I also combed through a century's worth of news articles, searching for the very first mentions of organizers and their work. These articles were often as entertaining as they were illuminating, and I draw from them heavily in the book's first two chapters, where I present the very first history of the organizing profession.

I'm not generally a fan of reality television, but for the sake of this project I watched innumerable episodes of organizing shows. Happily, other anthropologists and cultural critics have written a great deal about these shows, and I draw on their analyses in this book. I also read a number of short stories and novels featuring professional organizers, most of which depicted organizers in unflattering and, to my mind, inaccurate ways. I do not analyze these depictions at length in this book, but I do consider what they tell us about how the organizing industry has been presented and received in American culture.

Organization of the Book

I began this book with a story, that of Lauren and her many frames. Between the book's chapters, I've sandwiched additional vignettes detailing organizing jobs I participated in or was told about. I also refer back (and forward) to them as examples when I describe the organizing process in part II. I include these "organizing stories," as I think of them, because they show what organizing looks like and because they get at the heart of the organizer-client relationship: often intimate, sometimes transactional, occasionally contentious.[72] Together, these stories reveal how emotionally laden possessions— and the decision to keep or part with them—can be, and how organizers try to untangle clients' complex feelings around the organizing process. In short, I include these stories because they add texture to the information and arguments presented in the chapters themselves, and because I like them, and I think readers will, too.

This rest of the book is organized into two parts: part I concerns organizers' choice to do this type of work, while part II centers on the actual work organizers do with clients. As I noted at the start of this introduction, professional organizers have a lot to teach us about what's not working in the way Americans work today. The fact that so many people—especially women—have gravitated to this career over the previous decades tells us that, for various reasons, they see organizing as a better alternative than other available jobs. And so, the first part of this book explores what it is about organizing that has drawn practitioners to the field—both in its earliest years and today—and what it is about *other* jobs they hope to avoid by pursuing organizing.

I begin chapter 1 with a brief history of attitudes toward clutter and organization, noting that while ideas about culturally appropriate ways to deal with one's material belongings have changed over time, the expectation that such work should be performed by women has persisted. I then detail the rise of organizing as a profession in the 1970s and 1980s, highlighting some of the field's earliest female pioneers. At a time when many careers were closed to women, organizing was an area in which their gender actually worked to their advantage, since it was already seen as "women's work." Yet that same stereotype worked against early organizers as they sought to build their businesses and be taken seriously; both they and the work they did were dismissed as unskilled and of little value.

In chapter 2, I document the founding of the first professional association for organizers, which would eventually become the National Association for Productivity and Organizing Professionals (NAPO), by a group of Los Angeles organizers in 1983. Tired of having to explain and defend their work to people—especially businessmen—who derided and devalued it, organizers banded together to legitimize and publicize their growing field. They did so in ways that both drew on and denied their gender identity and that continue to shape the field to this day. For while organizers prize their collegial, female-led community, they also tend to accept, and even impose on one another, ideas about professionalism and what it takes to succeed as an organizer that marginalize and disadvantage certain groups of women, especially in terms of race and class.

Chapter 3 investigates what continues to draw new organizers to the profession in the twenty-first century. The occupation's appeal to women has endured, even as the successes of second-wave feminism have created more professional opportunities for women. I argue that organizing's growth must be understood within the context of the decline of traditional employment, rising insecurity, and the wide-scale entry of married women into paid employment. For many, organizing represents an attractive alternative to other kinds of work, jobs from which they were, or might be, laid off at any time, where they worked according to someone else's schedule and priorities, or did work they found trivial or tedious. In contrast, organizing offers flexibility, a low barrier to entry, and the opportunity to work for oneself. In this sense, many organizers are not so much *pulled* into this line of work as they are *pushed* into it by the failures of standard employment. This remained true even amid the tumultuous and unprecedented times of the Covid-19 pandemic, during which some organizers' businesses thrived and others floundered.

In part II, I shift my focus to the actual work of organizing. As much as the rise of organizing can teach us about the relative unattractiveness of other possible careers, the work organizers do with clients provides its own insights into the overdemanding nature of contemporary work and life. Organizers may have opted out of more traditional forms of employment, but most of their clients have not. When they work with clients, organizers focus less on people's stuff than on how they *feel* about the stuff, which itself connects right back to those feelings of overwork and overwhelm I touched on above.

All organizing jobs are different, but they tend to share certain similarities in terms of the overall process. In chapter 4, I sketch out what that process looks like in general terms, drawing from my time as an organizing assistant and interviews with organizers and clients. I consider the different strategies organizers use to encourage clients to part with more items, all of which involve shifting the client's way of thinking about their possessions. This work, which at core focuses more on people themselves than on their stuff, often challenges people's typical orientations to their belongings and, sometimes, to the community around them. I also outline what organizers see as the ultimate goal of the organizing process, which has little to do with pretty boxes or color-coded bookshelves. Instead, framing themselves more as teachers than "doers," they focus on creating tailored, sustainable systems and educating clients on how to use and maintain them. Along the way, I note the ways in which real-life organizing differs from how it's been presented in organizing TV shows; these differences create their own challenges for organizers, who often have to manage clients' misperceptions and unreasonable expectations of the organizing process.

Chapter 5 then zeroes in on the organizer-client relationship and the work organizers do to forge and maintain that relationship. Because in order to help clients, organizers must first connect with them. They do so by building trust, listening empathetically, and managing their and their clients' emotions. I argue that these relationships, rather than sorting or purging or filing, are what lies at the heart of the organizing process. Organizers use these connections to help clients get organized, but also to push back against the overwhelming demands society places upon households and the women who typically lead them. In this way, I argue, organizing can be understood as feminist work, as it aims to reframe and reduce the untenable burdens women find themselves shouldering in these uncertain times.

In a brief conclusion, I consider what organizing can do for us, and also what it can't. There is value in the joy and meaning organizers derive from their work and the care, connection, and support they aim to offer clients. But there are also ways in which organizers' career choices and the work they do with clients may serve to normalize and preserve some of the most troubling aspects of contemporary American work life. Ultimately, I argue, theirs is not a perfect profession, nor can it cure what ails us most. And yet, through their work—what they do and how and why they do it—organizers can nevertheless point us toward more humane ways of working and living amid an era of overwork and overwhelm.

part I

THE RISE OF PROFESSIONAL
ORGANIZING

If you watch a lot of home makeover shows, you're familiar with the "big reveal," the moment when homeowners see their newly redesigned space for the first time. Neatly labeled belongings, clothes hung by rainbow color in immaculate closets, appliance-free kitchen countertops. There are usually gasps of surprise and, more often than not, some joyful crying. I tend to be skeptical of these moments, knowing as I do that, like pretty much all reality TV programming, they are highly choreographed to produce a certain emotional response in the viewer. It came as a surprise, then, when I found myself moved to tears during a real-life reveal.

I was assisting on the second day of a two-day job reorganizing the basement work space of Marcia, a fashion designer and mother of three. Marcia and her family lived in a large, brightly decorated home in a quaint, upscale neighborhood in central Los Angeles. The front yard was crowded with sunflowers and lined by a small white picket fence. The house looked happily lived in, clean and a bit cluttered, with worn wooden floors and charming arched doorways. The entryway held a jumble of shoes, jackets, bags, and sports equipment. Piles of paper lay atop the kitchen counter waiting to be attended to. Bookshelves stacked two rows deep lined a wall of the large living room, more books in piles beside them. A comfy-looking couch was draped with a colorful afghan and scattered with mismatched throw pillows.

A slender white woman in her mid-fifties, Marcia wore chunky black glasses and no makeup. Her mane of black hair, touched with gray, was corralled into two long braids that nearly reached her waist. She smiled often, thanked us constantly, and invited us to help ourselves to anything in the fridge if we were hungry.

Marcia had been designing clothing for different women's fashion brands for more than twenty years, mostly from home. She did most of her work in the home's surprisingly well-lit basement, which was also used for storage. The 300-square-foot space included a large drafting table and two walls of metal shelving, the kind you buy at a big box store and assemble yourself. On each shelf, Marcia's work supplies—drawing pads, pens, pencils, markers, paint and paintbrushes, glue, tape, artificial flowers, needles and thread, ribbons, fabric swatches, a dressmaker's mannequin, multiple sewing machines—vied for space with the miscellany of family life—off-season sports equipment, old CDs, home movies, vinyl records, framed movie posters, the kids' old art projects, shoe inserts, extension cords.

Starla, the organizer I was working for that day, told me in advance that Marcia was good at making decisions and parted with things easily. The first step in organizing the basement, deciding what should stay and what should go, went quickly. We organized items by type, tossed anything broken or unusable, and relocated the sports equipment and a few other items to the garage. Marcia made quick work of the record collection. She set a few favorites aside, packed up the rest, and headed off to Amoeba Music, a nearby used record store. (Once the decision to part with something is made, organizers usually encourage clients to get it out of the house immediately; otherwise, items intended for sale or donation become one more pile of clutter to be dealt with later.) On her way home, Marcia planned to run a few errands and pick up her daughter from dance class. That left the rest of us—Starla, me, and two other assistants—to organize the basement into a usable work space.

For each type of item, we chose an appropriately sized box or bin (Marcia already had many on hand), labeled it with a Post-it note, neatly packed the items inside, and found a logical spot on one of the shelving units. Nonwork items, such as DVDs or kids' belongings, were assigned to the shelving unit farthest from Marcia's desk, while items she needed on a regular basis were placed within reach. Larger categories of items, such as ribbons, were organized into subcategories—plain ribbon, fancy ribbon, holiday ribbon. Once we found homes for everything, we replaced the makeshift labels with permanent ones. (Starla banned me from printing any of the final labels, saying, not without cause, that my handwriting is terrible.)

It took about three hours, but by the time Marcia returned home, the basement was nearly finished. There's rarely a dramatic reveal at the end of an organizing job; clients usually participate in, or at least witness, the process from start to finish. Marcia had been actively involved in the sorting process, but when she left on her errands, the basement was still a mess, with everything taken out but nothing yet packed away or put back. We rearranged the shelving units and other large items so the room looked larger. We vacuumed the floor, dusted the shelves, and wiped down every single item. The drafting table, previously piled with random stacks of paper and design paraphernalia, was clean and bare. On the shelf behind it, facing Marcia while she worked, sat a row of colorful art and sewing supplies, arranged in neatly labeled bins.

As I wrote in my field notes that day, "It really was like on TV." Marcia started down the stairs into the basement and stopped mid-step. She cried out in surprise, lifting her hand to cover her mouth. "I can't believe it," she said, and started to cry. She continued into the room, walking from shelf to shelf, touching random boxes, quietly reading labels out loud. "Fake flowers! Fancy ribbon!" Then she sat down at her drafting table and let out a small sob.

"I've been a designer for twenty years," she told us, "but I never felt like a professional until I saw all this organized on the shelves like this. I always grabbed as I went, never organizing, but here it is." She hugged and kissed each of us, thanking us profusely. "I could never have done this," she told us, and thanked us again. And then I was crying along with her, as were the others, even Starla, who prides herself on being a "tough love" sort of organizer. It was a bittersweet moment—despite her long success in a competitive field, Marcia had never seen herself as a professional, something I suspect is true of many women who squeeze their work, physically and temporally, into the spaces left around their family responsibilities. It felt gratifying to have been a part of something that made her feel differently about herself and her work.

1

The First Organizers

Women Have Always Been Expected to Manage the Stuff

The first organizers were all women. For most, starting their own organizing business represented an alternative to the other jobs available to them—nurse, teacher, secretary, waitress, homemaker— and allowed them to do work they enjoyed that was compatible with their other responsibilities and priorities. They came to this profession independently but around the same time, each believing they were pioneering something entirely new by monetizing skills they already possessed. In many senses they were. Organizing had not previously been seen as a job in and of itself, although organizing spaces and things had been a component of *other* jobs, such as homemaker, secretary, or efficiency expert. Yet in other respects, early organizers were simply continuing a long history of women being held responsible for managing material belongings both at home and in the workplace.

This parallel between organizing and other forms of labor typically performed by women (for free and for pay) had its advantages, as people tended to assume that women were, by nature, well suited to this type of work regardless of their specific training or education. And yet, the association of organizing with other female-dominated fields such as housewifery, housecleaning, and secretarial work made it difficult for early organizers to persuade others, especially men, that theirs was skilled work that deserved both remuneration and respect. This chapter first details the longer history of ideas around clutter and its management, then tells the stories of these earliest organizers, the paths that led them to this new profession, and the initial steps they took to combat skepticism and legitimize organizing as real and valuable work.

. . .

On a crisp February morning, I arrived at Beverly Clower's Los Angeles condominium to interview her about her nearly thirty years' experience as a professional organizer.[1] Beverly warmly greeted me at the door, then sat me down at the table while she heated water in a kettle on the stove. She brought out six different varieties of tea for me to choose from along with a jar of honey, a small bottle of milk, and even a little dish for my discarded teabag. It was exactly as I'd always imagined dropping by for tea at a friend's should be. She returned with a plate holding a banana nut muffin, a glazed donut cut into four pieces, and a savory onion-flavored roll cut in two, all for us to share while we spoke.

Beverly had a round face and bright blue eyes. Her white hair was cut short and she wore a white turtleneck, slacks, and a rose-colored cardigan that she took on and off during the interview, depending on whether she felt too cold or too warm. She was then in her late seventies, although she seemed younger to me, and had been working for more than sixty years. She'd started as a medical secretary in Atlanta when she was just sixteen, still in high school. After nearly a decade she decided it was time for a change—the work was often dull and there was little opportunity for upward mobility—but she felt ill equipped for anything other than secretarial work. So, she took a secretarial position at a bank, which turned out to not be much of a change.

As she recalled when I interviewed her more than four decades later, it was after a particularly annoying workday when "suddenly this light bulb came on." She remembered a news article she'd read about an exchange program for secretaries where you could work as a temp in London for up to four months. She called the employment agency—"Western Girl Agency, I'll never forget it"—that very day and asked if they still had the program. They did. She filled out an application on Thursday, gave two weeks' notice at the bank on Friday, and "three weeks later I was gone." It was, she said, like "the heavens opened up and a red carpet rolled down."

Her four-month stay turned into nearly a decade abroad, during which she temped at various businesses and worked as a personal assistant for entrepreneurs, first in London, then in Amsterdam. It was, she said, "the best thing that ever happened to me." Growing up in the 1940s and 1950s, she'd always been reserved. "I was very quiet and I waited to be spoken to." Living abroad "was a bridge that I needed." She grew more confident in herself and her abilities. "It gave me a broader life experience and I just fell in love with the ballet and the theater. It was just magnificent."

While working temp jobs in England, she tried to always leave an office in better shape than she found it. People noticed and praised her for it. One day a fellow secretary told her, "'Beverly, you're very organized.'" The compliment took her by surprise. "I'd never thought of that word pertaining to me or anyone else, being organized or otherwise. It just wasn't a biggie in my life." She worked for two different entrepreneurs, one of whom was starting a new business. At the start-up, she had much more responsibility than in previous positions. "I got to do all the setup: the systems, order the machinery, the telex machines, the photocopier. And I had to be very resourceful because we were really working out of a house, not a real office, but we had to transform a couple of rooms into offices."

She enjoyed the work and decided that when she returned to the States she didn't want to be "just a secretary anymore." ("I had a bad habit," Beverly told me, "of saying 'I'm just a secretary,' and I came to have a lot more respect for that [role] in the future.") She wanted better pay, more variety, and greater control over her own work. Eventually, she decided it was time to come back to the United States, but she wanted to try somewhere new. She planned to visit a few different cities before settling down. Los Angeles was her first stop, and she never left.

At first, she stayed in secretarial work; it felt familiar and was easy to find. She took a few temp jobs then landed a permanent position.

In 1982, when that company went out of business, Beverly decided she'd had enough of working for someone else; it was time to start her own business as a "freelance office worker." She named her company Office Overhaul. Her first clients were her old boss and his partners, who called her in to set up or reorganize their offices. "I've always been more comfortable in the office than in the kitchen. And I thought I was the world's first and only office organizer, or organizer of any kind."[2]

Less than a year later, however, a new woman joined Beverly's singing group. During the break, the two began chatting. "And she said what she did and I said what I did, and we just looked at each other in shock that we were doing the same thing, and we both thought, 'Nobody else does what I do.'" Beverly laughed at the memory. "We didn't know whether to hug or to slap each other. I mean, it was a letdown and a big nice surprise, too."

As startled as they were to discover one another, the two were in good and growing company. Beverly didn't know it at the time, but while she'd been living abroad, a small industry had begun to develop in the United States, one that wasn't yet referred to as "organizing" but had nevertheless begun garnering attention in American media.

A Brief History of Clutter and Who's Responsible for It

Before delving further into the history of professional organizing, it's worth noting that concern about clutter is not new. The word "clutter" has been used as a noun since the 1570s to mean "things lying in heaps or crowded confusion."[3] Ideas about clutter and its connotations are historically and culturally specific; they vary by time and place as well as across boundaries of class, race, and gender.[4] And while it is tempting to paint certain historical moments as pro-clutter (the gilded 1890s, the patriotic consumerism of the postwar 1940s, and the "greed is good" 1980s) and others as pro-simplicity (the Modernist movement of the 1930s, the counterculture of the 1960s, and the post–Great Recession years[5]), the truth is that at any time in US history, there have been those who embrace the ideals of minimalism and anti-consumerism and those who celebrate their opposite.[6] For example, when Ronald Reagan was elected president in 1980, some took it as a signal that "you didn't have to be ashamed of what you have anymore."[7] Yet just a year later, Duane Elgin published *Voluntary Simplicity*, now considered a founding work of the simplicity movement.[8] Other eras reflect a similar ambivalence. Simple-living advocate Wanda Urbanska recalls, "When I first started talking about this in 1992, I was seen as a wacko zealot."[9] In the same decade, *Real Simple* magazine, with its promise of "beautiful, actionable solutions for simplifying every aspect of your life," garnered 150,000 subscribers before a single issue had been published.[10] Cultural beliefs and tendencies are always more varied and complicated than generational generalizations can convey. And yet, the idea that preventing or reducing clutter is women's work, both at home and in the workplace, has remained surprisingly consistent across US history.

In the nineteenth century, for instance, Victorian design ideals privileged coziness over simplicity. It was understood that women were responsible for implementing these ideas in the home, as middle-class women were encouraged to "personalize their homes with handiwork and bric-a-brac to foster creative expression, moral growth and notions of 'gentility.'"[11]

During the Progressive Era, in contrast, a new emphasis on efficiency and rationality helped shift domestic ideals and aesthetics away from comfy clutter toward more simple, functional designs. This era also ushered in the field of scientific management, in which "efficiency experts" streamlined systems and spaces in order to maximize productivity. In workplaces, the task of implementing efficient systems fell mostly to men—most famously Frederick Winslow Taylor and Frank Gilbreth of *Cheaper by the Dozen* fame.[12] Initially, women struggled to make the case that their domestic expertise translated to the workplace. Frank Gilbreth's wife Lillian, for instance, had a PhD in applied psychology and was a full partner in the couple's business and engineering consulting firm, yet after her husband's death, their major clients canceled or failed to renew their contracts with her.[13]

Lillian Gilbreth had more success, however, in the budding female-led field of home economics, which rebranded the unpaid work of managing a home under the new moniker "domestic science," or "domestic engineering."[14] Famed suffragist and author Charlotte Perkins Gilman, for instance, wrote in 1898 that "The female housekeeper has crowded her limited habitat with unlimited things . . . and the labor of her life is to wait upon these things, and to keep them clean."[15] Reformers like Gilman sought to reduce homemakers' workloads and increase their status by applying the principles of scientific management to the home, although their critiques of poor housekeeping were often directed squarely at the poor, people of color, and new immigrants.[16] Their ideas caught on; by 1913, the *New York Times* was encouraging female readers to rid their houses of "clutter" in order to make their home more attractive, save money, and reduce time spent doing housework or managing servants who do it.[17] Whether cluttered homes were in or out of fashion, women were the ones expected to do the work of aligning domestic spaces with the aesthetic and cultural ideas of the moment.

As more and more women moved into secretarial work over the early twentieth century, women's decluttering endeavors began to be valued outside the home as well, as "office wives" (a common term for secretaries at the time) carried aspects of domesticity into previously all-male workplaces.[18] In a 1928 speech to the Soroptimist Club, the president of the San Francisco League of Business and Professional Women attributed the birth of the modern filing system to women's move from housekeeping jobs into office work, leading the *Los Angeles Times* to report that "Feminine Hands Have Taken Dirt and Clutter Out of Offices."[19] In a sentence too ridiculous not to quote, the article began: "Women's invasion of the realm of business is one of the reasons why it was yanked out of the doldrums, had its face and hands washed and a new ribbon tied into its curls."[20] Even as women's contributions to the workplace were being celebrated, the word "invasion" and the metaphor of beribboned curls suggest that stereotypes of female frivolity remained firmly in place.

The trend toward simpler, clutter-free spaces continued as the rise of Modernist architecture and design between the two world wars ushered in "an ocean of shining chrome, tile and white plaster," furthering the (often racist and classist) association of clutter with degeneracy and disease.[21] Although Modernism was short-lived, its assumptions and aesthetics remained influential, as did the idea, firmly grounded in middle-class norms and privileges, that "cleaning out a space makes it more livable, and makes the person within it more productive, happier, and calm."[22] It wasn't just the women performing this labor who were said to benefit from its results. In 1944, one designer predicted "an urge toward simplification in both design and decoration" following the end of World War II, as "after life in an Army barracks," soldiers returning from war would "be ill at ease in rooms that are filled with too much furniture and nicknacks [sic]."[23] His forecast was spot-on. Maintaining a clutter-free home became yet another thing wives were expected to do for returning veterans, in addition to surrendering their war jobs, tolerating his "outbursts," giving "him lavish—and undemanding—affection," submerging their own sexual desires, and avoiding unfeminine characteristics such as "a preference for colorless nails, slacks, and economic independence."[24]

Within a decade, the clutter-free home was consistently being described not just as an aesthetic, antiseptic ideal or veteran-friendly strategy but as a timeless and intrinsic good. Echoing the domestic engineers of previous decades, the 1949 article "Clutter Deplored" reported that "clutter in the kitchen is one of the homemaker's surest routes to fatigue and fluster."[25] Similarly, a 1951 article suggested ample closet and storage space as a design approach that "naturally cuts down household chores and eliminates clutter."[26] And, in 1952, a profile praised one woman's decision to make "a clean sweep of all the clutter" in her home and "strip down to essentials, to eliminate sentimental attachment to things" because "clutter is for squirrels, not for human beings who need simplicity, quiet, a place to relax from chaos and confusion."[27] As early as the 1950s, clutter was understood as a source of more work *and* more stress, while decluttered spaces were cast as the solution to the busy, chaotic nature of life outside the home.

At this time, a clean, well-decorated home also became a means of achieving social mobility, as "family status [was] elevated through beautification of the home."[28] In mid-twentieth-century America, clutter was generally understood among the middle class as a mark of poor housekeeping, a specifically gendered form of failure attributed solely to female household members.[29] One writer at the time was "perfectly willing to admit" she was "not an excellent housekeeper," because when she looks at what her husband refers to as "clutter," she sees not clutter but "a pile of interesting old magazines and overdue books with which I cannot bear to part."[30] In case others weren't as sure where they fell on the good-housekeeping scale, a 1962 newspaper article invited female readers with "wall-to-wall clutter and a futility room piled high with dirty laundry" to take a "tricky but scientific" quiz to determine exactly how poor a housekeeper they really are.[31] Those who scored low were offered a list of "Five Tips for Bad Housekeepers," including "Get Help: Beg, borrow, steal—but hire some household assistance. Enlist the rest of the family. Sacrifice luxuries to pay for professional cleaning or laundering. Or, get a part-time job to finance it."

The idea that one might pay someone to keep them organized and clutter-free was of course not new. There have always been people who organized other people's things for pay—butlers, maids, housekeepers, secretaries, personal assistants, efficiency experts, architects, and interior designers, among others, not to mention the unpaid work of homemakers. In each of these cases, however, decluttering and reorganizing were *components* of a job, not the job itself. It was only in the 1970s that the organizing and winnowing of personal belongings began to emerge as an occupational category of its own, one that, from the very start, was populated primarily by women.

The First Organizers

In 1975, *New York Magazine* published a special home furnishings issue titled "Get Organized! Neatness Counts." The cover depicted a large bank of small, square orange metal lockers like you might see in a school corridor. Some lockers were closed, others opened to reveal household items—shoes, yarn, a bowl—and, disturbingly, a woman's body subdivided between a column of lockers.

The issue profiled "New York's most organized people," recommended storage solutions in the form of high-end designer

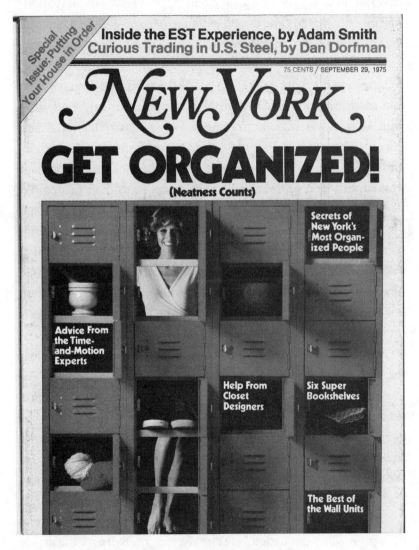

September 29, 1975, issue of *New York Magazine*, featuring the cover story "Get Organized!" Courtesy of *New York Magazine* and Vox Media, LLC. Photo: Harold Krieger.

bookshelves and wall units, and featured advice from time-and-motion specialists. The article "The Second Most Satisfying Thing in the World: Getting Organized" consulted "three sophisticated specialists" on how to deal with "everyday, low-grade environmental disarray."[32] These were not interior designers, whose "glossy, cosmetic solutions . . . should really be the last step in the reorganization process, not the first," the article proclaimed, but organizational experts. The piece included time management expert Alan Lakein, environmental systems designer Robert Propst (inventor of the cubicle), and "systems analyst" Stephanie Winston.[33]

Lakein and Propst worked within the established fields of time-and-motion studies and industrial design, respectively, both fields with roots in scientific management; Winston's occupational category was less clear. A Barnard graduate and former freelance book editor, Winston clarified that she was neither a decorator nor a "neatness expert," but someone who helps people sort their belongings, decide what to keep or discard, and develop systems to get "the specifics of their life" in order.[34] Her company, the Organizing Principle, which she'd founded two years earlier, is described (along with Stella McBride's Denver-based firm Organization Plus) as part of "a new profession that may do for the individual what systems analysts have been doing for industry for years."[35] The new profession went unnamed.

Within three years, that had changed. A 1978 front-page article in the *Washington Post* Style section, "Sinking Under the Clutter: The Organizer Can Get You Out of It," introduced Winston as a "professional organizer" who had "pioneered a new service" when she opened her business in 1973.[36] Winston had the idea for the business, she explained, when a friend mentioned seeing a notice posted at the supermarket offering help with moving. "I suddenly thought, 'Eureka, maybe I can help people get themselves together on a larger scale.'" She wasn't sure it was realistic, but "everyone I spoke to thought it was a good idea."[37] They were right. By 1978, the article reported, Winston, who at the time charged $135 a day for individuals and $225 for corporate clients, was finding it "far more profitable to organize people than words."[38] "You have to admire Stephanie," a former client said, "for taking what sounds like a non-idea—using common sense to help organize people—and turning it into a profitable business."[39]

The use of the term "non-idea," even in the midst of a compliment, signaled a certain skepticism toward Winston's work, and her ability to get paid handsomely for doing it. Later in the article, Winston explains that organization, like diet and exercise, "should be simple so that people will stick with it." In response, the author questions why, if it's so simple, people even need Winston's help, especially "at $200 a day." It is worth noting that no such skepticism was directed at Winston in the previous article, which aligned her work with that of male systems analysts. Nevertheless, this sense that there was something slightly absurd, even a little exploitative, about organizing people for money—especially this much money—permeates early coverage of the profession and its practitioners, of whom there were at least a dozen by the end of the 1970s.

For although the *Post* article's title refers to Winston as "*The* Organizer," she was actually not the only one. That same article states that her success had "spawned a flattering group of imitators, the new breed of professional organizers."[40] Winston's book, *Getting Organized*, published in 1978, is generally recognized as the first professional organizing book, but the claim that other organizers were mere imitators is debatable. It's more accurate to say that, like Charles Darwin and Alfred Russel Wallace, who arrived separately but simultaneously at nearly identical theories of evolution and natural selection, other people were having the same "non-idea" as Winston at the very same time, and nearly all of them were running into the same skepticism that Winston had.[41]

By the late 1970s, New Yorkers had at least six professional organizers (all women) to choose from. Winston was described as "the longest established and most expensive of the city's organizers," but at least one other, Denslow Brown, had been running an organizing business since 1974.[42] Another of those early New York organizers, Barbara Hemphill, brought her business with her when she relocated to Washington, DC, in 1979. The year before, Hemphill and her husband had returned to the United States after five years in India, where they'd adopted three orphaned children. As Hemphill told me in a phone interview more than thirty years later, her husband's nonprofit salary wasn't enough to support their expanded family, so she needed to find a way to bring in money without taking a full-time job. She wanted to prioritize time with her family, plus she'd been a teacher previously and hadn't liked the rigidity of working set hours. The solution, she figured, was "to identify a problem in the world that I could solve, that people would pay me for." She'd heard people talk about their troubles with disorganization, "about how they hadn't eaten off the dining room table in months because it was piled full of papers, or they couldn't file their income taxes 'cause they couldn't find their receipts, or they were fighting with their kids about their cluttered room or their husband about stuff on the counter and they were trying to cook and just stuff like that." Organization had always been one of her strengths, so she decided to give it a go.[43] "And so I took $7 out of the grocery money [to pay for a newspaper ad], which is a big deal because I used to walk twenty blocks because I didn't have fifty cents for the bus. The ad said 'Disorganized? I organize closets, files, kitchens, you name it, call Barbara Hemphill.'"

The first three calls were from men trying to pick her up. The fourth was from a newly widowed woman whose husband, an attorney, had died and left behind two offices full of disorganized paperwork—one at home, one at his workplace. His wife had no idea what to do. "She didn't know that she was my first client," Hemphill told me, "and I didn't tell her. I just went in and started sorting things and saying, 'Okay, I need to talk to the accountant about this and the stockbroker about this and the attorney about this.' And that was kind of how I started." To promote her service, Hemphill began speaking at church groups, garden clubs, parent-teacher groups, anywhere that would have her.

When the family moved to Washington, DC, Hemphill decided to get some business advice. She'd never intended to start a business— "it was, to me, just like, okay, there's a problem. I know how to solve it. I need money and people will pay you money for this"—but now it seemed she had one. So, in 1979 she visited the Small Business Association and told them, "I have an idea for a business and I would like somebody to help me put a plan together because I'm a music major."[44] The all-male group "just laughed me out of the room," Hemphill recalled. "No way, lady," they said, "that's not a business."[45] They told her she was crazy, that no one would pay to have someone organize their closets and kitchens. Recalling the slight when we spoke by phone in 2019, Hemphill remembered how vindicated she'd felt when Julie Morgenstern, an organizer she'd helped train, received the Small Business Administration Outstanding Woman Entrepreneur Award in 2003.

Hemphill was not the only one who struggled to have her organizing work taken seriously. Convincing people to pay for services that had previously been provided for free by (usually female) family members, or subsumed within low-status jobs such as housekeeping or secretarial work, wasn't easy, especially for organizers who planned to work primarily in homes.[46] When Standolyn Robertson graduated from high school in Florida in the 1970s, she told me, she and some classmates were taken by a local business leader on a tour of his company.[47] He asked the students what they wanted to do after graduating. When Standolyn's turn came, she tried to convey the career she was envisioning. "I was explaining this *thing*," she told me, "I didn't use words like 'professional organizer.' . . . I said to him, 'I'm going to go in,' and I can't even say for sure that I used the word *organize*, 'I'm going to go in, I'm going to redo their kitchen.' And he said to me, 'Oh, you want to be a wife.'[48] I go, 'No, no, no! I want to do it and then *go home*.' That was the best way that I could explain it. That I was going to play house in someone else's house and then go home." The businessman couldn't seem to separate the *identity* of a wife with the *labor* often performed by wives, and remained unconvinced. So, for a time, Robertson dropped the idea. It would take a few more decades and many jobs across many different industries before Robertson finally created the organizing business she'd been envisioning since her teens.

Across the country, around the same time, other would-be organizers were having better luck. In 1979, a *Los Angeles Times* article offered a "sampling" of "individuals whose goal it is to make your life easier." [49] In addition to personal shoppers, party planners, and mobile disco units, the list included Beverly Hills organizer Maxine Ordesky. Ordesky, formerly a full-time homemaker, had been looking for something to do while her young sons were in school most of the day. The family didn't need money—her husband's income supported them amply—but "I was bored," she told me when I interviewed her in 2019. Ordesky describes herself as "not the type" to spend her days lunching and shopping. She'd worked in offices before she married but didn't want to go back; she needed a more flexible job so she could work around her children's schedules. It was actually her husband's idea that she go into organizing. She'd always been very organized, "to my husband's horror," she laughed. "I think he was hoping I'd spend all my organizing energy on other people."

Her husband had read a *Wall Street Journal* article about Stephanie Winston and told Maxine, "You should read this." "And I did," she remembered. "And I was really intrigued, but not intrigued enough to do anything about it." One morning soon after, her husband was watching *The Today Show* before he left for work and heard Winston being introduced. He recognized her name and called to his wife, "Come in, come in, watch this! There's a woman on here doing something you could do!" She watched the segment and thought, "I *can* do that."

She came up with a name, the Creative Organizer, and in 1975 she ran her first ad in the back of *Los Angeles Magazine*. "I never in a million years thought the phone would ring," she said, "and it did immediately. So I was off and running." She started out charging $15 an hour. One day a potential client called. "He was talking to me about coming in and organizing his office and we had this whole long conversation." At the end of the call, he asked how much she charged. When she told him her rate, he was silent. She worried he thought it was too high and asked, "Is there a problem?" "Well, yes," he told her, "actually there is. If that's all you're charging, you don't do what I think you do." Relating the story, she paused to ask me, shoulders raised, "What do you say to that?" She couldn't salvage the call and lost the client, but immediately raised her rates.

Within a few years, Ordesky met another Los Angeles organizer, Stephanie Culp. Tired of the secretarial and waitressing jobs she'd been working, in 1979 Culp decided to start her own business. At that time, she told me, "women just didn't start their own businesses. Women were not entrepreneurs. You had Mary Kay selling cosmetics or you had Tupperware housewives selling Tupperware. That was it in terms of entrepreneurial stuff for women. . . . I don't think today's young women can even imagine how it was back then." But Culp was determined to make it work. Billing herself as "The Grinning Idiot," she ran a classified ad offering all-purpose errand services: "Have your idiot work done by pros. Nothing is too moronic or mundane. Call The Grinning Idiot."[50] The ad worked. She walked dogs, cleaned up after parties, "whatever walked in the door," she recalled during our interview. One day at a client's house, Culp noticed the place was filled with moving boxes. She asked the client if she'd just moved in. The woman replied that she'd lived there a year and a half. "You know," Culp told her, "I could help you with this if you want." Thus began Culp's transformation from Grinning Idiot to professional organizer. Although she quickly found enough work to support herself through organizing, when she told her family what she was doing for work, they asked, "Why don't you get a real job?" Back then, she explained to me, organizers were perceived as glorified housekeepers. "It didn't matter how you explained it to them," she remembered. "They still equated it with hiring a housekeeper or a cleaning crew."[51]

Gender and the Struggle for Occupational Legitimacy

Despite the many differences between them—married or single, mothers or child-free, working for the money or just because they wanted to—the organizers I describe above encountered continual resistance to the idea that organizing is *real* work. Winston's business was described as a "non-idea" even by her own satisfied client; Hemphill's first callers wanted to date her, not hire her, then the men of the SBA dismissed organizing as "not a business"; a teenage Robertson struggled to convey to the local businessman how her dream job differed from housewifery; Ordesky lost a potential client because he assumed her low rates (and perhaps her gender) indicated a lack of ability; Culp's own family members told her to get a "real job." These reactions differ in detail, but they demonstrate the challenges facing new professions populated by women who aim to charge for household and related tasks generally understood as women's work.

Like homemaking and housekeeping, organizing is labor performed primarily by women, often in the home, that involves providing services to other people. This trifecta of characteristics is not an auspicious one for a budding profession; these overlapping categories—women's work, domestic work, care work, and service work—all tend to receive lower pay and status than other forms of work performed by other kinds of people.[52] Economist Adam Smith, the "father of capitalism,"[53] went so far as to designate as "unproductive" *all* labor that involved providing services to other people, effectively arguing that most of the work most women spent their lives performing, whether for love or money, has no value at all.[54] Thus, as others have found in their research among personal concierges and life coaches—both fields whose tasks sometimes overlap with those of professional organizers—practitioners in these types of new fields struggle to have both their *work* seen as something worth paying for and *themselves* seen as skilled professionals.[55]

Early organizers needed potential clients to understand what it was they did for a living, but they wanted their work to be understood in a particular way, one that conferred upon this new profession a legitimacy that would translate into higher pay and more respect. To make the case for the value of what they do, organizers in those early years employed two different, somewhat contradictory approaches. The first, less common tack was to reject the tendency to devalue domestic work and women's work more generally. Back in 1974, even before she was referring to herself as a professional organizer, Stephanie Winston tackled head-on the dismissive attitude many people had toward the work of managing a home.

Although she said she enjoyed all forms of organizing, Winston explained she was particularly interested in household organizing "because it's been neglected": "I believe that running a household is a true executive/administrative enterprise . . . People may sniff at housewifery but, frankly, I'd like to see the reactions of a typical executive were he or she suddenly faced with coordinating the activities of three to five or six different people, maintaining life support systems for them—and all this very often on top of a regular job."[56] Winston makes the case that running a household requires a complex set of skills—one many business elites, whether male or female, would be hard-pressed to master. She also nods to the fact that by the mid-1970s, many women running households were simultaneously working for pay outside the home. (Despite the popular mythology around the 1950s suburban housewife, American women's labor force participation rose steadily following the end of World War II.[57]) Other organizers similarly embraced the association of organizing with female homemaking, naming their businesses Major Mom, Your Wife's Wife, or the Occasional Wife, whose logo is a drawing of a slender woman wearing a 1950s-style party dress, apron, pearls, and heels.[58] While these names and images reinforce certain gender stereotypes, they do so in the course of celebrating, rather than rejecting, the value of women and their work as mothers, wives, and homemakers.

More frequently, however, early organizers leaned as far away from such gendered imagery as possible.[59] Leaving the gender and class stigmas around housewifery and domestic work firmly in place, they vociferously denied similarities between those jobs and their own, emphasizing that they were neither homemakers nor housekeepers. To support that claim, many organizers—both then and now—refuse to do more than cursory cleaning on the job. They might wipe down a shelf before they load it back up with books or do a quick vacuum at the end of the job to pick up any detritus of the organizing process, but they are emphatic that cleaning is not part of what they are hired to do.

Instead, early organizers emphasized parallels between organizing and higher-status professions. As early as 1979, one organizer described herself as "a physician for those who suffer from chronic disorganization."[60] In 1982, another framed herself as "a physician for messy people" and "a doctor for the disorganized."[61] As therapy and therapeutic language became increasingly common, other organizers referred to themselves as "clutter therapists" or "the paper therapist."[62] (I return to the relationship between organizing and therapy in chapter 5.) Both medicine and psychology are *professions*, rather than jobs, in the sense that they require specific degrees and credentials. As fields long dominated by upper-class men (although both are majority female as of 2023), medicine and psychology also carried with them a gravitas and legitimacy that homemaking and housekeeping lacked. By connecting their work to that of doctors and therapists, organizers sought to establish the legitimacy of organizing as a profession and themselves as professionals, albeit at the expense of potential solidarity with similarly female-dominated occupations.

Perhaps the most obvious step early organizers took in this direction was calling themselves "professional organizers," as opposed to just "organizers."[63] I once had a Who's-on-First-like discussion with a fellow anthropologist about the term "professional organizer." To her, it made intuitive sense that "professional organizers" would be those who organize businesses (professional spaces), while "personal organizers" work with individuals to organize their homes (personal spaces). I explained to her that all organizers who organize other people for money are "professional organizers"; the adjective "professional" describes the *person* doing the organizing—they are professionals, not amateurs—not the *kind* of organizing they do. As I reflect back on that conversation, it does seem like overkill to include "professional" in a profession's title. Doctors do not refer to themselves as "professional doctors," nor do we read about "professional lawyers" or "professional professors." Practitioners in these fields don't need to go to such lengths to signal their status—their disciplines' long and distinguished histories and specialized credentials do that for them. Early organizers had none of these things. Each woman was waging her own small, independent battle to be taken seriously by the people around her. In order for that to change, a critical mass of organizers would first have to meet one another. In 1983, around the same time Beverly Clower and her choirmate were debating whether to hug or duke it out, that's exactly what they did.

Not every organizing job is an intensely emotional experience. I had posted on the NAPO Los Angeles Yahoo group that I was looking for unpaid assisting jobs in order to better understand how organizers work. Lara, whose decision to leave corporate employment I describe in chapter 3, emailed me about a job unpacking and organizing a home for a family who had just relocated from the East Coast. I jumped at the opportunity, and on a midsummer morning found myself waiting in a long line of cars to enter the Oaks, the elite gated community in Calabasas where some of the Kardashians live. When I made it to the gatehouse, I showed my ID and the guard confirmed my name was on the list of expected visitors.

I pulled up to the house, which was easy to spot thanks to the large moving truck parked out front. Lara and her assistant Brittney arrived soon after. We were greeted at the door by Mark, father of two and husband to Cece, who was upstairs tending to the couple's newborn daughter. Their toddler son trailed his father as he gave us a tour of the large Spanish-style home. The job would take place over multiple days, but today's focus was unpacking the kitchen.

While Cece's newborn napped upstairs, Lara and Cece went through the empty kitchen, discussing how Cece liked to have her kitchen organized. As Cece explained her preferences, Lara placed labeled sticky notes on some of the drawers and cabinets ("utensils," "pots," "baking"). We would figure out the details as we went, once we'd seen how much space the items in a particular category would take up.

This job was unique in that there was no pressing need to discard any items. At more than 5,000 square feet, the house was much larger than the family's previous home. And although Cece preferred how the kitchen at her old home had been laid out, the new large, open kitchen had ample storage, plus a spacious walk-in pantry.

Our first task was to locate and gather all the boxes labeled "kitchen" or "pantry" from the main living room, where the movers had placed them, alongside the boxes destined for the other first-floor rooms, including the living room, dining room, and Mark's home office. This required a candid conversation with the lead organizer. I was fourteen weeks pregnant at the time and wasn't supposed to be lifting any heavy boxes. After a quick group hug at my happy news, Lara directed me to take over unpacking duty. She and Brittney brought the boxes in, and I started opening them to see what was inside. Most items were wrapped in packing paper, so I spent most of the day cross-legged on the kitchen floor surrounded by piles of packing material. Every so often I gathered up the surrounding mess and moved it to the recycling bin in the garage.

Once all the boxes were inside and opened, Brittney, Lara, and I set about organizing the various items into categories—glassware, mugs, dinnerware sets. For most of the day, Cece was out running errands or upstairs watching the children, so the three of us had the kitchen to ourselves. Brittney, a blond in her thirties, ran her own small organizing business, specializing in organizing photos and memorabilia. She'd been in business longer than Lara, but Lara's business had taken off so quickly she was regularly hiring Brittney and other organizers to assist her on big jobs. The two enjoyed working together; they were both "energizer bunnies," they told me—high energy and in constant motion.

As we chatted, Brittney and I occasionally interrupted to ask Lara's opinion. Should vases be stored in the kitchen or pantry? Should we keep dinnerware sets together or organize by item type (dinner plates, salad plates, bowls, etc.)? Would a drawer or cabinet be better for storing Cece's huge collection of Tupperware and other reusable containers? We set aside a section of items to confer with Cece about the next time she popped into the kitchen.

At one point, I was tasked with gathering together all of the family's mugs. There were multiple matched sets of mugs like the sort you purchase in a set of six or twelve from Crate & Barrel or Ikea, plus a random assortment—Best Mom Ever, one from Café du Monde in New Orleans, mugs featuring photos of the family, funny sayings about the lifesaving virtues of caffeine. The more boxes we opened, the more mugs we unearthed. Cece had directed us to store the mugs in a cabinet shelf just above the countertop where the coffee maker would live. The shelf was wide and deep enough for three rows of mugs, but it would prove a challenge to fit all these mugs into that one space.

The next time Cece passed through the kitchen, Lara asked her if she wanted to take a look and get rid of any of the forty or so mugs I had gathered onto sheets of newspaper spread out in a corner of the kitchen. Cece looked over the mugs spread out before her and said that no, she wanted to keep them all. Lara then suggested she might choose the mugs the family used most often for the shelf and store the rest in the pantry or a less centrally located cabinet. Cece considered the assembled mugs again and said the family used all of them regularly, so they should all go on the same shelf. So that's what we did. Stacked three rows deep, with a fourth row of mugs perched atop the others in the back row, we fit them all in. Did I believe that a family with two adults, a toddler, and a newborn could use more than three dozen mugs on a "regular" basis? I did not. But when you have the space, you don't necessarily have to make the same hard decisions about what to keep as you would in, say, a one-bedroom apartment with a kitchenette.

At the end of a seven-hour day, as we packed up to head home, Lara took out her checkbook to pay Brittney and me. I reminded Lara that working alongside her was part of my research, and that I didn't want to be paid. She insisted, and I declined again. Not one to go down easy, Lara grinned, handed me a check for $100, and said, "Then it's not a payment, it's a gift for the baby, and you can't say no to that." And with that, she had me. I accepted the check with thanks and drove home. When I arrived back at our condo, I opened the cabinet that held our mismatched coffee mugs, selected three of my least favorite, and set them aside to donate to the office kitchen at work.

2

Collaborative Competitors

The Growth of a Profession

This chapter details the rise of organizing's first professional association. I describe the steps organizers took to build a professional community and how they worked together to contest dismissive perceptions of them and their work. In some respects, the history of the organizing industry is a feminist success story that adds a new, yet untold chapter to the history of women's work in the United States. Together, organizers worked to build a female-dominated professional community that was inclusive, collegial, and fun, rejecting what they saw as the stodgy, cutthroat nature of other, male-dominated professions. In doing so, they positioned their gender as an asset, or at least not a liability. At the same time, early organizers bought into certain established ideas about professionalism—especially those that privileged full-time work and drew rigid boundaries between work and family responsibilities—that actually worked against them as female business owners and continue to cause divisions among them. As well, while organizers rallied together against gender discrimination, they minimized the impact other differences—especially class and race— had on individuals' ability to succeed in this new career. Ultimately, the profession organizers built serves as a model for what a female-led, collaborative occupational community can look like while also reminding us how challenging it can be, even with the best of intentions, to escape the constraints of the culture in which you're operating.

· · ·

By the early 1980s, professional organizers were cropping up in large cities across the United States. Some knew of each other, often because friends and family mailed them news clippings about people doing similar work in other places. A few, like Maxine Ordesky and Stephanie Culp in Los Angeles, had forged friendships and were already sharing leads and strategies for growing their businesses. Many others were, as freelance secretary Beverly Clower had been, still under the impression they were "the world's first and only" of their kind.

In 1981, Karen Shortridge, a former business manager with a master's degree in counseling psychology, started her San Diego company, Organizers Unlimited. During a bout of unemployment, Shortridge had been looking for "a way to make ends meet."[1] She also wanted a "job that brought together as many talents as possible. And allowed her to be her own boss. And gave 'strokes' in a way that the 'sterile environment' of a large corporation no longer could."[2] Organizing checked all the boxes, so she gave it a try. She was profiled on the front page of the *Los Angeles Times* less than a year after she began organizing and began to receive an avalanche of calls from potential clients as well as from others looking to start organizing businesses.[3] Soon after, Shortridge met another California organizer, Susan Rich, who was "'fit to be tied' at the thought of new competition."[4] After a "somewhat guarded" meeting over lunch, the two decided to bring together the people working in, or hoping to work in, this new field. In 1983, when a local paper wrote an article about her, Shortridge added a notice at the end inviting others interested in organizing to a meeting later that week at Rich's home.

Within a year, ten to twelve organizers, all based in Southern California, most of them white women in their thirties to fifties, were meeting monthly at one another's homes. At those early meetings, Southern California organizers got to know one another and talked about their work. It was exciting, attendees recalled, to connect with others who were not only organized, like themselves, but also hoping to create a business out of that skill. Working with people who are disorganized can be stressful, even overwhelming at times, as can running one's own business. Coming together allowed organizers to sympathize with and support one another while also exchanging practical strategies and advice, building a new community around their nascent profession.

For some attendees, like NAPO co-founder Ann Gambrell, these early meetings were life changing. When I interviewed Ann at her clean, cozy Los Angeles home in 2014, she greeted me at the door, saying, "You have just passed Organizing 101—you're on time!" Born just outside Chicago in the 1940s, Gambrell, who passed away in 2022, said her job options were limited growing up. "The only professions at that time for women," she recalled, were "teaching, nursing, and hairdressing." She chose nursing and spent twenty-three years as a psychiatric nurse. In 1964, she moved to Torrance (a suburb in LA's South Bay) with her husband and young children. She started nursing at a local hospital and helping her husband with his insurance business.

Nearly two decades later, a women's group she'd joined hosted a guest speaker on organizing. "All the while she was talking," Gambrell recalled, "I was improving on her talk in my head. I was not a speaker, but I was thinking, 'Oh, I would have said this. I would have given this example or told this story which would have made that point.'" That night, on the drive home, she decided to become an organizer.

She began teaching organizing classes at a local adult school to promote her business. She also joined Leads Club, a networking group for female small business owners started a few years prior by image consultant Ali Lassen, a single mother of five.[5] At a Leads Club meeting, a woman told her about a group of local organizers who'd been meeting. Gambrell found their number, called, got the address, and drove up to Los Angeles for the meeting. She was intimidated by how much more experienced they seemed to be—"I was such a novice," she said. "I had no idea what they were talking about! But I knew that it was something I wanted to do." When she arrived home from that first meeting, Gambrell told me, she called her husband into the bedroom. When he asked how the meeting went, she told him, "I don't know where these women are going, but I'm going with them." She laughed, remembering that moment three decades later: "I mean, that's exactly literally what I said. 'I'm going with them.'"

In some respects, these early organizers were a varied group. Some had the financial support of working spouses. Others were single and entirely self-supporting. Some had children, some did not. Some were wealthy, others barely scraping by. Some worked primarily in residential organizing, helping individuals and families reorganize and declutter their living spaces. Others worked mostly in workplaces, setting up new offices, creating filing systems, and streamlining information flows and work processes.

In other respects, they had a lot in common. All were white women, mostly thirty or older. All had completed high school and most had some additional schooling, whether college or secretarial or nursing school. All had worked in other jobs previously, including those who'd stopped working when they had children. As the stories in the previous chapter attest, they all made a conscious decision *not* to stay in or return to their previous occupations; some needed a job they could integrate with parenting responsibilities, others craved work that was more fun, more varied, or more meaningful than what they'd been doing before.

And of course, they all loved organizing. As one organizer who attended those early meetings remembered: "You walk inside that meeting room and all of the sudden you feel like you've come home. Everybody in the room is just like you and we've been the odd man out, the oddballs forever. . . . We've been the perfectionists that nobody respected or appreciated except when it came down to bringing them success. You know, we were never paid for the talents, the skills that we possess. So being in the same room with like minds, that blew my socks off that first time." While their individual strengths and temperaments varied, most organizers at these early meetings shared what organizer Maxine Ordesky calls "a generalized personality." Organizers "tend to be perfectionists," Ordesky told me. "They tend to be caring people, and outgoing. They tend to have strong personalities."[6]

Those strong personalities occasionally clashed. One attendee complained that these early meetings often devolved into what she called "coffee klatches," entirely social gatherings with no clear direction or agenda. Within the first year, a divide emerged within the group between those who wanted to formalize their gatherings into a professional association and those who did not. Some organizers preferred to spend their time and energy building their own businesses; others may have been hesitant to ally with their own competitors. But for many new organizers, starting a professional association was an important step toward establishing legitimacy for their new occupation, one other once-new occupations—such as realtors, interior designers, and home economists—had used to help define, oversee, and advocate for their young fields.[7]

And so, in 1984, a group of about a dozen organizers separated and officially founded the Association of Professional Organizers (APO), soon renamed the National Association of Professional Organizers (NAPO).[8] In 1985, the group elected its first slate of officers—Beverly Clower, Stephanie Culp, Ann Gambrell, Maxine Ordesky, and a former accountant named Jeanne Shorr—who are now referred to as NAPO's founders.[9] At the time of NAPO's founding, there were already many all-female professional associations in the United States—the National Federation of Business and Professional Women's Clubs was founded as early as 1919, the National Association of Bank Women just two years later.[10] Yet although NAPO's original members were all women, most if not all of them white, the group never restricted membership by gender, race, or any other identity (which is not to say all people feel equally welcome in the group, a topic I return to later in this chapter). And so, while men have never accounted for more than 5 percent of the group's membership, and usually far less, NAPO was consciously created as a group defined by the nature of the work they were doing, not the sex of the people doing it.

In its early years, NAPO focused on generating awareness of professional organizing as a whole. As the members saw it, broader exposure for the field would be a rising tide that lifted all of their boats. After all, if a potential client didn't even know organizing existed, it didn't yet matter which organizer she'd choose to hire. There was still a long way to go before people stopped equating organizers with house cleaners or confusing them with labor organizers. To that end, the founders each played to their strengths. Those who enjoyed public speaking gave talks and led meetings; the writers among them published books and articles about organizing, careful to include mentions of NAPO and often promoting one another's businesses. Those with accounting and business experience handled the finances, set up bylaws, and secured 501(c)(3) status as a nonprofit organization. The more outgoing and diplomatic among them interacted with event attendees and new members around the country. The most tenacious waged a three-year, eventually successful battle with the California Yellow Pages to include an entry for "professional organizers" in the telephone directory.[11]

In 1987, they held the first-ever professional organizing conference. They invited organizers from around the country to gather in Los Angeles. The group had grown rapidly since its founding, from around a dozen to more than a hundred, but membership was still small. NAPO leaders worried that conference attendees would be dismayed at the sight of an empty conference room, undermining their efforts to present organizing as a serious and growing occupation. "We wanted to look like we were somebody," Ann Gambrell recalled. They invited friends and family members, she told me, "to bulk up the room." "We padded it with some of our friends," Stephanie Culp said in our interview, "because we wanted it to look successful. We wanted it to look successful, and it did look successful, and it was successful."

At the last minute, keynote speaker Fritz Coleman, a local weatherman, canceled. (Struggling to remember Coleman's name during our interview, Gambrell called out to her husband, who was watching television in an adjacent room. He supplied the name. "He's my memory," she told me. "If he dies before me, I'm going to kill him.") They found a last-minute replacement in comedian George Wallace and the show went on. Within a few years, the conference became an annual event, growing from around fifty attendees at that first gathering to more than 500 in recent years.

NAPO's membership also continued to grow, more than doubling every year from 1985 to 1990.[12] In 1988, those seeking a directory of members could send a business-sized self-addressed stamped envelope (39 cents postage at the time) to a California PO Box.[13] (A year later, the same directory would cost five dollars.[14]) And of course there were many organizers across the United States, successful ones with long-standing businesses, who might not have been NAPO members but who nevertheless benefited from the organization's efforts to increase the field's visibility.

Collaborative Competitors

From the start, NAPO's leaders sought to build a professional community that was more collaborative than competitive. In those early days, "we were very generous with each other," Stephanie Culp recalled in an interview with me. "We didn't have the sense of competition at all." In part, this was a strategic decision. A professional association was envisioned as a mutually beneficial endeavor, one that would earn publicity for the field and for organizers' individual businesses. "We were never competitors," Beverly Clower told me. "NAPO members were colleagues," she continued, "and we were all trying to build our businesses. And we recognized very quickly that if we built our business and helped other people build their businesses, that's how people are going to know that we exist." Those who disagreed with this approach, one founder posited, wouldn't have joined the group in the first place. "If you're afraid to share," she explained to me, "you're not going to join NAPO, because they are a group of very committed professionals who share what they know with each other because we know it's for all of our own good."

Thinking back to her business's early years, Clower wonders whether she might have given up and taken another secretarial job if she hadn't met that other organizer at choir practice and eventually found her way to the group that became NAPO. "We really were stronger together," she told me. "Together we were better, together we were stronger, and it helped individually as well as the association." As another longtime organizer put it, "it's not about getting a bigger piece of the pie, it's about making the pie bigger." With such statements, organizers reject the neoliberal idea that economic success depends on unfettered competition. Instead, they envision a collaborative approach where practitioners in the same industry can succeed together, rather than at one another's expense.[15]

Many organizers explicitly contrasted NAPO's female-led, collaborative culture with that of other, male-dominated professions. One early NAPO member worked "in the corporate world" for twenty years before starting her organizing business. In her previous jobs, she said, "it was all cutthroat and sarcastic and politics, and I was sick of it, just sick of it. Get me out of here!" Coming to NAPO, she remembered, "really did feel like I was coming home, because it was warm, it was generous, lots of hugs." Another organizer echoed this description of NAPO's "huggy" culture, saying she didn't imagine a conference of accountants, for example, "would be all that touchy-feely" (although she added a disclaimer that her own accountant is actually a very nice guy). In this respect, NAPO functioned not just as a vehicle to advance the profession but also as a safe, affirming space for its female members.

Another longtime organizer, when describing NAPO's culture to me, referenced an episode of the show *Downton Abbey* that aired a few days before our interview. In that episode, two male obstetricians had conflicting diagnoses and a female patient died as a result of their prideful refusal to collaborate or compromise. "That would never happen in NAPO," she said. "They would collaborate, and they would not be antagonistic towards one another, and they would not put the other one down. It is a cooperative thing that you do for the good of your client, or for the good of each other." Although she saw this cooperative approach as characteristically female, she quickly noted that male NAPO members had embraced the "collaborative competitor" ideal as well. Here, the benefits of collaboration are expanded to include the good of organizers' clients, in addition to organizers themselves.

I don't want to overidealize organizers' collaborative approach. I occasionally heard stories of organizers who stole clients or ideas from one another or otherwise behaved in unethical or un-collegial ways.

For the most part, though, my experience of NAPO in the twenty-first century aligned with the founders' ideals. Organizers do tend to be, as one journalist described them, "a cheerful and orderly tribe."[16] I was the beneficiary of many welcoming hugs at NAPO meetings and conferences, which were usually lively, friendly affairs.

Despite ostensibly competing for the same client base, organizers today still regularly cite other organizers as their biggest source of clients: overbooked organizers pass jobs to less established peers; people who land big jobs hire other organizers to assist them; clients who require a type of assistance one organizer is not able or willing to provide—organizing computer files, for instance, or managing an estate sale—are handed off to specialists in that area. I lost count of the number of times different organizers told me it simply wasn't necessary for organizers to compete with one another, because there was more than enough work to go around.[17] In this respect, NAPO still functions as it was intended, as a space for organizers to connect with, support, mentor, and educate one another while enhancing the reputation and visibility of their individual businesses and their shared field. At the NAPO Los Angeles meetings I attended, for example, conversations between organizers might cover how cute someone's outfit was or how one's kids were faring, but they were equally likely to concern how to handle an especially challenging client, how to price organizing packages, thoughts on manila folders (a more divisive topic than you'd imagine), or who needs assistants for an upcoming project. In these exchanges, organizers both inform and connect to one another, strengthening their professional community while helping each other manage the emotional and pragmatic challenges of owning a small business.

In rejecting overt competition and fostering affectionate, mutually beneficial relationships between members, NAPO's early leaders challenged certain male-dominated ideals of what professionalism, and professionals, look like. They built an association that fit the sort of work they did and the sort of people who tended to do it, creating a novel space for (mostly) female entrepreneurs. In this sense, the history of organizing is part of the larger history of American feminism;

it shines light on the accomplishments of groups of women that have gone unnoticed or been minimized in a society that doesn't tend to value women or their work. Regardless of whether early organizers thought of themselves as feminists—some did, some didn't—they built an occupation founded, led, and mostly populated by women. They did so by employing skills and strengths typically attributed to women and insisting on the value of themselves and their work.

Despite these impressive gains, there were drawbacks to the way organizers went about trying to legitimize their field. They discarded old beliefs about competition and collegiality, but held on to other vestiges of a male-dominated model of professionalism, especially when it came to women with children. Nowhere is this tendency clearer than in organizers' discussions of "the dabbler."

The Dabbler

I heard the same story multiple times from multiple organizers about a businessman—his name and industry were never specified—who'd been invited to speak at one of NAPO's early conferences. Addressing the assembled organizers, nearly all of whom were women, he told them they would need to behave in a more businesslike manner if they wanted organizing to ever be anything more than a "cottage industry."[18] The story was often accompanied by an eye roll at this sexist guy who talked down to organizers at their own conference. At the same time, nearly every time the story came up it was being used to illustrate why organizers *do* need to take their businesses seriously, why they *do* need to behave in a "professional" manner. As annoying as this fellow may have been, his comments were taken seriously, even decades later, and even by those who bristled at his criticism. I think the story still circulates, long after the man's name has been forgotten, because it gets at the heart of an enduring sore spot within the profession, namely the idea that people won't take organizers seriously if they don't act more like typically male professionals. It's an ironic standard for a profession led by women, yet one that some organizers still choose to enforce upon each other.

From NAPO's earliest days, organizers and guest speakers at chapter meetings and national conferences have regularly emphasized the importance of behaving professionally and treating your business "like a business," as opposed to a hobby.[19] In the name of professionalism, organizers have been exhorted to join NAPO, set up a website, ensure their business follows the NAPO Code of Ethics and, after the program was established in 2007, become a Certified Professional Organizer (CPO),[20] among other things. Failure to do so was generally understood as a lack of professionalism, one that was often framed as a gender-specific flaw. For example, many new organizers struggle to make the leap to charging for their services, especially after organizing for free for friends and family.[21] At a NAPO conference session for new organizers, the female presenter suggested this was a challenge unique to women. "Women," she generalized, "need to talk about money more. Women are not comfortable talking about money." That's something you need to get over, she explained, if you want to run a business. Role-playing an organizer who'd done the math and arrived at a hypothetical hourly rate, she looked down at her imaginary rate sheet and turned to the crowd, hunching her shoulders with a worried expression. "Is that too much?" she asked, cringing away from the audience. The mostly female audience erupted with laughter, recognizing in her performance their own discomfort around charging for their work. The presenter straightened up and squared her shoulders. "If you want to do charitable work, go do that. But don't run your business as a charitable organization. Try to take your insecurity out of it and think in a linear, logical way about the value of your business." It went without saying that she saw this insecurity, this illogical desire not to offend or overreach, as, like not talking about money, a woman thing.[22] "Your neighbor," she concluded, "will always see you as a neighbor. Your sister will always see you as a sister." By charging them anyway, even at a low rate, "*You'll* see yourself as a professional." In this instance and many others, while professionalism was framed as a non-gendered set of beliefs and behaviors, *unprofessionalism* was understood as the province of women. This distinction became especially relevant when organizers set out to defend their occupation and its reputation against perceived threats in their midst.

In theory, credentials like NAPO membership and CPO certification serve as "marks of distinction" that allow organizers to differentiate themselves from people they see as less qualified and less competent, such as amateur organizers and house cleaners.[23] In practice, few clients have heard of NAPO, let alone CPO certification. Even organizers who believe strongly in the value of certification say not a single client has ever asked whether they were certified, nor, for that matter, whether their business was insured, nor, in most cases, how many years' experience they have.[24] As well, many of the most experienced organizers are not certified because their businesses were well established before the credential even existed. In short, until NAPO is able to "educate the market" as to the value of CPO certification, anyone can call themselves a professional organizer.[25]

But if all organizers are "professional organizers," experienced organizers have few concrete and consistent ways to distinguish between themselves and even the least experienced practitioners.[26] As a result, many organizers turn to other means of identifying the "unprofessionals" among them. In doing so, they rely on established models of professionalism that privilege certain kinds of workers over others, the same sort of standards male business leaders had used to disparage early organizers and their chosen profession.

If "professional" is the height of what most organizers aspire to be, the "dabbler" is its opposite. Dabblers, multiple organizers told me, are people who did not take the work seriously.[27] Working part-time, neglecting to create a website, using earnings as "pin money" (rather than income to sustain a household)—these are the traits of a dabbler.[28] And, although it was rarely stated directly, there seemed to be a sense that single women working as organizers were, by definition, *not* dabblers, while female organizers married to men were more suspect, especially if they had young children.[29]

One married longtime organizer with a working spouse told me she has noticed that other organizers seem very interested in her husband's occupation and income. When another organizer asks her what her husband does for a living, she says she can't help but wonder why they're asking. "Where did that question come from? You don't even know him!" Occasionally she'll respond, "Well, when you meet him, why don't you ask him?" These sorts of questions hurt her feelings, she says, because "You can see that's what they're getting at: Do you have to work? They're defining you as a businessperson, do you have to do this? Are you dabbling, or are you serious?" She continued, "I love what I'm doing and I really feel that I bring value to the table, but I am not sitting there going 'Oh no, if I don't get another client, I'm not going to be able to pay the rent.'" And yet, she said, "Does that make me less of an organizer because I don't have to do it if I don't want to do it?" Here, she pushed back against the assumption that having a high-earning spouse, or otherwise being financially stable without income from organizing, makes one any less of a professional at her craft. And yet, she, too, described dabblers as a problem for the industry—she simply wanted it understood that not *needing* to work did not, in itself, qualify one as a dabbler.

Dabblers, I was told, were a problem because they make the profession look bad, undoing the work generations of organizers have done to be taken seriously. One longtime organizer with a background in corporate America told me: "Dabbling does not reflect well on those of us who this is our way of living. The term 'professional organizer' means a great deal to us and no, we don't like that people who are not serious about it call themselves a professional. Doctors are professionals. They don't do it part-time, they don't do it when they feel like it, they don't only help their friends." This organizer was not antagonistic toward less experienced organizers; she was well liked by her peers and beloved for her willingness to mentor new organizers. For her, the key distinction between dabblers and professionals was not how long they had been in the business, or even how good an organizer they were; it was about whether they were actually trying to build and grow a profitable business. To her, being a professional means working full-time, whether you feel like it or not, for people beyond your own inner circle. Invoking doctors as a model for what professionalism looks like (although many doctors now do, in fact, work part-time), she reaffirms a kinship between organizing and more established elite professions.

And yet, while the description above suggests a clear divide between dabblers and professionals, the reality is much blurrier. When describing dabblers and the threat they posed to the industry and its reputation, no organizer named names. No one told me, "Jane just dabbles in organizing," or "Sherri over there gives the field a bad name." The only times specific organizers' names came up in discussions of dabbling were as *exceptions*: "Of course, so-and-so has only ever worked part-time, but she's very successful." "That organizer doesn't need to work full-time—her husband's rich—but she's one of the best there is."

In fact, many of the most respected members of NAPO's Los Angeles chapter, where I attended monthly meetings for more than a year, arguably fit the definition of a dabbler. Some (including one of the few male organizers I interviewed) worked part-time by choice because they were raising young children or near retirement and no longer wanted or needed to work so many hours. Other well-liked organizers who held leadership positions in the chapter worked mostly as assistants to other organizers, never bothering to formalize or advertise their own business. Some founding members of NAPO still had no online presence because their client base was established before the internet was. Other organizers never made a website because word of mouth and referrals already brought them more business than they needed. None of this seemed to undermine these organizers' credibility or damage their reputation among other organizers.

The fact that no specific organizer was ever described to me as a dabbler might be explained as the product of NAPO's huggy, collegial culture—if you can't say anything nice, don't name names—but I'd argue something different. I think there are few if any identifiable dabblers among NAPO's organizers because the dabbler is a bogeyman, or in this case a bogeywoman, a cautionary tale that functions to scare new organizers into taking their work, and the work of other organizers, seriously. How many hours an organizer works, how much money she makes, whether she "needs" the money or not, whether she wants to grow her business or keep it nice and small, none of these factors actually seems to carry much weight within the organizing community. For one thing, few organizers know for certain how many hours other organizers work or how much they earn in a given year. (One organizer told me how shocked he was to discover that one especially quiet, unassuming organizer he knew through NAPO was earning well over six figures a year through her work with celebrities and other wealthy clientele.) For another, my observations suggest that if an organizer is invested enough in the field to join NAPO, attend meetings and conferences, and connect with others in the field, she has adequately demonstrated her commitment to the profession to her peers, and thus removed herself from the dabbler category regardless of hours worked or money earned.

There is, however, another level of significance to the specter of the dabbler. The traits of the dabbler are gendered ones. Women are more likely than men to work part-time. Women are less likely than men, especially at the time of the organizing profession's founding, to be the main breadwinner in opposite-sex marriages.[30] And work performed by women, regardless of how lucrative or beneficial, is more likely to be dismissed as a hobby, as opposed to a career, than work performed by men.[31] When organizers decry the dabbler, they seek to distance themselves from the sexist stereotypes that were levied against them in the occupation's early days.

This tendency is clearest in another piece of organizing lore I heard multiple times over the course of my fieldwork. In this story, an experienced organizer gets a message on her voicemail (or answering machine, in some especially dated versions) from a woman seeking advice about starting an organizing business. When the organizer returns the call, the woman's child answers the phone. Sometimes, the organizer telling the story played the character of the child, raising her voice to a high, whiny pitch: "Mommmmmy! Someone's on the phone!" At this point, the storyteller usually paused or tipped her head, eyebrow raised, as if the problem with this scenario is so obvious it went without saying. The listener was supposed to understand, without being told, that allowing her child to answer the phone when a client might be calling was so unprofessional as to disqualify the child's mother, regardless of her organizing skills, from being taken seriously by clients or colleagues alike. "How many clients has she lost that way?" one teller asked rhetorically. "Okay, somebody's got a hobby." Another told me, "The first thing I said to her was 'If you want to be in business, you have no business having that phone answered like that.'"[32]

When I heard this story, it was usually from experienced organizers who'd been working in the field for at least a decade. Each time the account was told in the first person, as an encounter that happened to her. The odds of this same event happening multiple times to different organizers are slim; more likely, some tellers have mistakenly or intentionally appropriated for themselves a story that happened to someone else. Whether the account is true is less significant than how and why it circulates among organizers. The fact that I was hearing this story in the 2010s—when most people had cell phones and were unlikely to answer anyone's phone but their own—suggests its point is more moral than practical.

In the story, the would-be organizer's downfall is her inability to separate her business identity from her identity as a mother. She hasn't failed as an organizer, she's failed as a *professional* because she has not performed a certain *kind* of professionalism, one that keeps the boundary between work and home, business and family life, clearly defined and rigidly guarded.

What professionalism looks like is a social construct, one that changes over time and across cultures, groups, and occupations. In the nineteenth and twentieth centuries, middle-class Americans embraced a model in which full-time, waged employment was the standard for professional success.[33] It was a model built on certain class, gender, and racial privileges. But professional positions weren't available to most Americans, including immigrants, men of color, and women of all races. The elite white men who had access to these positions were able to work in them because they made high enough salaries either to support a stay-at-home spouse who managed all or most domestic and childcare responsibilities, or to hire other people, usually women of color, to perform this work.

When that businessman at the NAPO conference envisioned business professionals, he likely imagined himself and other middle-class, white-collar businessmen who adhered to the Organization Man model of the mid-twentieth century.[34] And when he looked out at that sea of female organizers and imagined what it would mean for them to professionalize, he assumed it would look the same for their businesses as it did for his. But organizers have never fit the model of professionalism he was likely envisioning, and they probably never will, because it wasn't meant for them. His model of professionalism was never intended to accommodate working women, especially not working mothers, or two-earner families. It's a testament to the determination and optimism of NAPO's founders that they took on the challenge regardless, striving to succeed within a system rigged against them. As they fought tooth and nail to be taken seriously, it's understandable—if still unfortunate—that they were worried that organizers who violated the norms of male-dominated professional culture, like the nameless mom in the story, might undermine the progress they had made. As one longtime organizer put it when we discussed the tale of the toddler on the telephone, "I don't believe in treating anyone ugly for any reason, but some of that [criticism] was probably fair, like, come on, work with us, we're trying to get out of this whole 'cottage industry' [stereotype] and you're not helping if your three-year-old answers the phone."

Nevertheless, when organizers decry the dabbler, when they suggest it is unprofessional to work part-time, rely on a partner for income, or blend wage-earning with caregiving—all things women are more likely to do than men—they reinforce a system wherein working women, especially working mothers, are at an inherent disadvantage. This is especially unfortunate for a female-dominated occupation that holds a special appeal for women looking to blend paid work (and paid caregiving) with unpaid work (and unpaid caregiving), something I expand on more in the next chapter.

There are organizers who resist the profession's privileging of this particular version of professionalism. As noted in the previous chapter, Stephanie Winston, one of the very first organizers, celebrated the tie between organizing and housewifery, a profession she believed was unfairly devalued. In my own research, I encountered other organizers who openly rejected their colleagues' tendency to denigrate organizers who failed to model certain kinds of professionalism.

One such organizer specialized in organizing large families, and was herself the mother of eight children. After her last child was born, the organizer's husband asked if she could think of a way to bring in an extra $100 a day to help support their large family. She considered returning to teaching, her previous profession, but didn't want to go back to full-time work so soon after having another child. A friend came over to meet the baby and, commenting on how neat her home was, asked if she would be willing to come over to show her how to get her own home organized. The organizer happily agreed. Their "session" went so well the friend suggested she turn this into a business, so she did. When we spoke, she'd been organizing for fifteen years, always part-time, "because that's the way I like it."

This organizer had been a NAPO member since she started her business. She knew, she said, that "Some of my colleagues would be a little bit upset or something because I was using my home phone. My kids would answer my home phone." But for the clients she wanted to serve, that wasn't a problem. "My clients liked that," she said, "because they were looking for that. They wanted something a little bit out of the box. They wanted someone they can relate to." Being a mother working for mothers also allowed her to run her business the way she wanted. "I didn't have a problem saying, 'I've got to leave now. I have to carpool.'" She knew some other organizers would say that was unprofessional, but it suited her and it suited her clientele.

As far as I know, this organizer was not the one whose kid answered the phone in the oft-told story, but she might as well have been. But rather than undermining her business, as she saw it, the "unprofessional" move of allowing her children to answer the phone when clients called actually enhanced her appeal for her target market. She openly flouted the model of professionalism she knew her colleagues embraced, asserting instead a model of professionalism tailored to the nature and priorities of her own business. Doing so does not seem to have hindered her business or her reputation within NAPO, where she was an active and vocal member.

I tell her story as evidence that not all organizers accept the male-dominated model of professionalism they inherited from twentieth-century American business culture, but also as a reminder that there are other ways of conceptualizing what it means to be a professional or to take one's business seriously. Early organizers were in the tricky situation of trying to make their work legible as a career in a context where both what they did and who they were worked against them. That so many organizers have held on to this particular set of beliefs around the inherently unprofessional nature of combining mother-hood with paid work, despite their profession's emphasis on inclusiv-ity and cooperation, shows how difficult it can be to shirk off old ideas when building something new. Even as organizers have kept moving forward, those cultural holdovers have persisted.

Unequal Barriers to Entry

In describing what it takes to succeed in their field, organizers' emphasis on professionalism, in all its incarnations, also obscures the extent to which factors beyond an individual organizer's control also influence their likelihood of success.[35] Many organizers celebrate the field's unusually low barrier to entry. Technically, you can start an organizing business without spending a penny, in contrast to many businesses that require more seed capital or specific credentials. A new organizer might design a website, print business cards, join NAPO,[36] or pay to incorporate her business and secure insurance, but she does not *have* to. This can be a double-edged sword; many expe-rienced organizers lamented to me that anyone can call themselves an organizer and, voilà, they are one. That is true, but how easy it is to succeed as a self-employed organizer can vary dramatically depend-ing on the resources—financial and social—an organizer brings with her into the profession.[37]

As I've noted, most organizers' first clients—paid or not—are usu-ally their own friends and family. Most often, their business builds from there, by word of mouth supplemented by whatever forms of marketing and advertising they employ (usually a website, giving talks in the community, and perhaps offering discounted organizing packages through sites like Groupon). How quickly your business grows, and how much you are able to charge, depends a great deal on who makes up your network, and how much disposable income they have.

Jamie, a Manhattan organizer I interviewed, left a lucrative job in consulting when she had her first child. She found she was good at managing the day-to-day logistics of parenthood—sleep training, organizing the nursery, figuring out a nap schedule that worked—and that many of her mom friends were not. At many playdates, she ended up advising friends on how to handle this or that, even helping declutter their closets or reorganize the changing table with them while the kids napped. No one paid her for it; she was, she said, "just kind of amusing myself." She stayed in touch with her colleagues from the consulting firm. When one of them became pregnant, she told Jamie, "I want you to come set up my house like you set up your house." Jamie agreed but refused to be paid for her time. "You're my friend," she said. "You'll take me to lunch." Jamie describes the friend as "one of those people that is just hugely networked," so when the job went well, "She loved it and she told three people. And one of the three people told five people, and I have never advertised. I mean, it was just total word of mouth." When we spoke, she'd been in business eight years, had still never advertised, and charged $200 per hour ($400 on weekends). She was also booked solid for the next three months.

Jamie was not the only well-networked organizer I met, but it's not just that her network was large—it was also wealthy. "I feel," she told me, "like I lucked my way into a very affluent group of women and men who have the resources to pay for this." The kind of people, she says, who have a trainer, a stylist, a driver, and an organizer. "I am that organizer for this group of people."[38]

I met other organizers with similar success stories. One actor-turned-organizer was organizing Los Angeles celebrities within months of opening his business. When we met, he'd been organizing professionally for less than two years, had already been featured on national television programs, and was charging $1,600 a day—far more than many organizers with much more experience. Part of this good fortune had to do with the unique nature of Los Angeles, home to Hollywood and many very wealthy people, famous and not. Many of the organizers I met with backgrounds in film and television leveraged those connections to good effect. From my conversations with them, it seemed that once you'd pleased one extremely wealthy client with your organizing skills and your discretion, referrals to other wealthy clients started rolling in. This happened as well to some organizers who were not themselves wealthy; one organizer I interviewed, a middle-class single mother, happened to share a massage therapist with a big-name celebrity. The therapist recommended her, the celebrity loved her, and from that point on she was regularly hired by people so wealthy that even their nannies earned more than six figures; some clients flew her across the country, even around the world, to help organize their numerous estates.

Being well networked mattered even when your network wasn't especially prosperous. When New York organizer Maggie launched her business, she created a website and emailed the link to everyone she knew. Luckily, she said, she knew a lot of people. "I have been here [in NYC] for I think sixteen years, so I have an extensive network of people, friends and people I've worked with and people who trust me. I immediately got some clients and that was exciting."

Other organizers struggled more in the early days of their business, especially organizers of color, whose personal and professional networks tended to be smaller or more financially constrained. They had to work harder to locate clients and market their business. Organizer James Lott Jr. started his organizing business at age forty.[39] His children were grown (he'd had them young) and he was ready for a change. "I was like 'This is my turn now,'" he told me. He moved back to Los Angeles after twenty-two years away and made a list of the pros ("not pros and cons," he emphasized, just the pros) of every job he'd ever had—nursing, acting, hosting, voice-over work, housecleaning, cashier, store manager, event planner, and more. Looking at the resulting list, he knew, "there's a business in there, but I don't know what it is." Lott had never heard of professional organizing, then he read organizer Julie Morgenstern's *Organizing from the Inside Out*. "This book tells me," he said, "this could be a business." And yet, he hesitated. "Entrepreneurship was for somebody else," he remembers thinking, "not me. I usually got jobs. You work for ten years. Do it myself? Just me, myself?" Then, on a housecleaning job, he realized he was already doing organizing for the client, in addition to cleaning. He decided to go for it and was still organizing when I met him thirteen years later.

Starting a new business in a new city hadn't been easy, he didn't have much of a network to draw on, but he found his way. "I'm old school," he told me. He printed 500 postcards and two t-shirts with the name and logo of his new business. "I picked areas in LA that I wanted to work," he said, and he started walking for exercise down those streets, handing out postcards to people he passed. "I got another client, then another client, and I started targeting areas that are kind of left out. Being a Black man, as you can see," he told me via Zoom, "I'm Black and Latino, I'm also Puerto Rican. I speak Spanish. So, I started targeting those communities." More than a dozen years later, he says, "I literally have two clients still to this day [from that early canvassing], semi-regulars that still call me for stuff." Since then he's expanded his social media presence and used a wide range of networking and promotional techniques but, he says, "Sometimes old school's the best way."

Like James, Hilda, a Mexican American organizer, was interested in organizing for members of her own community. Hilda grew up the oldest of seven children, each just one year apart, in "one of those crazy typical Hispanic families," she says. She worked in fast food throughout high school and college, then moved into banking soon after earning her bachelor's degree. She stayed at the same bank for twelve years, through two pregnancies, and became known for organizing the stockroom shelves, corralling the myriad Post-its and pencils. While her kids were young, Hilda saw work as a way to make money, but her focus was on her family. As her children got older, Hilda still needed to work to help support the family, but she wanted to start doing work she loved and that felt more personally meaningful. One day, Hilda's therapist suggested she consider becoming a professional organizer. Hilda, who had never known organizing existed, attended one NAPO meeting and was hooked.

Her new business was growing slowly. "I've been trying to figure out," she told me, "how I could market to the Hispanic community, because there's such a huge need because of hoarding and clutter and all that stuff." There's a lot of shame around hoarding and clutter in American culture generally, but Hilda believes it is even stronger within certain groups. "Hispanic communities, they're so tight-knit. They don't let other people in, because I think in some aspect they think they should be able to do it on their own."[40] Her mother, a "social butterfly," recommends Hilda to her friends, but few reach out to her. They worry, Hilda thinks, "What are they going to charge?" When they do hire her, she says, Hispanic clients often refuse to recommend her to their friends because "They don't want people to know they use a professional organizer." She thinks they worry that people will wonder, "'Why can't you take care of your own stuff?' Because it's a reflection on you. It's a bad thing." A Black organizer I interviewed described a similar hesitancy with the Black community toward hiring organizers. "A lot of times in our culture," she said, "you kind of feel like you have to do it all on your own, like you can't outsource, you can't have someone do this for you." For organizers looking to serve communities of color—most of whom, like James and Hilda, are people of color themselves—these attitudes can present additional barriers.

Organizers of color also described to me instances of racism they experienced from white clients. One Black organizer told me he was working in a white client's Los Angeles home when the client's white boyfriend returned home and began yelling racial epithets, saying he didn't "want any [n-word] touching [his] stuff." The client apologized for her boyfriend and tried to pay the organizer, but he told her to keep her money and left. When another Black organizer showed up to a job she'd been recommended for by a white organizer, the client opened the door and said, "Oh, she didn't tell me you were Black." Another Black organizer noticed that clients who reach out to her after viewing her website are usually people of color. She told me she sometimes wonders how many white people have looked at her website, which includes a photo of her, and decided not to work with her on the basis of race. She imagined them thinking, "This one's Black, so I'll work with this [white organizer] because I'm more comfortable with this because this one looks like me." This sort of racial preference among clients works the other way as well. Multiple Black organizers told me that when Black people *do* hire organizers, they often prefer to work with organizers of the same race. They believed this was because Black clients wanted to support Black-owned businesses and because they expected Black organizers would be less likely to judge them and more familiar with the sorts of things they owned. However, because Black people are a statistical minority in the United States, and because systemic racism has led to dramatic racial disparities in wealth and income, clients' tendency to self-select organizers of the same race generally works in favor of white organizers and against organizers of color.[41]

Some organizers believe these sorts of racial disparities also explain why so many Black organizers continue to work full-time jobs while running their organizing businesses. One Black organizer told me, "A lot of our Black organizers want to do organizing full-time but for whatever reason, lack of money or lack of support, or whatever the case is, they're holding other jobs." She suspected white organizers were more likely to "have the support of their family, the generational wealth, a supportive spouse or something along those lines."[42] In this way, too, Black organizers and others who lack financial reserves find themselves at a disadvantage when they set out to build and grow their businesses. This echoes research on other occupations, in which workers from more economically privileged families tended to have stronger financial safety nets that allowed them to endure economic precarity, and cultural, educational, and social capital that helped them achieve more stable work in their chosen field.[43]

Like organizers of color, male organizers are also a minority in the industry, but this actually seemed to work to their advantage. Within the organizing community, likely because there are so few of them, male organizers tend to garner a lot of praise and positive attention. The addition of any new male organizer at a NAPO meeting or events tends to be noted and celebrated. (This presents an interesting contrast to the experiences of Black women organizers, who, as I explain in a moment, sometimes felt unwelcome at NAPO events.) Male organizers may also benefit from the "glass elevator" effect, in which professional men, especially white men, entering female-dominated occupations tend to advance more quickly and earn more money than their female peers.[44]

Until recently, organizing also fit a broader pattern in which men are the most visible and celebrated practitioners of types of work performed mostly by women. For instance, while women do the majority of home cooking in the United States, most professional chefs are male, especially the most highly regarded among them.[45] Similarly, one of NAPO's founders told me the industry's stark gender imbalance makes it all the more irritating to her that male organizers seem to draw disproportionate media attention. "The vast majority of organizers are women," she said. "Women started it at a time when women didn't have their own businesses. But the press now is going to men." She brought up organizer Peter Walsh, the lead organizer on *Clean Sweep*, one of the first organizing shows, who went on to became "Oprah's organizer," appearing regularly as a guest on *The Oprah Winfrey Show*. "He's *always* getting press," she sighed, "and it's like 'Where did this guy blow in from?' Now that we've built it, brought it along, guys are stepping into it." While she and other female organizers welcomed and even celebrated men joining the field—I suspect because it added legitimacy to the occupation, although no organizer ever said that directly—they resented the outsized attention their male colleagues received and the way it minimized the work women had done to grow and legitimize the field.

These inequities, and the obstacles they create for certain groups of organizers—especially women of color—were rarely discussed at

NAPO meetings during my fieldwork in the 2010s (although some regional NAPO chapters may have been more attuned to these issues than others). My initial interviewees included numerous women of color, but with a few rare exceptions, the racial composition of the organizing industry seldom came up during my interviews or observations. As well, although multiple organizers talked with me in private about the challenges of aging in this profession, which can be quite physically demanding, I never heard it publicly acknowledged that people with physical disabilities, age related or not, might face unique obstacles to building an organizing career.[46] Instead, the presumption seemed to be that a good organizer's potential is limited solely by her willingness to work hard and run her business "like a business," dedicating ample time and resources to training, networking, and marketing. At a NAPO session for new organizers I attended, for instance, organizers were told, "Schedule yourself to go to work Monday, Wednesday, and Friday 9–12, no cheating. Put your butt in the chair and work—outreach, marketing, etc. Going to work will generate the clients." This isn't bad advice, but its effectiveness depends a great deal on other factors, ones no amount of butt-in-chair time can fully compensate for.

NAPO leaders are hardly alone in overestimating the degree to which individual agency can overcome social inequalities. That's a favorite American pastime, one grounded in long-held ideas about individualism and the almighty work ethic and bolstered by neoliberalism's romance with entrepreneurship.[47] As sociologist Erin Cech has argued, "Individual hard work is not the answer to structural barriers."[48] Suggesting it is places extra burdens on those who face additional obstacles, such as organizers of color or those with limited financial resources.

The general lack of attention to race or the experiences of organizers of color that I witnessed at NAPO also echoes the broader embrace of colorblind ideology within the United States, in which not acknowledging a person's race is seen as evidence of being "not racist."[49] Like so many organizations, NAPO presented itself as "race neutral," equally welcoming to all organizers, despite its overwhelmingly white membership and leadership. "This way of thinking," as sociologist

Victor Ray argues, "reinforces the fallacy that only people of color have race, and obscures the broad, everyday dynamics of white racial power within organizations."[50] From its inception, NAPO set out to be equally welcoming to all, but its overwhelmingly white membership and leadership sent a different message. Thus, regardless of NAPO leaders' inclusive intent, these assumptions and omissions nevertheless shaped NAPO's culture, resulting in a space that, as huggy as it may have been, didn't feel especially welcoming to many organizers of color. That has begun to change in recent years, however, spurred by the efforts of Black organizers and America's broader public reckoning with racial inequality and injustice.

"I Just Didn't See Enough People Who Look Like Me"

Organizer Dalys Macon took her first NAPO class in 2005, thirteen years before she actually launched her business. She found the course intimidating, in part because at the time she had young children and a full-time job and wasn't sure she was up to everything running a business entailed. But she continued organizing for free for friends and family and kept informed about developments in the organizing industry. Every January, she told me, she'd run out to purchase the "organizing special editions" of magazines that came out at the start of the new year. Macon, who is Black, loved reading about organizing and the people who were making a living doing it. And yet, she told me, each new year "I was so disappointed with the lack of representation for women of color and other minorities."

Macon finally started her organizing business in 2019 after surviving a bout with breast cancer. After cancer, she told me, "you start looking at life differently." She decided the time had come to finally start the business she'd long dreamed of. She kept her corporate job and started organizing on weekends. In January 2019, one month after Macon finally launched her business, she bought her annual organizing magazine and saw that of the dozen or so organizers profiled, "not one of them was either a woman of color or any minority, for that matter. And I thought, 'my goodness,' here we are, thirteen years later [after her first organizing class] and the face of organizing has *still* not changed."[51]

Macon decided that needed to change. She arranged to meet with some other Black organizers in the Washington, DC, area. The meeting was a success. "I learned so much in that two-hour meeting," Macon told me, "that I thought, other women needed to hear this!" She decided to create "a platform where I could just spotlight other women of color," and in 2019 the Instagram account Black Girls Who Organize (@blackgirlswhoorganize) was born.

Initially, Macon told me, "I set out to do one lady per month. I figured I would meet twelve and that would be the end of that." After all, as Macon wrote in her first post, after years as an organizer she had only encountered "a few" other Black organizers.[52] It turned out there were way more Black organizers out there than Macon had realized, so many she had to up her posts to two per week. By the time we spoke in 2022, she had spotlighted close to 150 Black organizers, some from other countries and continents. "It's been overwhelming," she says, "but amazing."

Although Macon didn't realize it at the time, a few years before she started Black Girls Who Organize, other Black organizers had been similarly concerned about the position of Black organizers within the industry. When Naeemah Ford Goldson launched her Atlanta-based organizing business in 2013, she attended a few NAPO meetings. Although now a NAPO member, Goldson was initially hesitant about joining the organization. "I didn't really feel all that welcome at NAPO," she told me. She didn't experience any overt racism, but "I just didn't see enough people who look like me."[53] Worried this lack of representation might discourage other Black women from pursuing careers in organizing, Goldson started Professional Organizing Sisters, a Facebook group for Black, Indigenous, and other people of color (BIPOC) working as professional organizers. "I purposely made sure that it's only for BIPOC women, because we don't want our voices to get drowned out, you know, because it is an industry that's dominated by white women. So we need a safe space where we can kind of chat and we can talk among ourselves about how we feel and everything."

She started messaging other organizers of color she knew or had seen on Facebook. Some joined, some didn't, but those who did quickly told their friends and the group grew rapidly via word of mouth.

In 2017, Goldson and other Atlanta-based members of the Facebook group decided to meet in person. Over brunch they shared their experiences as organizers of color. "It was great," Goldson remembers. "Everyone kind of had the same experience where they felt overlooked [at NAPO meetings or online organizing forums], or maybe they didn't start their business when they wanted to start their business because they didn't see enough people that looked like them and weren't sure if they would get hired."

Of that initial group in Atlanta, a few decided to keep meeting regularly and, just like those earliest organizers over three decades prior, started their own association. Founded in 2017, the National Association for Black Professional Organizers (NABPO) was intended, according to Goldson, as "a safe space" for other organizers of color, one where they could connect with and receive mentoring from other BIPOC organizers around the country. NABPO also created an online membership directory where clients could search for organizers of color by location and area of expertise. As Goldson explained, this was intended to let the Black community know, "Hey! We're Black professional organizers, and you can hire us!"

Both #BlackGirlsWhoOrganize and NABPO function as "counterspaces," safe, supportive environments outside the mainstream where members of underrepresented communities can learn together, vent frustrations, and share stories of isolation, microaggressions, and overt discrimination.[54] Such spaces are crucially important to build connections, combat isolation, promote members' mental wellbeing, and foster success. In both cases, in addition to functioning as counterspaces, these groups also increased Black organizers' visibility, both to potential clients and to other people of color considering a career in organizing. Their efforts were successful—both groups grew steadily, if slowly—but their existence didn't necessary impact the broader professional organizing community, which remained mostly silent around issues of race and inequality.

All that changed with the murder of George Floyd.

The Black Lives Matter movement started in 2013 in response to the acquittal of George Zimmerman for the shooting death of Trayvon Martin, a Black teenager who'd been walking unarmed through Zimmerman's gated community. But it was the police murder of George Floyd in 2020, recorded in a heart-shattering nine-minute video shared around the world, that turned Black Lives Matter into one of the largest social movements in US history. In addition to the massive online and in-person protests that followed Floyd's murder, his death also "resulted in a lasting shift and a more vocal and engaged online public" around issues of racial justice.[55] This seismic shift occurred while most Americans were sheltered at home mid-pandemic, following the news more closely than ever; it reverberated throughout US culture, impacting every corner of American life, even the professional organizing industry.

In 2022, I reinterviewed Michaela, a Black organizer I'd assisted on a few jobs back in 2013. She'd recently been asked to serve in a leadership role in her local NAPO chapter and found the timing suspicious, coming as it did amid the resurgence of Black Lives Matter. Remembering the summer of 2020, she said, "Everybody all of a sudden was like 'Oh my god, we need Black people!' Like, honestly, every time I watch the news now . . . every specialist is Black." She saw a similar tendency among her clients, many of whom said they hired her specifically because they wanted to support a Black-owned business. So, when a white NAPO leader contacted her about taking on this new position, Michaela couldn't help but wonder if her race had something to do with it. She asked, "Did you approach me because I'm Black?" The woman replied, "In all honesty, that was part of it, but before that you met all the other criteria."

Other Black organizers found themselves similarly in demand. One described to me a trend on Instagram where white professional organizers were "silencing their [own] voices," using their accounts to promote Black organizers' businesses instead of their own. One Black organizer was suddenly invited to speak in multiple forums about his experiences as an organizer of color. An unintended consequence of this expanded visibility was that a lot of Black organizers learned about one another—and about NABPO—for the first time. The group's membership swelled to more than 100 members.

Black organizers noticed a shift within NAPO as well. One organizer told me that while she had not encountered overt racism at NAPO meetings and events, she had never felt especially welcome, either: "I think [after Black Lives Matter] a lot of the community overall—Blacks, whites, everyone—through introspection, they really just said, 'You know, we've kind of had our blinders on, not intentionally, but we kind of had our core group of women in our circle and we never chose to go outside that circle.' So now they found themselves trying to make a more concerted effort to go across the board, regardless of color, to collaborate, to create friendships." As she saw it, the organizing community was finally asking how their industry could become more inclusive. "Because, quite frankly," she told me, "as you probably know, it's just been older, mature, white women that pretty much dominated the industry."[56]

NAPO continues to take steps toward inclusivity and racial awareness. In 2020, the NAPO Board included Diversity as one of NAPO's five strategic initiatives for the year. The group's annual conference included a session on "Incorporating an Anti-Racist Mindset and Practices to Build your 21st Century Business."[57] Black and white organizers alike told me they were pleased with NAPO's increased efforts at inclusivity. They also had some concerns. One white organizer who led her chapter's Diversity, Equity, and Inclusion (DEI) committee told me that "NAPO's trying to step up to create a national dialogue on diversity, equity, and inclusion," but also noted that these DEI sessions tend to be poorly attended. "I just think there needs to be more, a lot more."

Another Black organizer I interviewed was pleased that NAPO's website now included information about NABPO and Black Girls Who Organize. "I think that's a big start in the right direction," she told me. She was more ambivalent about the organizers who've reached out to her saying they "want to do something special for the Black girls who organize." She wants to tell them, "That's not really what it's about.

I understand your heart, but it's still creating some alienation." She doesn't want what she calls "special treatment" or to have white organizers collaborate with her just "to check a box." Instead, she wants to build real, lasting relationships with other organizers, and to see Black organizers recognized not for their race but "because of their skill set and because of their knowledge."

When I asked another Black organizer whether she thought NAPO had become more inclusive in recent years, she replied, "I think they're trying, but I think it's going to take time." She continued, "Because, I mean, they've been doing things how they do it for so long and I feel like it might be so ingrained, but they don't even realize." Sighing, she said, "That's fine, but I just think it's gonna take a while."[58]

The same can be said, in a broader sense, about the organizing profession as a whole. They've been doing things "how they do it" for a very long time, in ways that have served them well and also not so well. In their dedication to growing and publicizing their new field, early organizers overcame significant obstacles, particular in terms of legitimizing themselves and their work in the face of gender stereotypes and dismissive attitudes to women business owners. At the same time, they reinforced cultural ideals around professionalism that penalize those—especially mothers—who cannot or will not maintain strict boundaries between their home and work lives. Organizers' single-minded emphasis on hard work has also obscured some of the hard realities about what it takes to succeed in this industry, especially the extent to which a would-be organizer's class and racial background—rather than her work ethic—impact her ability to locate clients, quit her day job, and feel welcomed and represented in the industry's professional spaces. Despite these challenges, the field has only continued to grow since NAPO's founding, in numbers and renown. This has a lot to do with the work early organizers did to promote the field, and with more recent efforts to diversify the industry. But it's also a product of other, larger shifts, ones that have made other jobs worse, especially for women, thus increasing the appeal of professions like organizing.

I'd never been to an estate sale before, and I'd been expecting something fancier. The word "estate" conjured something grandiose, a manor house, or something with white columns in front. Instead, the estate sale I was assisting on was in a home that looked a lot like the one I grew up in, a brown ranch house on a small cul-de-sac, flower bed out front spotted with violas.

Inside I found Michaela, the organizer I was assisting, and her friend Lizzie. The two had arrived early to set out the bright yellow signs I'd seen pointing my way along the last few turns into the neighborhood. Michaela, a single mother who specialized in moves and estate sales, sat at a small folding table just inside the entryway. On top of the table sat a metal money box, a stack of her business cards, some black Sharpies, and many sheets of small round stickers for pricing. Lizzie, whom Michaela met back in her acting days, was also assisting that day. She was crouched nearby, unloading books from boxes and lining them up along the front of the brick fireplace.

The home we were working in belonged to a woman who had recently died. She was single and had no children. Her sister and nephews had hired Michaela to clean out the house and sell what she could. One of the nephews, a tall redhead in a baseball cap and cutoff shorts, was helping us set up. He trimmed a few bright-red roses from the back garden and placed them in a small crystal vase, which he set next to the money box.

The front room was full of six-foot folding tables covered in an assortment of dishware, linens, and home decor. There were Buddhas, lots of Buddhas—red plastic Buddhas for a few dollars, large white stone Buddhas priced at $35 to

$45 each. There was a 1970s-style set of matching brown glass plates with at least twelve complete place settings, plus serving dishes. A small cabinet in the corner housed a collection of giraffes—crystal giraffes, glass giraffes, ceramic giraffes, carved wooden giraffes, paintings of giraffes. A few dozen unopened boxes of candles sat atop a pool table, which was also for sale.

In place of a dining table there was a large conference table, like you'd find in a corporate office, surrounded by eight black office chairs in good condition. The kitchen was closed off with caution tape and a handwritten "do not enter" sign, but the bar that ran alongside it housed more glassware, tiki-style barware, and serving items for sale. There was a small set of matching glass swizzle sticks, each with a colorful bird perched atop. (I eyed these all day and should have purchased them when I had the chance; they sold at some point when I was out of the room.) Through the sliding glass doors you could see two sets of patio furniture, also for sale.

A long thin hallway connected the living room to three bedrooms, each with a full bedroom set. Clothes still hung in the closet, shoes lined below them and hats on the shelf above, all unpriced but also for sale. Even the leftover toiletries were for sale—half-empty shampoo bottles, used makeup compacts, an open bag of cotton balls—as were the cleaning products stored under the bathroom sink.

Michaela was worried from the start about how this sale would go. When we opened at 9 a.m., not a single person was waiting outside. Her sales usually have a line of fifty or more buyers by the time she opens the doors. She advertised on the same sites she usually did, the ones estate sale buyers know to check (those signs around the neighborhood, she told me, rarely bring in customers). She listed a few bigger-ticket items for sale on Craigslist—the pool table, patio sets, an antique bedroom set, the Buddha collection. She said the poor turnout was likely because there were few things of especially high value for sale—no tools, designer clothing, or mid-century furniture.

Just a few people trickled in throughout the day, browsing a lot and buying little. Some were regular buyers Michaela knows well. She often sets specific items aside for collectors or resellers she knows might want them—antique watches for one, Bakelite jewelry for another. One older couple came to all her sales. They were especially charming, joking with Michaela and each other. "You know he's going to want that mirror," the woman said, rolling her eyes, as her husband examined a bejeweled mirror leaning against the sliding glass door across the room. They bought two potted plants, a set of small cocktail glasses, and the mirror. Another of her usual buyers came, did a quick circuit around the house, and left without buying anything. One woman offered $100 for one of the patio sets, which was priced at $150. It had some damage, she said, and she'd need to fix it up. Michaela stayed firm on the price, saying $100 was too low for a five-piece set. After the woman left empty-handed, Michaela said, mostly to herself, "I'm not taking a hit on my profit so you can make more when you resell them."

Often when customers arrived, they asked at the door whether there were any of a particular type of item for sale—tools, fishing rods, old toys. Most were disappointed at the offerings and left soon after. One man told Michaela there were a lot of estate sales that day, which might be why hers was so quiet. Around noon, three hours after the sale opened, Michaela told Lizzie to go home, that she wouldn't make enough that day to pay her for any more hours of work. Lizzie was a friend, Michaela told me, and fine with working a half day, but she'd hired a different assistant for the next day who she'd have to pay no matter what. If tomorrow's sales were equally slow, she might actually lose money on this job after paying her assistant.

The poor turnout, she told me, was making her question her choice in agreeing to work this sale. Some organizers specialize in high-end sales, she told me. She'd done those—earning $10,000 in a single weekend on one—but it wasn't her specialty. Even small sales with enough items can make good money, although this clearly wasn't one of them. She'd taken the job because last month had been slow, and she jumped at the chance for a job, any job.

Around 2 p.m., Michaela decided to call it quits. Altogether there had been fewer than a dozen purchases in the five hours since we opened, totaling less than $50. Michaela gets just 40 percent of that for her fee. She'd return the next day with another assistant and hope for better results. She planned to post more photos of individual items on Craigslist that night in hopes they'd generate more sales tomorrow. Whatever didn't sell then, the family intended to put out for a garage sale the next weekend.

She locked the front door behind us, the money box tucked under her arm. As she was uprooting one of the yard signs and placing it in the back of her SUV, a lime-green VW Bug pulled up in front of the house. A young blond leaned out the window and asked if the sale was still open. Michaela told her we were done for the day. The girl asked her to please reconsider, explaining that she and her mother had driven all the way from Ventura, nearly two hours away, to check out the Buddhas for sale. "We'll give you a nice smile," she said jokingly, "if you'll let us in the house!" Michaela laughed. "I don't need smiles, I need money," and she turned to unlock the door to let them in.

3
Alternatives to Standard Employment, Especially for Women

In organizing's early days, gender discrimination limited the career options available to women. Nurse, teacher, secretary, waitress—these were the types of jobs early organizers felt they had to choose between, and so they built themselves an alternative in organizing. And yet, in the decades since the occupation's founding, women have broken through glass ceilings in countless fields. While gender discrimination unquestionably persists, especially for women pursuing careers in traditionally male industries, women today simply have more options to choose from when deciding which jobs to pursue.

This opening up of previously restricted careers has diminished the allure of some female-friendly jobs working women once flocked to. For much of the twentieth century, for example, waitressing offered women a living wage that enabled them to support themselves and their families. Yet as Candacy Taylor has documented, the daughters and granddaughters of these career waitresses, or "lifers," don't want to follow in their footsteps. The work is physically grueling and low status, and the proliferation of chain restaurants has eroded servers' earnings; as a result, the job has less appeal for women with better options to choose from.[1]

That hasn't happened to professional organizing. Running a small business is time consuming and risky, and organizing can be physically and emotionally challenging. Yet the field has continued to grow since the 1980s, attracting people, mostly women, with a range of education and work experience. In this chapter, I consider why that is. Why, in the twenty-first century, when second-wave feminism has opened up so many professions to women, does organizing continue to appeal to so many women? What is it about this job that draws them in, and what is it about the other jobs available to them that makes organizing look so good in comparison?[2] And finally, if organizers are choosing the risks of entrepreneurship over the realities of standard employment, what does that say about the jobs they're leaving behind, and the people left doing them?

• • •

The idea that people should make a living doing something they love has gained cultural traction in recent years, offering an alternative to old ways of thinking about work as primarily an obligation, form of self-discipline, or means to social and financial mobility.[3] And indeed, I could fill an entire chapter with organizers' descriptions of how much they love organizing. After a meeting of NAPO's Los Angeles chapter, I joined a group of organizers for dinner at a nearby noodle shop. I overheard one organizer tell a newcomer to NAPO, "I feel blessed. I get to do what I love." One of NAPO's founders said her husband often tells her that she "was the luckiest person that he knew, because I loved what I did and I made some money at it." In the introduction to her book *Making Space, Clutter Free*, organizer Tracy McCubbin asks, "You know how some people get really excited about squeezing pores or tweezing eyebrows and will ask everyone in the dorm if they can do theirs? I get that excited about creating order out of chaos."[4] Another organizer told me, "I love figuring out easy ways to do things. I love to do that. It's almost like I do little feasibility studies. How can we make this more efficient? I love doing that."

Most organizers' love affair with organizing started young. I lost count of the number of organizers I spoke with who described regularly reorganizing their bedroom furniture as kids and alphabetizing their childhood bookshelves.[5] A newspaper article titled "Organization Is in Their Blood" says most organizers "describe themselves as meticulous, born organizers." The article goes on to quote NAPO founder Stephanie Culp: "Most organizers can't remember a time when they weren't concerned with order; their first memories often involve organizing their toys as children."[6] One organizer I interviewed told me that in kindergarten, when she couldn't sleep during nap time, she'd help the teacher organize her desk. Japanese organizer Marie Kondo tells a similar story from childhood: "At school, while other kids were playing dodgeball or skipping, I'd slip away to rearrange the bookshelves in our classroom, or check the contents of the mop cupboard, all the while muttering about the poor storage methods."[7] Another organizer describes her organizing skills as going "back to her childhood, when she enjoyed emptying toy chests and linen closets so she could put them back in a more useful way."[8] When asked how long they've been organizing, regardless of how many years they've been in business, many organizers reply "my whole life."[9]

Of course, the idea that some people are "born organized" needs to be unpacked. Girls tend to be socialized from a young age to help with domestic tasks such as cleaning and decluttering.[10] By organizing their homes and classrooms, and developing a fondness for it, these girls were operating well within cultural norms around gender and work. As sociologist Erin Cech has argued, whether we realize it or not, the types of tasks we find interesting and meaningful—and therefore opt to pursue as careers—are shaped by our social positions.[11] A passion for organizing might seem like an individual quirk, but it's also the product of having been socialized into a culture that sees this as women's work. Female organizers themselves are well aware that their talent and inclination for this field has likely been shaped by the culture in which they were raised.

When I asked why so many organizers are women, one organizer in her seventies told me: "I don't know if it's culturally that the women feel like this is something for them, or they're more comfortable maybe because they handle and touch most of the things like laundry and groceries and keeping the cupboards organized and all that stuff. I mean, there are not a lot of men who do those things, because the men historically went out and made the living and the women stayed home and made the home." This version of American history is of course partial at best. The idea that men go out to work for pay while women toil for free at home dates back only to the mid-nineteenth century and has never reflected the reality of most American families. (Consider, for example, what enslaved women, women in farming families, or working-class women who perished in the Triangle Shirtwaist Fire, among many others, might have to say about these claims.) Yet this narrative, versions of which I heard from multiple organizers, reflects the continued assumption, even well into the twenty-first century, that women are both naturally and culturally suited to this kind of work, which explains in part why so many women are drawn to this field.

As I've said, men have never made up more than a tiny percentage of organizers. As one male presenter announced to a sea of mostly female organizers, "Welcome to the NAPO Conference, where there's never a line for the men's room!" It's also worth noting that not a single male organizer I interviewed described having been especially organized, or interested in organizing, as a child. Instead, they were likely to say that they wanted to start a business doing something, and organizing seemed like a viable field that aligned with skills they already possessed. Nevertheless, the existence of male organizers complicates gendered explanations of what draws people to work as organizers. And yet, the female organizers I interviewed describe their male peers in ways that serve to normalize men's presence in the field while also reaffirming cultural scripts around gender and work.

I heard multiple times that male organizers were especially valued—by clients and other organizers alike—for their physical strength, as organizing jobs sometimes involve heavy lifting. A female organizer in the San Francisco Bay Area, for instance, said that male organizers were especially in demand as assistants to other, female organizers. One new male organizer she'd met was "booked solid" with assisting jobs, she said, because "he's wanted by every organizer because he's a man. So, he is really good at organizing, but he's also the heavy lifter." Another stereotype of male organizers—one my own observations bear out—is that most specialize in more "manly" subfields, such as organizing garages or managing moves. Thus, the presence of male practitioners is explained in ways that leave firmly intact the idea that organizing, especially in the home, comes more naturally to women (despite the fact that a majority of organizing clients are also women who clearly weren't "born organized").

It's also a common belief among organizers, male and female alike, that most male organizers identify as gay. One straight male organizer told me he asked his organizing mentor before his first NAPO chapter meeting, "Am I going to be the only straight guy?" She replied, "Yeah, you will be." He told me that when he met a second straight male organizer at a NAPO meeting a few months later, the man's first words to him were "So you're the other one!" Some female organizers explained the presence of gay men within their field by stereotyping gay men as inherently more feminine, more like women, than straight men. "Maybe I'm pigeonholing," one straight female organizer in her seventies told me, "but gay men have such a feminine side that they for some reason can identify with this and they can work in homes with moms." A lesbian organizer suggested gay men are attracted to organizing because "there is a different kind of genetic makeup in this," suggesting that organizing ability is not only inborn, but genetically determined, as if gay men are somehow more genetically similar to women (straight or gay) than to straight men. In this way, organizing's appeal continues to be seen as a gendered one, regardless of the gender of the people doing it.

Organizers' love of organizing is certainly a key part of the field's allure, as is the cultural understanding of such work as culturally appropriate, even biologically suited, for women. That organizers love organizing so much also has definite benefits. Loving what you do and having fun doing it, as noted in the introduction, is a major indicator of job satisfaction, far more important than level of pay.[12] It also provides emotional fulfillment, reduces work fatigue, and offers individuals a sense of purpose, as I describe in more detail in chapter 5.[13] Doing work you feel passionate about can also offer a sense of continuity and agency amid a precarious economy where old models of career paths no longer apply.[14]

And yet, as scholars have noted, there are downsides to the "do what you love" approach to work.[15] First, as I note above, what we love is inextricably linked with our social identities and the culture in which we were raised, so encouraging folks to follow their passion when choosing a career ends up further entrenching occupational segregation, as large numbers of women—and very few men—just happen to be passionate about female-dominated types of work. As well, the opportunity to turn your passion into a profession isn't equally available to all. The people freest to take the risk of pursuing work they feel passionate about are typically those who "already enjoy the greatest economic, racial and gender privileges."[16] With organizers, we see this in the unique barriers faced by organizers of color (racism, a lack of generational wealth, unequal representation in media coverage) as well as the distinct advantages of organizers who enter the field with ample cultural and economic capital.

The cultural emphasis on doing what you love also places a heavy burden on individuals, who are expected to either successfully parlay something they enjoy into a sustainable career or find ways to "fall in love" with the work they're already doing. Because if you're dissatisfied at work, that becomes your own fault—either you're not good enough at what you love or you went about it the wrong way or you chose the wrong passion to pursue in the first place. Either way, the focus stays on the individual, rather than on broader structural issues or systemic problems around work, thereby stifling the sorts of critiques and collective action that might otherwise occur.[17] In short, if we focus only on how much organizers love organizing, we risk ignoring why and how much they *don't* like—or don't imagine they'd like—the other jobs they might be doing instead.

Independence, Anxiety, and Entrepreneurship

Organizing was not a first career for most of the organizers I met and read about.[18] They came from pretty much every field you can imagine. They'd been teachers, nurses, bartenders, accountants, movers, artists, professors, administrative assistants, personal assistants,

freelance writers, historians, screenwriters, sound technicians, electrical engineers, computer programmers, management consultants,
environmental specialists, university administrators, website designers, actors, producers, nannies, paralegals, sales assistants, nuclear
weapons specialists, and the owner of a scrapbooking store.[19] Some
had loved their previous jobs, others not so much, but all had decided
organizing was a better fit for them at this particular point in their life.
Rather than framing that "better fit" as the product of individual preference and priorities, it's worth examining what exactly it was about
their previous jobs and industries that no longer worked for them.

For some organizers, standard employment didn't lose its appeal, it
never had any in the first place. Leila, a San Francisco organizer in her
mid-sixties, told me that growing up in her family, self-employment
was the norm. "On both sides of my family, everybody was always
self-employed. I think that that's kind of ingrained a little bit. With
the six children in my family, only one works for somebody else." She
tried working for someone else early in her career. "The longest I ever
lasted on any job was two years," she told me. Working for someone
else was easier, she said—"I wasn't necessarily working that hard.
I'd have plenty of free time in the evenings"—but it wasn't for her.
"After usually about a year I'd be bored to tears, there are no challenges. You walk into the office, you're already tired." She opened a
small bookstore, which she ran for more than a decade. When a rent
increase forced her out of business in the early 1980s, she decided her
new business would be helping other people run their own small businesses. When we spoke, she'd been a professional organizer focusing on business organizing for more than twenty years. "My goal,"
she told me, has always been "to make enough money to do what I
want." It hasn't been easy, she said, but she wouldn't have it any other
way. "When you're self-employed," she explained with a wry smile,
"you're free to work any eight days of the week you want. I've never
worked harder in my life; I've never had greater job satisfaction. I
can't imagine doing anything for as long as I've done this."

For Leila, working hard wasn't a problem, nor were the long hours
some jobs demand. What she couldn't handle was the monotony of

standard employment, the lack of variety, the mindlessness of the work, the feeling of exhaustion *before* the workday even began. Running her own business was harder and more time consuming than working a full-time job for someone else, but the freedom to "do what I want," rather than being told what to do, outweighed everything else. Leila wasn't looking for *easier* work, she was looking for *better* work, and, in organizing, she found it. This emphasis on freedom—to do what you want, when you want, and how you want—came up again and again in my interviews with organizers.

When thirty-five-year-old organizer Sophia was a child, she told her mother, "I'm never going to have a job where they are going to tell me how many vacation days that I'm going to have." Her mom replied, "Good luck." But Sophia has managed exactly that. After graduating from college on the East Coast with a degree in film studies, she moved to Los Angeles to work as an assistant to a well-known movie producer. For the next few years, she worked for a number of high-profile directors and producers. When one of her bosses moved into a new home, she offered, "I can help you do that." She unpacked the entire house, then went out and bought all the new items they needed to fully furnish it. She was good at it and enjoyed the work, so in between jobs assisting on movies she started helping clients organize their houses. "I kind of realized," she told me, "that I liked doing houses a lot more." It's one thing, she said, to help one person with their life, as she did during her assistant jobs. "But being able to work with all of these different kinds of people with different situations and to be able to do an immediate change, to come into someone's house, they haven't seen their kitchen countertops in ten years, and in one day I can make that different. It's exciting!"

Like so many of the organizers quoted earlier in this chapter, Sophia loved organizing, the process itself and the high of making a visible impact in a relatively short time. She was also drawn to the variety of the work, something she enjoyed about her time in the film industry as well. She decided to make the shift official and moved back to New York, where she apprenticed for a few years under one of the best-known organizers in the business. When she felt ready, and with the encouragement of her organizing mentor and former clients, she moved back to Los Angeles and, in 2008, opened her own organizing business. Starting her own business was "definitely scary," she said, "and as a single woman, I just didn't know if I could live on it . . . there weren't a lot of people who were doing it full-time and making the amount of money that you could live on, especially in LA." At the same time, that sort of uncertainty wasn't altogether new to her. "I think that I was kind of prepared for this life, too, because I came from the freelance background in film, in which you have a job, you do a movie, and when the movie ends you are unemployed." Her previous jobs had prepared her, she said, "not to go to work nine to five." By the time we met, she'd been organizing full-time for more than four years and had moved up to charging $100 an hour. "There are some months where I only have two days off, so it's been pretty crazy. It's been really busy and then all of a sudden it stops for a week and it's quiet, and the next week it's crazy again." This variability is scary at times, she explains, "because you don't have the security" of a regular full-time job. And yet, she mused, "nowadays with the jobs the way that they are, there isn't a lot of security anyway." She's grateful, then, that "the film career definitely prepared me for that, with having a job and [then] not having a job."

As Sophia notes, her experience in an industry characterized by short-term contracts and cyclical unemployment made the leap to starting an organizing business less intimidating. She also benefited from a strong network of fellow organizers and former employers. Not knowing when or how much she'd be working (or earning) in a given month was stressful, but she suspected that, these days, organizing wasn't that different from any other job in that respect. She didn't know that firsthand, having never worked a typical nine-to-five job. Other organizers did, and it was their experience in the very sorts of jobs Sophia and Leila had avoided that propelled them toward organizing work.

Maggie, an organizer in her early thirties, lives in Brooklyn with her partner Rachel. We spoke on the heels of Hurricane Sandy, when much of the city (my hotel room included) was still without power.

Trained as an artist, after earning her BA, Maggie took a full-time job at a nonprofit dedicated to supporting the arts. Maggie had never thought of herself as especially organized, but her colleagues praised her skill at organizing the large amount of information—both paper and digital—their work required. One of their partner organizations was so impressed that they hired Maggie as a consultant, on top of her full-time job, to implement new filing systems for them. "I was twenty-two, maybe, at the time," she recalled. "That was the first time that someone had paid me professionally to just actually, literally, go in as an organizer. I didn't think of myself as a professional organizer at that time."

Maggie eventually left that job to earn a master of fine arts degree. A self-described "queen of side jobs," to support herself during graduate school Maggie worked as a governess, house cleaner, art teacher, and tutor, among other roles. Employers continued to notice her organizational skills; she earned extra money organizing closets for house-cleaning clients and helping a boss manage his mail and organize his home office. Just after she completed her MFA, the school where she'd been teaching part-time told her she would have to switch to full-time or lose her health insurance. Some people would welcome the stability of a full-time position, but, as Maggie told me, "I didn't really want to spend the rest of my life being a high school teacher. That wasn't what I had envisioned for myself."

She hadn't necessarily planned to be a professional organizer, either. "When I came to organizing as a profession," she said, "it was not because I was like 'This is the ultimate career for me. This is what I've always wanted to do.' It was much more 'This is where probably I'm going to make the most money on my own terms, being self-employed, using the skills that I have.'" What she didn't want, she knew, was a full-time job. In her mind, she explained, taking a full-time job would mean a loss of freedom. "This is all, like, 'freedom' in quotes," she clarified, "because you're not any more free working for yourself and working three part-time jobs than you are necessarily having a full-time job." Nevertheless, her brief experience in full-time work, even at a job she'd enjoyed and found meaningful, was enough to convince her that was not the life for her. Thus, while she knew that whatever freedom she'd gain would need to be secured firmly within air quotes, at some core level, she still knew it *felt* freer, at least to her.

In the two years since she started organizing full-time, Maggie's time working with corporate clients has only confirmed her impression of standard employment. "I do really like variety," she said. "When I go in and work at [corporate client offices] and I see these people, I do not envy them at all going to the same place every day and having a boss. I think that might be something I also don't want—a boss. They just all seem really miserable." When organizing work is slow and finances are tight, "there are moments when having that stability seems really, really great." In those down times, she takes on as many side jobs as she can find, and she's grateful for her partner's steadier income, but she's uncomfortable not always being able to pay her full share of expenses. She's even talked with her partner, she told me, "about how I should just apply for a full-time job and let all this craziness just go away and just go to one place every day." And yet, ten years have passed since Maggie and I first spoke, and she still hasn't opted to return to full-time employment.

For Maggie, a brief taste of full-time work and occasional forays into corporate environments were all it took to compel her to start her own business. For others, the decision to leave full-time employment took much longer and, when it came, was not entirely voluntary.

At fifty-three, organizer Lara had spent most of her adult life working for someone else. Originally from the East Coast, she moved to California in the 1970s to attend college but dropped out to work full-time as a receptionist at a large financial services company. Her attention to detail and straightforward manner earned her a quick promotion to secretary, then personal assistant. She started attending night school and, upon earning her associate's degree, was promoted to office manager, a position she held for nearly twenty years. In 2010, she was laid off without warning due to budget cuts. Lara's husband also worked, but she'd always earned the bigger income. "Not working," she told me, "was not an option. I had to get to work." But after three decades of working for someone else, she was dreading the idea of going back to corporate America. "I just did not want to sit behind the desk anymore. The most important thing to me was that I didn't want somebody else to have control over me for the rest of my life—[to control] when I get a raise, if I got a raise, when I went on vacation. I just needed to have some independence." Lara might not have wanted to lose her job, but once she did, she couldn't imagine going back.

In this regard, Lara resembled many of the laid-off high-tech workers I met in my previous research on white-collar unemployment. Even elite tech workers who had plenty of financial reserves and strong professional networks cringed at the thought of ever again putting themselves in a position where someone else got to decide whether or not they had a job. Even after he found another lucrative, high-level position, one interviewee's "underlying anxiety" that he might be laid off again never went away.[20] The "dread" Lara speaks of about returning to corporate work suggests a similar anxiety, one that led her to make a dramatic midlife change of profession.

Lara had always imagined she'd be good at running her own business, and around the time of her layoff she'd learned about professional organizing when her cousin mentioned NAPO to her. "I thought that they were teasing me," she said. "They know I have OCD," she continued—she'd been diagnosed with obsessive-compulsive disorder years before—"and I'm an organizing crazy person. I thought it was a joke." Her cousin assured her NAPO really did exist, and Lara attended a meeting of the Los Angeles chapter. "That," she said, "is when I realized that people could actually do this for a living." She launched her business the next day. Within two weeks she had her first client. "I didn't have time to stop and think, 'What if this doesn't work out?' It was never an option. It was always, this is going to be what I am going to be doing for the rest of my life."

Two years into running her own business, Lara rises most days by 6 a.m. Between organizing sessions, emailing, scheduling and confirming appointments, and attending networking events, she works ten to twelve hours a day. "Then at ten o'clock," she sighed, "I fall into bed and that's it. It's a long day and that goes on six days a week. That is a lot of hours."[21] She's always been a hard worker; that part is not new. What *is* new is the insecurity of not earning a steady paycheck. Her husband recently quit his job to start his own business, so the couple's spending has scaled back dramatically. "The first two years," she told me, "we watched everything. There were no vacations. I immediately traded in my car. I immediately stopped spending. It's a huge adjustment, but [we're] getting used to it, realizing what is important, what's not." Early on, she'd hired an accountant and figured out exactly how much money she'd need to make a year—minus business insurance, assistant fees, and taxes—to cover her share of family expenses—as she said, "to pay my bills and keep my home." She saw a profit her first year in business and doubled it in her second. When we did our first interview in 2012, she was close to earning her target annual income for the first time. She was, she said, "working my way to get back to that financial security that I need and want." "I'm not there yet," she told me, "but I'm hoping by the end of this year I will be able to breathe."

Not being able to breathe sounds pretty awful, but, then, so does the dread Lara experienced at the thought of returning to corporate work. Compared to traditional full-time employment, self-employment may feel like freedom, but it's no walk in the park. Sophia, Maggie, and Lara were all managing to support themselves, to varying degrees, through their organizing work. To do so, they tend to work long hours, longer even than they did in their "full-time" jobs. All three also described the stress of not knowing where or when their next paycheck will come from. The Covid-19 pandemic only exacerbated that uncertainty, as some organizers, especially those who specialize in moves, found themselves busier than ever, while others ceased work entirely for months on end. To weather these cycles, some organizers are able to draw on savings, unemployment assistance,[22] small business loans,[23] a spouse's earnings, or alternate income streams.[24] Others have none of those options, akin to the one in three Americans who, in a financial emergency, could not come up with $2,000.[25] Despite the long hours and constant uncertainty, Sophia, Maggie, and Lara all chose to stick with organizing; as of 2023, they'd all been in business for more than a decade, and organizing remains their primary source of income.

In an era of rising insecurity, when even so-called permanent jobs can disappear without warning, the choice is not so much between security and insecurity as between different *kinds* of insecurity.[26] Organizers' decision to pursue self-employment should thus be understood as a strategy for obtaining security, rather than a willingness to sacrifice it.[27] And yet, it's a strategy with significant drawbacks, and not just for organizers.

For although these organizers have freed themselves from monotonous and restrictive corporate jobs, they've also placed responsibility for their financial well-being entirely on their own shoulders. That's a trade-off they and other organizers were willing to make in return for the freedom to schedule their own vacations, set their own rates, and do work that was varied and fun. It also allowed them to escape from the monotony, power dynamics, and insecurity of corporate employment.[28] But it's a trade-off nonetheless, one that leaves organizers and their households bearing heavy burdens while employers are off the hook for providing secure, livable, rewarding forms of work. I'll return to this line of argument at the end of this chapter, but before I do, I want to first turn to organizers' other central complaint with standard employment, namely that it is incompatible with the other, unpaid work they are also expected to perform.

Pursuing Flexibility

When I interviewed Becky, a married organizer with two children, I had just learned that I was pregnant. I can't speak for other anthropologists, but one of my favorite parts of fieldwork is the opportunity to step into other people's homes and lives, to glimpse, even if only briefly and incompletely, the inner workings of another household. In this case, stepping into Becky's two-story, 1960s-style home, tucked away on a dead-end road at the foot of the Hollywood Hills, was also a chance to witness the life of a working mother, a category I would soon be joining.

We settled down at a large, well-worn dining table. Photographs of her children taken over the years lined the wall behind me. As Becky made herself a cup of coffee and me a mug of tea, I watched her boys grow from newborns to toddlers, kindergartners to middle schoolers, all across the stretch of a single wall. When she returned, bearing freshly baked cinnamon muffins, Becky told me how she'd come to start her organizing business six years before.

After graduating from a small liberal arts college in the Midwest, Becky started working behind the scenes in television, first in set design, then as a stage manager. When she was in her late thirties, she met her husband at work. The two were soon married and expecting their first child. Becky had always assumed she'd go back to work. Work had always been "super important" to Becky. She loved her job and the people she worked with. Working in TV, she said, "is fun and fabulous." And so, when her first son was five months old, she returned to her job at a local television station. "I lasted two days," she told me. "I said, 'I cannot do this.'" Despite having found a great childcare provider, she said, "I just could not be away from him. It was just too hard. And I had the luxury of my husband having a good enough job that I could stop working."

Becky was aware how fortunate she was to be able to leave her job in order to focus full-time on parenting; without a working spouse with a high-enough income, it simply wouldn't have been an option, no matter how hard it was to leave her infant son each day.[29] Nevertheless, she hadn't *wanted* to leave her job; she'd been pushed to because she couldn't take any more leave but she just wasn't ready to be away from her baby all day. Had Becky lived in one of the many countries that offer extended paid parental leave, she might have happily gone back to her old job after a bit more time at home with her child. (Sweden, for instance, offers 480 days of paid leave to be shared by both parents; France allows both parents to take paid leave until their child's third birthday.) But Becky doesn't live in those countries; she lives in the United States, one of just six countries in the world that don't guarantee paid parental leave.[30] And so, she gave up that "fun and fabulous" job she'd loved. Even so, Becky was fortunate to have had a choice, albeit a limited one between less-than-ideal options. Another organizer I met left a similarly demanding media job when she had her first child. When she tried to find a new position after eight months home with the baby, no one would hire her, a common experience among women with children.[31] "Isn't that crazy?" she asked incredulously. "It was just eight months!"

After a few years Becky had another son and decided to stay home until both her children were in school. She wanted that time with them when they were young, but she loved and missed her work in television and looked forward to contributing financially to the household again. But when the time came, she couldn't find a job that fit her new life as a working mother. She'd expected to return to her old industry, but "it turns out there's really not something you can do in entertainment that doesn't have crazy hours and doesn't want to take that first high-priority place in your life. And I didn't want to do that." As is the case for many professional women returning to work after a career break, Becky's priorities and work preferences had shifted, but the nature of her job and what it demanded of her had not.[32] And while the entertainment industry may be uniquely demanding in some respects, other jobs weren't much better when it came to combining them with responsibilities of primary parenting.

As she considered new career paths, Becky realized, "I can't just go work for somebody. Everything I found was like 'Well, what happens when my kid's sick and I have to skip work?' Not necessarily possible." Just as the lack of paid parental leave shaped Becky's decisions around work, so did employers' lack of flexibility in case of family emergencies. (Although most OECD countries offer paid caregiving leave—ranging from a few days to as long as three years in the case of a critically ill child—the United States has no national family caregiving or medical leave policy.[33]) Her husband's job required frequent travel and did not allow him much scheduling flexibility either, so the responsibility for managing both the day-to-day parenting and any specific crises fell squarely on Becky. She could have hired a nanny or after-school childcare, she said, noting how fortunate she was to even have those options, but the whole point of stepping back from her career had been to spend more time with her children, so that didn't feel like the right choice either. Ultimately, she decided, "running my own business seemed like a great plan." The only question was what sort of business it would be.

Becky's friends and fellow school volunteers noted how organized she was, and told her, "You should do that for other people." Like so many other soon-to-be organizers, she had no idea that job existed. She researched the field—"how to market, how to build the website, what kind of licensing do you have to have, contracts, business plans, all that kind of stuff." She also considered "how it will affect my family's finances, good or bad, all those kinds of things." Their family could get by on just her husband's income, so the plan was that Becky's earnings would, ideally, cover the cost of two college educations (not a paltry sum in the United States today). Her approach, she says, was "Okay, let's see logistically if it will work and if it sounds like something I want to do." Ultimately, she decided, "Yes, I can do that."

Unlike Leila and Sophia at the start of this chapter, entrepreneurship wasn't something Becky had been dreaming of or aiming for all her life. And unlike Lara and Maggie, Becky didn't dislike her experience working for someone else—the only "freedom" she was after was the freedom, if we can call it that, to be the kind of parent she wanted to be: engaged, present, available in a crisis. Had she been provided a longer leave, had jobs in her field offered shorter or more flexible hours, had there been better support systems in place in case of family emergencies, had her husband's job allowed him more flexibility to share the work of parenting or had he moved to one that did, she would have stayed in her old industry. But none of those things happened, and so, like so many women in similar positions, Becky was forced to consider alternatives to standard employment.

Although she was good at it and enjoyed organizing, for Becky, the job's major allure was that, in her view, "it fits really well with being a mom." Her choice of the gendered word "mom," rather than "parent," is apt. Despite women's gain in the workplace and the narrowing gap between men's and women's earnings, women nonetheless continue to perform the majority of household chores and caregiving.

The "rightness" of this divide is reinforced by cultural attitudes; as of 2023, most Americans still believed that society values women's contributions at home more than their contributions at work, and that the opposite is true for men.[34] Thus even in opposite-sex marriages with two working parents, the burden of combining paid employment with household responsibilities falls more heavily on women. The ability to manage one's own working time outside the constraints of a standard job is thus one of the major draws to self-employment, especially for women.[35]

By no means is self-employment a magic bullet that alleviates the challenges of managing paid work and caregiving. Becky's initial plan, for instance, was to work Monday through Friday, 8 a.m. to 2 p.m., while her sons were at school. She was up-front with clients about the fact that she didn't work weekends and her weekday hours were limited. As a result, her business grew more slowly than she'd have liked. During the first two years, she recalls, "I spent a lot more time marketing than I did actually organizing, trying to get my name out there." She often found herself passing along attractive jobs to organizers she'd met at NAPO who were willing to work weekends. If she'd needed her organizing income to support her and her family, she'd have had to fold the business long before it became profitable. Over time, though, her business has grown to the point that she regularly works six to eight hours a day, four days a week. She even takes weekend jobs, on occasion, although she charges a higher rate for those ($85/hour vs. $65/hour on weekdays) to cover the cost of childcare. She expected the higher rate would deter clients, but it hasn't seemed to. "I have found," Becky continued, "that the busier I've gotten, there just aren't enough hours in a day to book all the clients."

Just a few weeks before our interview, Becky's sons had begun attending an afterschool program two days a week to allow her additional afternoon hours for work. The arrangement wasn't ideal. Becky prefers being free to pick her boys up from school. "I like them to come home and have that downtime and playing-together time and play-with-me time." She'd recently told her husband, "My worry is if

I do these two [long work] days, then it's going to be three, and then all of a sudden they'll be in [aftercare] five days." And that, she said, was exactly what she *didn't* want when she started the business. "The more your business grows, it's fabulous, I can't say anything bad about it, except that it's hard to stop it where you have to stop it. So that's the trick—I'm right in the middle of trying to figure that out."

The challenge for Becky is to manage her desire to grow her business and earn more money with her desire to spend a lot of time with her children, which was the very reason she wanted to start her own business in the first place. I spoke with many organizers in a similar boat. Some, like Becky, were in two-income marriages, and thus able to keep a reduced schedule without derailing the family finances.

Vanessa, for instance, a forty-year-old married mother of two, has been organizing for more than a decade. She was single and self-supporting when she started her business, then continued organizing after she got married and had children. "What I love about my organizing path so far has been that I organized for so many years before I had kids. And I had kids and I was able to maintain my business." That's not to say her business didn't change as a result of becoming a parent. Before having kids, Vanessa says, she returned business emails immediately and worked whatever hours her clients needed her. Now, she returns work emails within twenty-four hours, rather than right away, and, like Becky, she tailors her schedule around caring for her two young daughters. She'll occasionally work longer days if the job requires it, but "those days are not often," she says, because "I just know I'm going to be tired and I'm not going to see them [her daughters]." Her husband, an entertainer, usually works evenings, so he's able to look after the girls during the daytime hours when they're not in school. This was especially helpful during the Covid-19 pandemic, when Vanessa and her husband coordinated their work schedules to oversee their daughters' virtual schooling. (Vanessa continued to work with existing clients during the pandemic; she wore masks, stayed socially distant, and, thanks to Southern California's generally mild climate, was able to do most of the sorting at folding tables set up in clients' yards.)

For Vanessa, any income lost as a result of her limited hours is well worth the benefit to her family and well-being. As Vanessa says, "I kind of feel like I have the best of both worlds. I get to do a job that fulfills me and I get to still be present for my kids when I need to be. So, I feel like I'm super lucky that I found a job that does that for me." Nevertheless, Vanessa sometimes struggles with the limitations she's placed on her business in order to make time for her family. Reducing her work hours and responding to work emails within twenty-four hours, rather than right away, required adjusting her own expectations as well as her clients'. She told me she has to remind herself sometimes, "This is my life and this is okay. I'm still running a good business. I'm still there for my clients."

That Vanessa needs to reassure herself that it's "okay" for her to work less and be less available to her clients reveals ongoing tensions around what it means to run a good business, the same tensions we see in Becky's worries about the slippery slope toward longer work hours. To some degree, Vanessa and Becky have both internalized the idea that working long, unrestricted hours and being constantly available to clients is what it takes to run and grow a successful organizing business. At the same time, that model of success doesn't fit with their role as engaged parents. Both women—and many others in their shoes—are struggling to live up to two mutually exclusive ideals, what Beckman and Mazmanian call the "ideal worker" and the "perfect parent."[36] The ideal worker puts in long hours, is always available, and is totally dedicated to his work. The use of the masculine pronoun is intentional here, as the ideal worker is traditionally a masculine role, regardless of whether the people inhabiting the role identify with the gender attached to it.[37] The perfect parent, in this case a role gendered feminine, dedicates her entire self to the project of child-rearing, putting her child's needs before her own and engaging in extended and enriching "quality" family time.[38] Neither of these ideals is actually attainable—it is impossible to be consistently, one-hundred-percent perfect as a worker *or* a parent, let alone both. And yet, the ideals themselves are powerful and persistent cultural beliefs, ones working parents have to grapple with whether they fully subscribe to them or not.

Despite these tensions, Vanessa wasn't the only organizer who described herself as "lucky" to have "the best of both worlds" in combining her work as an organizer with her role as a parent. Carol, a married mother of two, used the exact same language to describe the organizing business she started in 1995 when her younger child was in kindergarten. She hoped to supplement her husband's larger and more stable income by $1,000 a month working part-time, which would allow her to be home with the kids when they weren't in school.[39] If she couldn't meet that target, she reasoned, "then I had to go and get a real job," drawing that familiar distinction between "real" and "part-time" work. She exceeded that goal, eventually earning enough to put both kids through private school, at $30,000 a year, from elementary through high school, all through part-time organizing. "I think that's what most moms want," she told me, "to be able to have the best of both worlds, be able to make a living and have something of their own."[40] Looking back, she's glad that "I had my own life. I had my own career and I didn't miss any soccer games or plays. So, I was really lucky that way."

Although Carol and Vanessa both frame their ability to combine organizing and parenting as the product of "luck," it is of course more complicated than that. Married organizers with children like Becky, Vanessa, and Carol have spouses to help them carry the twin burdens of work and parenthood, allowing them to work flexible, limited hours without derailing the household's finances. In Vanessa's case, her husband also shares childcare responsibilities. The three are from different racial backgrounds (Vanessa is Black, Becky and Carol are white), but all three are middle to upper class and all completed some higher education (Becky and Vanessa have bachelor's degrees, while Carol attended secretarial school). Rather than "luck," it was thanks to these combined advantages that, for these women, starting a business wasn't as risky as it might have been for others, because their households weren't dependent entirely on their income.[41] For organizers who lacked these sorts of supports, organizing's "flexibility" had a sharper double edge.

Michaela, a single mother in her forties, is raising her elementary-school-aged daughter on her own and prizes the flexibility organizing allows her. A Black woman with an associate's degree, Michaela decided to start her organizing business following a layoff from an office manager position. She didn't choose to leave that position, but she prefers working for herself anyway. At her previous job, she said, "I couldn't even ask for some time off to see my daughter [perform] in something at school. . . . I wouldn't even ask for the time because I knew the answer would be no." Now that she is self-employed, she said, "I have the freedom and the flexibility. I have nobody over my head, I have nobody being nasty to me." Her experiences working in offices were so bad, she says, that she won't even take business-organizing jobs. Not even the generally higher prices corporate gigs pay could lure her back into that toxic, overly restrictive environment.

When we first spoke, Michaela had been in business for six years. That year had been her most profitable yet, but it had ended with a month-long dry spell that had her worried. "I was disillusioned also," she recalled, "because I [had] thought I'm on the steady upwards spiral, like it's not going to stop. And then it stopped and I was like, now what? It wasn't the best feeling, that's for sure." I asked how she handled those challenging times. "After I cry," she said, "I have to forge ahead. I don't have a choice. I don't have any family that I can rely on. There is nobody there that I can say, 'Let me borrow this X amount of dollars.' I have a child that depends on me, so I have to go ahead." Michaela tries to schedule her clients while her daughter is at school. Otherwise, she says, it starts to feel like she's only working in order to pay for the babysitters she hires to allow her to work. "Because what is the point of making money," she asks, if she has to spend it on babysitters? Michaela's double bind makes clear the limits of flexibility in the absence of affordable childcare or a partner who can (and will) share in childcare responsibilities. She needs the flexible hours as much as, if not more than, the other working mothers described above, but unlike them, she can rarely afford to trade potential income for more hours at home with her child. In this sense, the promise of flexibility is more elusive for organizers with limited financial and familial support.

Thus, while a flexible schedule is one of organizing's major draws, especially compared to the rigid hours of traditional full-time employment, that same flexibility can work against organizers with limited financial and familial support, who feel they need to take every job they can get, no matter how inconvenient the hours. This mirrors the way in which flexibility tends to operate in employer-employee relationships, where the most privileged workers enjoy the positive aspects of flexible work while the less privileged bear more of its burdens.[42] In the latter case, flexibility can at times be experienced as just another form of control and insecurity.[43] As a result, as many organizers attest above, choosing self-employment over working for someone else is really just trading one form of precarious work for another. But does it have to be?

Organizing Better Jobs

Over the previous half century, the United States has seen a dramatic decline in secure employment, even for those privileged workers who once took it for granted. Large numbers of Americans are jobless; even more work part-time only because they cannot find full-time work; still others do the work of full-time employees but are technically temporary or contract workers, refused access to the rights and privileges of employees. Those who do manage to land full-time work have seen the benefits long associated with such arrangements dwindle, as pensions disappear, costs of health insurance rise, and new technologies allow work responsibilities to occupy more and more of workers' time outside of regular work hours.[44] Even the most elite American professionals report deep dissatisfaction with their work. Apparently, as journalist Charles Duhigg has argued, "there is no magic salary at which a bad job becomes good."[45] We are thus living at a time when working for someone else is both more elusive *and* less attractive than in previous generations.

In this context, the appeal of working for oneself has grown, especially for those, like women, particularly women of color, who have traditionally been denied access to the best jobs anyway.[46]

Self-employed people, especially women, report high levels of job satisfaction, experience a greater sense of control over their work, and are more likely to believe they are regularly putting their strengths to use at work.[47] Financially speaking, median income for self-employed workers is about the same as for those who work for employers, not counting benefits (a significant exclusion).[48] And yet, while we live in a cultural moment in which all people, not just business owners, are being urged to see themselves as entrepreneurs[49]—to embrace risk, competition, and self-reliance—it's clear that for many people, the decision to start a small business is less an expression of nascent entrepreneurship than a response to a precarious labor market and unsatisfactory work arrangements.[50] In this respect, as anthropologist Dawn Rivers argues, self-employed small business owners are "neither entrepreneur nor entrepreneurial," at least not in the risk-taking, aim-for-the-stars sense that entrepreneurship tends to be understood.[51] Most of them "would happily return to a traditional job if they could find one that would allow them to find the same meaning and structure they have created for themselves" through self-employment.[52] Having been unable to find such a unicorn of a job, many Americans, organizers included, have turned to self-employment in an effort to gain control over the work they do, how and when they do it, and who they do it with.[53]

Thus, while organizers may be pulled to this work by their love of organizing, they're also pushed to it by the failings of the other work arrangements available to them. They've chosen organizing as an alternative to jobs in which they were treated poorly; worked long hours on someone else's schedule; performed monotonous, unsatisfying tasks; missed their kids; endured discrimination; and generally felt their work lives were out of their own control. Through organizing, they have worked to craft livelihoods that, while still stressful, demanding, and uncertain, offer a reprieve from some of the worst aspects of their previous careers.

And yet, although leaving standard employment has arguably improved many organizers' lives, it hasn't done anything to improve the jobs and industries they left behind. The problems with work that organizers, and so many others, seek to escape through self-employment aren't gone, they're just someone else's problem. Because becoming an organizer—like starting most other small businesses—is harder for some due to class and racial inequities, the people likely to be stuck in the least appealing jobs are those with the fewest financial and other resources. Consider, for instance, the Black organizers described in the last chapter who organize only on weekends because they can't afford to leave their full-time jobs. This is the problem with individualistic solutions to systemic problems; they leave the system itself unchanged. As Michal Pagis has argued, "Paradoxically, while trying to improve their work conditions, workers use strategies that end up supporting the reduction in workplaces' responsibility for employee satisfaction."[54] In this case, the "strategy" of going to work for oneself abdicates employers' responsibility for providing workers—especially women—with secure, satisfying jobs that accommodate their professional and personal priorities.

One can imagine a scenario in which, rather than giving up on standard employment entirely, disgruntled workers might ask more of their employers, rather than less. They might demand more security, more variety, more freedom in how they accomplish their work and how they schedule their work lives. They might insist on paid parental and caregiving leave, a limit to work communications outside of regular working hours, and better and more easily transferable benefits.

Even after they've made the leap to self-employment, organizers and others might ask more of their communities and their government in order to reduce the burden on themselves and their households. They might demand free or inexpensive high-quality childcare so they don't have to pay the babysitter most of what they earned in a day's work. They might champion a universal basic income, a regular cash allowance to all citizens regardless of individual need, to help them endure the inevitable slow periods when work is harder to come by.[55] They might insist that social supports like healthcare, pensions, and disability and unemployment insurance be delinked from standard employment and made equally available to the self-employed.[56] They might envision all sorts of changes, large and small, that make it easier for them to do their jobs while also living fuller, more reward-ing, less stressful lives.[57]

To be clear, what I'm suggesting is not a return to the "good old days" of secure employment. Such calls often rely on misplaced nostalgia—the old days weren't good for everyone. Some peo-ple never had access to those jobs in the first place. As well, part of what made standard full-time jobs work so well, for employees and employers alike, was the unpaid or underpaid labor of others. The nine-to-five workday was built for men whose wives (and sometimes housekeepers and nannies) managed the work of maintaining the home and family.[58] Even if those "good" jobs magically reappeared—which seems unlikely—they wouldn't work for today's workers any-way, many of whom are single parents (usually mothers), couples who require two incomes, or individuals who want work that is more varied, meaningful, and socially beneficial.[59] Rather than lamenting the decline of secure employment, as so many have done to so little effect, it makes more sense to consider how Americans' work might be remade anew: safer, more stable, more equitable and accessible, more rewarding, both personally and financially.[60]

I'll return to this subject at the close of this book. But first, in part II, I'll turn my attention to the actual work organizers do with clients. Because, as it turns out, a big part of organizing involves helping cli-ents manage the same sorts of challenges organizers themselves have faced, how to deal with the competing, overwhelming demands of the work they're supposed to do and the gendered expectations of the society in which they do it.

part II

THE ORGANIZING PROCESS

One summer Saturday I joined Marilyn, a thirty-year-old organizer, on a job working with Nan, an elegant executive in her fifties who had just relocated from Texas
to Los Angeles for work. Nan's employer was paying for her three-bedroom
apartment, which was a lot smaller than the home she'd moved from. Marilyn
and Nan had already been working together for a week, sorting through Nan's
belongings, discarding or donating some items, and figuring out how to arrange
what remained in this new space.

Marilyn likes to start each session with a meditation, which Nan was open to.
After the meditation, Marilyn asked me to gather Nan's shirts into one place so
Nan could begin sorting through them. Nan was still in the process of moving in
and her clothes, a mix of high-end professional attire, workout gear, and casual
wear, were stored in multiple spots—two dressers, one short and one tall, a wall-
length mirrored closet, and at least five suitcases of varying sizes stashed in a
corner behind her bed.

While I worked in the bedroom, pulling t-shirts from drawers and blouses from
hangers, I could hear Marilyn and Nan sorting through materials in the home
office. Before they'd started in that room, I'd separated Nan's large collection of
office supplies into categories—pens, pencils, pads of paper, staples, and so on.
Now they were working through them, deciding which to keep, which to throw
away, and where to store those that remained inside and atop the large mahog-
any desk Nan had inherited from her father.

When I'd last passed by the office door, they'd been working on pens and it
seemed to be going slowly. I asked Marilyn about it later. "Every client's different,"

she told me. "I've had clients tell me 'Anything that's office related, throw [it] away,' and I just threw away more than half the room. Then this client, she has to look at each individual item, tell me about its history, and then talk about if she needs it or not, if she needs to fix it, and then [she] decides. So, if we're talking about that much time for one thousand, two thousand items, that's the time it takes."

This was what was going on with the pens. "First," Marilyn described, "she had to test each one to see if they work. And each one had a story." Of one pen, for instance, Nan said, "I love this pen. I usually use it for crafting," before setting it in the keep pile. "She had to tell me the story for each one and touch it. Each pen, each pencil." Typically, Marilyn explained, "when people touch something they're more likely to hold on to it." In such cases, Marilyn "manages the situation" by not letting the client touch anything. Instead, she holds up each item herself and the client tells her yes or no without ever laying hands on it.

Nan didn't have trouble letting things go, but she did seem to need to talk through each decision aloud with Marilyn before doing so. Even replacement ink cartridges had to be touched one by one, but Nan "promptly threw some of them [away] after the story was told." Ultimately, Nan discarded or donated about half of the office supplies.

I continued gathering tops while the two took a short break. By this point, the king-sized bed was covered with piles of shirts, some stacked more than ten high. Even so, the closet, drawers, and suitcases were still more than half full with the categories I hadn't yet touched—pants, dresses, pajamas, sweaters, jackets, and more.

After their break, Nan came into the bedroom to begin sorting. Although she'd been warm and enthusiastic up to that point, she was curt when I asked how she'd like to proceed. She eyed the pile on the bed, lips tightly pursed. She walked around the room, looking into the open closet, opening and closing drawers. Then she walked out and I heard her speaking to Marilyn in hushed tones. After a few minutes, Marilyn came back and asked me to help with a different task, wrapping and boxing Nan's delicate crystal and china pieces before we stored them high on a shelf in her hall closet.

As we worked, I quietly told Marilyn that I thought I had done something to upset Nan, who was now on the phone in another room. Marilyn confirmed that Nan was distressed, but said I shouldn't take it personally. "She was very, very, very overwhelmed," Marilyn said, "because she saw the whole contents of the room out, all her clothes, all that she had. It just looks so much bigger when you're in a smaller space." When Nan saw the shirts piled on the bed, Marilyn continued, "she said that it was more stressful than when it was unorganized. Because she didn't know that she had that much."

This, Marilyn said, was "where the tricky part comes in for the organizer." As she'd explained to Nan, "It's a process. You can't go around it without getting all the stuff out. So, she's going to have to go through the uncomfortable stage." Marilyn said this happened in a lot of organizing jobs. "There's that little hump," Marilyn explained, "and it's always right in the middle of the project." The organizing process "really sheds light on every single piece, every single item that you have." When Nan saw that pile on the bed, "everything fell upon her and it was too much to deal with."

The good part, Marilyn had reassured her, was that this "little hump" would pass. "When you release it, or when you decide on a home for some of this stuff, and make sure everything fits, then that's where the transformation comes in." I asked whether she thought Nan would be able to pare down her wardrobe as she had her pens. "Definitely," she replied. "I think she's totally ready. By the time she called me, it had just gotten to that point. She's totally ready to get rid of stuff."

The two had decided to start fresh on the clothing in the morning. The job was already over budget, and Nan was not happy about it. To reduce costs, Marilyn had offered to give Nan "homework," organizing tasks to complete on her own before we returned the next day. Nan declined, telling Marilyn, "No, I want to do all of this with you here." Later, as we loaded her supplies into the back of her car, Marilyn told me, "It's interesting when they want to get everything done so fast, but they also want you to be there for every decision. They just want to talk to you."

4

Sort, Purge, Put Back

The People-Changing Work of Managing Things

Up to this point, you've read a lot about *why* organizers do what they do. In part II, I turn to *what* organizers do when they work with clients. This chapter presents a fine-grained look at the organizing process—what it involves, how organizers manage it, and what it aims to achieve. Doing so requires some generalization, but I try not to ignore or minimize the extent to which clients, jobs, and organizers differ. To paraphrase anthropologist Clifford Geertz, I work to expose the similarities between organizing jobs without reducing their particularity.[1]

As organizers often say, every organizing job is different, but not *that* different. At core, they tend to involve the same key steps: sort, purge, and put back. In this chapter, I walk readers through those stages, noting the challenges that can arise along the way and the strategies organizers employ to avoid or overcome them. Some of this material builds upon the many organizing stories sandwiched between this book's chapters. (You already know, for example, that organizers often start by grouping like with like and that they rarely if ever force a client to part with a belonging.) I also bring in additional examples from my fieldwork and, occasionally, my own experiences of organizing my home and belongings.

In contrast to how organizing has been represented in popular culture and previous scholarly critiques, the organizers I worked with understood their role as one of respectful collaborator, rather than enforcer of specific ideals around order and aesthetics. And yet, their work often necessitates encouraging clients to part with possessions,

something organizers achieve through a variety of sometimes contradictory approaches, including physically distancing clients from their
possessions; encouraging clients to focus on their present-day needs
and priorities, rather than imaginary future ones; creating space for
clients to dwell on their feelings about a particular object—to tell its
story—before releasing it; and asking clients to consider who might
need or enjoy a specific item more than the client themself, thus
transforming the act of discarding unwanted goods into a gesture
of generosity and compassion. Through these and other strategies,
organizers engage in the work of transforming not just clients' homes
but also clients themselves. They help clients re-envision their relationships to their belongings, teaching them to think more, and differently, about the things they own—their purpose, potential, and the
price we pay for them, financially, environmentally, and emotionally.
In doing so, organizers offer a glimpse of other ways we might relate,
to our things and to each other, ways that diverge from the capitalist
default of accumulation, competition, and waste.

After laying this foundation, I move on to chapter 5, where I shift
my focus from clients' relationships to their belongings to their relationships with organizers themselves, including the complicated
work organizers do to forge and navigate those relationships.

• • •

In some respects, every organizing job is different. Some of this variety has to do with the wide range of specializations that fall under the
umbrella of professional organizing. Some organizers love working
with paper, others hate it. Some specialize in digital clutter, others
don't even have a website. There are organizers who obtain certifications specifically for working with clients who struggle with conditions that impede their ability to get and stay organized, such as
hoarding, obsessive-compulsive disorder, attention deficit hyperac-
tivity disorder, and traumatic brain injuries.[2] Other organizers consciously avoid such clients, either because they feel unprepared to
work with chronically disorganized clients or because they simply
prefer other sorts of jobs. Other organizing specializations include

photos and memorabilia, closets, garages, relocations, senior moves, filing systems, time management, space planning, estate sales, and organizing for feng shui, among others. Some organizers never set foot in private homes, preferring instead to work solely with businesses. The skills and tools a job demands naturally vary across such specializations. A photo organizer, for instance, might meet with a client once or twice then complete the job on her own at home, while an organizer working with a chronically disorganized person would rarely do any organizing without the client present.

The settings in which organizers work are as diverse as their areas of specialization. One Los Angeles organizer described the variety of her work this way: "One day you're in a celebrity's home and the next day you're in somebody's home who can't even afford to keep the power on, who saved up for months just for you to come over for four hours." Los Angeles organizer Vanessa told me, "It's still—after all these years—a little bit shocking how different your life can be when you're working as an organizer. One day you're helping a teacher clean out a garage and another day you're in Malibu looking at the ocean, cleaning out what was already pretty clean." She enjoys that variety, but Vanessa admitted that working with exceptionally wealthy clients can sometimes throw her for a loop. "There have been certainly some places where I have been in and thought, 'Holy mackerel!' We're going through people's closets and here's a $5,000 shirt or something, and it's just sort of unreal to me, even though I see it all the time." As I detail in the next chapter, working in such disparate settings, and for clients in such varying class positions, can require organizers to take on a chameleon-like quality, adjusting their emotional style and strategies to the specifics of a given job. And yet, on a practical level, organizing a closet of $5,000 designer shirts isn't all that different from organizing a closet of $15 t-shirts.

Despite the disparate settings in which organizing sessions can take place and the varying quality and quantity of items organizers are asked to assist with, the steps of the organizing process tend to be, at core, quite similar. One organizer told me that when she first began organizing, "I read a ton of books and did the research thing on organizing. Got every magazine [about organizing] and pretty quickly realized pretty much everyone does it the same way." Organizers might vary in the specifics, she said, endorsing different filing systems or favoring baskets over bins, but otherwise, the process tends to look about the same: "It's sorted into categories, we purge as much as we can, and then we put it away neatly. That's basically the same for everybody." Other organizers, she said, "probably wouldn't like me saying this, but yeah, there you go." Despite her suspicion that other organizers would disagree, or at least wouldn't want this said aloud, other organizers I interviewed tended to agree that the organizing process is usually predictable—group like items together, then purge, sort what's left, and put a new system in place.

Understandably, this isn't something you'd broadcast if you were an organizer trying to market a new book or show about organizing; in those cases, an organizer needs to distinguish their unique system from all the other ways of getting organized that people have already tried. (I'm thinking here of Marie Kondo's KonMari system, Julie Morgenstern's S.H.E.D. process, or the Home Edit's signature rainbow aesthetic.[3]) This is a key difference between what organizers do and what books about organizing *tell* people to do. Because a book or blog or TV show can't be tailored to each individual reader or viewer, the process has to be pitched as both novel and one size fits all. In real-life organizing, the opposite is the case. The process itself is usually pretty standard and straightforward; it's in *tailoring* that process to the individual client that things get complicated. For this reason, before the organizing process even begins, organizers tend to carefully weigh which clients they decide to work with.

Determining Fit through Consultations

Whether free or for a fee, in person or by phone or Zoom, organizers describe using consultations to determine whether a job is a good "fit," in terms of both the work involved and the client for whom they'd be doing it. One pair of organizers who co-founded a business told me their typical workday begins with responding to potential clients who'd called or emailed the day before. This is partly to beat out other organizers who might be competing for the job, they say, as "whoever calls them back first and whoever they establish rapport with the best, that's who they're going to work with." But there's another reason for responding promptly that has to do with the collaborative nature of the organizing process. "It's important for us," one of them explained, "to get back to someone as soon as possible, because I really feel like there's a psychological window for someone to be open to the idea of having a stranger come into the house and organize them." Thus, if the call goes well, they schedule a free, in-person consultation soon after because "we want to get in there at that moment." As in other personal service professions, such as personal training or life coaching, organizing usually requires a cooperative, invested client. If I hire someone to walk my dog or repaint my home, the mood or mindset I'm in when they arrive, or whether I'm there at all, is unlikely to interfere with their ability to complete that task. It's different for organizers. If a client doesn't feel like organizing or gets cold feet about working with an organizer, there's usually little the organizer can accomplish on her own. It's important, then, for organizers to assess a client's mindset and level of motivation to get organized *before* showing up to start organizing.

Another organizer who offers free in-person consultations explained that she always speaks with the potential client by phone before agreeing to meet them in person. Even from a brief phone call, she said, she can tell whether a client is likely to actually hire her. If a client seems overly anxious or doesn't seem to have thought through what they actually want to hire her to do, she suggests they call her when they have a clearer sense of the job. "I don't really want to go for the free assessment and waste my time if it sounds like it's not a client that's actually going to happen. So I'm pretty picky about that. That being said, most people who call really are ready to do it." For her, phone calls function as a pre-consultation consultation to save her time, especially in light of the long commutes that tend to be involved in Los Angeles, where she and most of her clients live. Other organizers solve that problem by charging for consultations, having found that people willing to pay for a consultation tend to be serious about actually hiring an organizer.

Organizers also use consultations to determine the nature of the job, the readiness of the client, and whether it's one they want to take. Organizer Hilda told me that when she goes to a potential client's home, "I can tell if someone's ready within the first half hour of talking to them. One red flag is when they say what they want to do but they never let you in the rooms." If just the thought of letting an organizer *look* at their space puts them "on edge," Hilda said, "they're not ready." In those cases, Hilda always explains why she is declining the job. "I say, 'You know what, I've really thought about this. We can't work together. As much as you really want to, you need to go get some kind of [psychological] help for it because we're never going to get anywhere.'" As an example, Hilda described a potential client who called her for help with the "paperwork chaos" associated with her family business. "But the minute I picked up one Post-it and moved it to this side," Hilda remembered, "she lost it and she went into the kitchen and closed the door." After that day, Hilda told that client, "I can't work with you. You need to go and work with a [mental health] professional to let you accept that you need help. You just want me to hold your hand and I can't do that." The woman asked her to reconsider, but Hilda held firm. She could have accepted the job, knowing it was unlikely they would make any real progress organizing the women's paperwork, but that felt both immoral and unproductive to Hilda. If she couldn't really help, she didn't feel right taking the job. As I describe in a moment, this reflects an agreement across the organizing profession that the client's best interests should outweigh the organizer's potential financial gain.

Sometimes, organizers say, the problem is not that the client is not ready, but that their family members may not be. DC-area organizer Yazmin offers potential clients what she calls a free "discovery call." "It's important to me," she said, "to have the whole family's buy-in" before she takes a job. "I can tell," she explained, "when a woman is like 'Okay, I'm up to here and I really want to do this' but the spouse is saying, 'I think it's fine as is.'" Some organizers might take that job, she said, but she would not. "I would not work with that client. I would have to have the buy-in from both because, at the end of the day, the home should be representative of both of them." Otherwise, she feared there might be resentment on the part of the unwilling spouse, which would make the job unpleasant or impossible. Here again, organizers aim to work with clients they feel they can actually help, rather than anyone willing to hire them.

In other instances, organizers felt ill equipped for the type or extent of work a job would involve. Lara, a Los Angeles organizer who told me she rarely turns down jobs, described one job she did decline. She'd been hired by the client's niece, who'd been appointed conservator of his estate. (That in itself was uncommon; most organizers don't allow their services to be "gifted," or purchased on behalf of someone else, without confirming that the recipient is open to working with an organizer.) "I went in," Lara said, "and the guy definitely didn't want any help. . . . He was just not ready, he was elderly and abrasive and strong." It was also a hoarding situation, which Lara said "was just way out of my comfort zone." She continued: "I believe that people who work with people that hoard should have a lot of training, maybe work with a therapist, but I didn't have that training and it just wasn't something that I was qualified to do, nor is it something that I want to be qualified to do. You learn what your strengths are and what your weaknesses are. You learn what to refer out. There's an entire pool of great organizers that will do something that you either don't want to or can't do, which is awesome." For Lara, the client's disposition was a challenge, but not an insurmountable one. However, once the nature of the job became clear, she decided it was outside her area of expertise and referred the client to a NAPO colleague who specializes in hoarding.

In cases like the one Lara describes, on-site consultations are also important because people's perceptions of their own situation can be unreliable. Terri, a research-scientist-turned-organizer, describes her initial calls with potential clients. "I try and gauge, you know, do you have a few piles around? Do you have lots of stuff? Do you have a pathway that you can walk to it?" A client might describe themselves as "a hoarder," but what that means on the ground can vary radically.

"People's perception of how messy or neat they are is wildly all over the net." One client told Terri, "I'm just such a mess. I'm terrible. It's awful. It's just the worst thing ever. I really need your help." When she arrived at the client's home for the consultation, Terri said, "I went into her office and she had this one stack of paper that was maybe half an inch thick on her desk. Not even that. It was just basically a few bits of paper on her desk and she's like 'I can't stand it. It's driving me nuts.'" On the other hand, she said, there are clients who tell her on the phone, "Oh no, it's not too bad." Then when she arrives at their home, "they've got piles of paper all over their desk and they've got paper behind them on the floor." As a result, she says, "When people say, 'I'm a mess,' well, I have to qualify that. I have to find out how much of a mess you actually really are, because you might not be as much of a mess as you think you are." Once Terri has a sense of how much "mess" is actually involved, she can determine whether she feels comfortable taking the job and how much time and expense it will likely involve.

I did hear of a few cases where organizers declined to work with clients who seemed dangerous or unstable. One organizer, for instance, told me she arrived on time for a consultation with a potential client and he answered the door in a towel, then seemed in no rush to get clothed. She cut the consultation short, she said, because the man gave her "a bad vibe," and later told him she would not be able to work with him. Many organizers told me they text a friend or family member their location every time they go on a job, in case something goes wrong. When organizers mentioned this, it was usually in the context of a job when a female organizer was working alone with a male client in the client's home. I didn't hear of any instances when an organizer was harmed by a client, or vice versa, but organizers' vulnerability in entering strangers' homes alone was openly acknowledged within the professional community, something I expect is less common in male-dominated professions that involve entering clients' homes, such as plumbing or pest control.

Whether they opt to take a specific job or not, the fact that most organizers feel they have a choice of which clients to work with distinguishes them from many service providers, who have far less agency in choosing their clients. This signals the relatively privileged position most organizers occupy and, as I discuss in the next chapter, shapes the nature of their relationships with the clients they do opt to work with. That said, I don't want to overidealize organizers' willingness to sacrifice financial gain for the good of their clients. There are undoubtedly organizers who'll take any job that pays, and if they did they might be unlikely to admit that in an interview. Organizer Yazmin, who had been in business for four years, told me that "when something within my gut tells me this is not the right client for me, I can respectfully say to them, 'I think what you might need includes more than I am able to provide to you at this time. And I would like to provide you some other recommendations of people that may be better suited to address your concerns.'" Yet she acknowledged that this response "takes growth, because initially when you're starting, you're just so happy to have clients, to have business, that you're like 'I'll do it!'"

That said, Yazmin and other members of the professional organizing community are openly critical of organizers who take any job that comes their way. At multiple meetings of the Los Angeles NAPO chapter, new organizers were warned not to take jobs they were ill prepared for, whether because the job was large and complicated or because it involved issues of hoarding or dangerous working conditions. For example, during a Q&A following a presentation at a NAPO meeting, one organizer noted she was in the process of starting her business and asked for advice on a job she'd just taken working with a man she described as a hoarder. She had no experience in this area and was feeling overwhelmed. Immediately, other organizers suggested she consider passing the job to a more experienced organizer, and perhaps assisting that organizer on the job in order to gain experience. The new organizer seemed annoyed by these suggestions. Newly divorced and with two children to support, she said she couldn't afford to "give the job away." Her response was met with concern from other organizers in the room. If she wasn't willing to give up the job, one told her, she might at least bring on a more experienced organizer as a partner. Otherwise, a few organizers worried aloud, she might do real harm to the client and make his situation worse, not better. At the meeting's close, multiple organizers approached the new organizer to offer their assistance or urge her to reconsider tackling the job on her own.

This and similar instances I witnessed or heard about suggest a strong consensus among organizers that the good of the client, and the reputation of the profession, sometimes necessitate placing the client's interests above the organizer's financial gain.[4] Once they accept and begin a job, organizers continue to navigate that tension between prioritizing the client and getting the job done, as they work to move the organizing process forward while respecting the intimate, often fraught relationships people have with their belongings.

Bring It All Out

As I noted in the story that opened this book, about Lauren and her frames, organizers usually defer to clients in terms of which area they want to work on, choosing to start with whatever area or areas the client is most bothered by. However, when a job involves an entire home or a large portion thereof, organizers make strategic decisions about where to start. That usually means focusing on one area or type of item at a time in order to avoid overwhelming the client. That's in part because, in organizing, things usually get worse before they get better. If you want to organize your junk drawer, for instance, the first step is to dump it all out so you can see everything. Only when you can see it all, organizers say, can you make informed decisions about what to keep and, in turn, how large and what type of space you'll need when it comes time to put everything back. Laid out in front of you, items tend to take up a lot more space than they did when tucked away in a drawer, cabinet, or closet; seeing everything laid out in front of you also brings home the reality of how much you actually own. For this reason, organizers generally recommend starting small, choosing to "warm up" with a space that can be worked through rather quickly and won't need to be left unfinished overnight. This has logistic and psychological benefits. It creates less mess, and it allows clients to see the results of the organizing process and to feel a rush of accomplishment that will hopefully help them power through the work yet to be done. In contrast, if you tackled every single room all at once, it would be difficult if not impossible to complete it all in one shot, and the client would be left with an unlivable space and without that motivating feeling of progress.

Sometimes, the gathering process requires first searching through an entire space to collect together all items of a single type. This was the case in the organizing story that precedes this chapter, in which I culled through Nan's closets, drawers, and suitcases to assemble all of her shirts in one place, or when I gathered all the empty frames from around Lauren's apartment. Although this process can sometimes be distressing—as was the case with Nan, who was upset at having to witness how much clothing she actually owned—its purpose is to allow clients to make informed decisions about what to keep and what to let go of. On one job I worked, the client said she didn't want to get rid of any sheets, because they were all "good sheets" in matching sets (fitted sheet, flat sheet, pillowcases). Once we took everything out of the linen closet, though, she could see that she had about a dozen sheet sets for an apartment with two beds. Together, she and the organizer discussed how many sheet sets she actually needed for her home. They decided on six, allowing for two on the beds, two in the wash, and two extra, just in case. The client then chose her six favorite sheet sets and donated the rest to a local animal shelter. I watched the same thing happen with other sorts of items—pens, towels, coffee mugs, spatulas, black V-neck t-shirts, you name it. Once they saw how many of an item they actually owned, rather than assessing each item individually for its quality or usability, people were more willing to cull what they now saw as surplus items. This didn't always work, as the stories I've shared about Lauren's frames and Cece's mugs attest. Sometimes this wasn't a problem. If the client has enough space to store everything, then having a dozen sheet sets or fifty mugs isn't a problem. Similarly, even a space jam-packed with items doesn't necessarily require attention if it's not bothering the client.

A room that feels crowded to one person might feel comfortable, even spacious, to another, depending on their "clutter threshold."[5] What constitutes "clutter" also depends on cultural norms around household design and decor.[6] Some believe clutter has been unfairly maligned in the contemporary United States. Contrary to the adage that a cluttered desk is the sign of a cluttered mind, some argue that clutter is a mark of, even a catalyst for, creativity and efficiency.[7] Others see clutter as a privilege, one rarely available to immigrants and refugees. "If our life is made from the objects we collect over time," one author writes, "then surely our very sense of who we are is dependent upon the things we carry."[8] Still others contend that narratives of clutter as a cultural threat have less to do with the mental health and safety of people living with clutter than with Americans' obsession with pathologizing difference and tendency toward moral panics.[9] Despite stereotypes of organizers as anti-stuff (one short story features an organizer who isn't happy until the client's home sits entirely empty, "not even a chair to sit in"[10]), organizers tend to agree with such critiques, regularly emphasizing that clutter is only a problem if a client thinks it's a problem.[11] In this way, organizers position the *client* as the expert on whether a space is in need of reorganization. As I explore more in the next chapter, this presents an interesting contrast to other practitioner-client relationships, such as doctor and patient, where the doctor's role is to determine both whether a problem exists *and* how to go about solving it. In organizing, the organizer's expertise comes in only *after* the client themselves has decided there is a problem in need of fixing, at which point organizers employ a range of strategies to help clients navigate the process of parting with some, or many, of their possessions.

Letting Things Go

Although organizers are grateful for the attention organizing shows have brought to their profession, many have serious qualms about such programs. They told me stories about producers *adding* objects to a room before the filming began to make it seem more crowded than it actually was, or leaving half the client's furniture on a tarp in the yard in order to get that perfect "after" shot of a sparsely decorated, well-organized room. Organizers also complained that such programs convey a misrepresentative sense of the time and effort involved in organizing a home. Even the briefest organizing sessions last longer than an hour-long episode, and most televised organizing efforts involve days of unseen, and expensive, labor. As one longtime organizer told me, thanks to organizing shows, potential clients often "think that in two hours we're going to do this wonderful makeover. They don't see that there are fifty people behind the sets [on organizing shows] and they were filming for hundreds of hours to make it a thirty-minute program." People who watch such shows thus end up with unrealistic expectations of real-life organizers, which organizers then have to manage as they pitch, price, and carry out real-life organizing sessions.

The biggest complaint organizers had about organizing shows, hands down, was how clients are treated on these programs, especially when it comes to the "purging" part of the organizing process, which many clients find quite difficult. Organizer Becky, for instance, told me she finds it "hard to watch how people are treated" on organizing shows. She described an episode of one show where a husband and wife were asked to choose one prized possession from among their belongings then play a silly game; whoever won the game got to keep their possession, while their spouse had to get rid of theirs. "Why would you ever do that to someone? It's their most prized thing. That's just not the way to do it." As Becky and other organizers told me, that's not how organizers interact with clients outside of the reality TV screen. "I treat my clients with respect," Becky said, "and I won't tell them they have to get rid of something." Some organizers explicitly note in their contracts that the client, not the organizer, retains ultimate control over the organizing process, and that all final decisions about what items to keep or discard will be made by them. This clause aims to allay any fears clients might have about being forced to part with items against their will, while also protecting the organizer should a client later regret the decision to get rid of (or keep) specific items.

Forcing people to give away their belongings or treating them harshly is not only unkind, organizers say, it's also ineffective, even counter-productive.[12] Organizer Eileen was especially critical of programs that involve cleaning out the home of someone who hoards, which she describes as "mental illness as entertainment." "Within six months of a clean-out," she told me, such homes "are usually back to where they were, and worse." Organizer Tess was equally critical of "clean-outs," whether televised or in person. Quick fixes don't work, she said, because you need to "honor" clients and allow them time to process the decisions they're making. Otherwise, she said, "they're going to be traumatized and go right back to where they started." In contrast, she and other organizers emphasize that organizing has to be an entirely consensual process that focuses on what the client can and wants to do, rather than what the organizer—or anyone else—thinks they *should* do.

Some clients are frustrated when an organizer refuses to make decisions for them. One organizer recalled an instance where a client was "really stressed" about sorting through her mother's belongings. Holding up one item, the client asked, "What should I do with this?" The organizer responded by asking questions about the item, what it meant to the client, whether or how she might use it. After some back-and-forth, the client said, "I hired you to tell me what to do." The organizer apologized, telling her, "I'm sorry, but it's not my nature to tell you what to do." Organizing, she later told me, "is not about enforcing anything." Instead, in yet another parallel to the therapist-client relationship, organizers see their role as guiding clients in making their own thoughtful, informed decisions, not making those decisions for them.

This organizer's use of the term "enforce" is significant. Organizers have indeed been described as "enforcers of order"[13] who are "scornful of—and hell-bent on correcting—their clients' apparently 'irrational'" relationships to their belongings.[14] But scholars like myself who have spent time with professional organizers have found that organizers are both aware of and sensitive to the deep, complicated relationships people have to their belongings.[15] Their object in working with clients is less to deny the connections we feel to our possessions than to help clients understand and navigate those connections in the course of achieving other goals.

And yet, as much as organizers are emphatic that they never make a client get rid of anything, there is no denying that a significant part of what they do involves helping people "let go" of things, which generally means to donate something, recycle it, or throw it away. For some jobs, purging items isn't all that important. In the organizing story about the mugs, for example, Cece wouldn't part with a single one of her dozens of mugs, but that was fine, because her large kitchen had space to store them all. But the vast majority of organizing jobs require that at least *some* items—often many items—be removed from a space: the contents of a three-bedroom house have to be winnowed down before a move to a one-bedroom condo; room has to be made to park a new car in a chock-full garage; or, as in an organizing story yet to come, costly storage units have to be emptied entirely. In such circumstances, it becomes difficult for the organizer to do their job if a client is unable or unwilling to part with many, or even any, items. This gets at an inherent tension in most organizing sessions: although organizers won't *make* a client part with something, their work often involves convincing clients to *choose* to part with more items than the client might initially want to.

In the course of doing so, organizers have ample cultural discourses on which to draw. As anthropologist Katie Kilroy-Marac has noted, the concept of "letting go" is pervasive in self-help and wellness culture more broadly, where it is understood to be a means of "relieving distress and achieving well-being."[16] We are encouraged to let go of the past, let go of toxic people, let go of negative emotions, all in the name of self-improvement and happiness. In this cultural moment, most clients are already primed to understand, and experience, letting go of objects as an act that benefits their emotional well-being. That still doesn't mean letting go is always easy, which is why organizers employ a range of strategies aimed to help clients part with their belongings.

Don't Touch It

While they sometimes do marathon jobs that last eight or more hours a day for multiple days, most often organizers schedule their sessions in three- to four-hour increments to avoid fatigue, for clients and for themselves.[17] What can be accomplished in a single session varies widely depending on the individual client. This can make it difficult for organizers to estimate how long a job will take or how to price it. Some organizers charge a flat rate per hour or session (often with a reduced per-session cost the more sessions you book), while others price by the job.[18] Each has pros and cons. When charged by the hour, organizers explained, some clients try to rush through the process to save money, or they suspect the organizer of moving slowly in order to log more hours. Pricing by the job can be tricky, because it's difficult to estimate how long a job will take, even after an organizer has visited the space in question. When people ask her to estimate how many hours a job will take, one longtime organizer said: "I always tell them, 'I never know until I work with you. Because it really depends on how fast you can make a decision.' Some people can look at something, and I'll say, 'Well, what about this? Is this something that you need? Or want to keep [it] for family? Donate it?' And they'll go, 'Yeah, get rid of it,' and 'No, no, I don't need that. Oh, yeah, I want to keep that.' And other people go, 'Oh, I don't know, I don't know,' and they can't make a decision. And they could ponder over [the item] and then go, 'I don't know, let's set it aside.'" Because every client works at a different pace, a stack of papers that takes an hour for one client might take six hours for another. It thus behooves the organizer to find strategies that both speed up the process and help fewer items land in the keep pile.

One strategy organizers employ is to physically distance the client from the item itself. When sorting through a stack of books, for instance, the organizer will hold one book up at a time and ask the client what they want to do with it, rather than having the client touch each book themselves. In her research on Canadian professional organizers, anthropologist Katie Kilroy-Marac describes this technique

as "blocking the 'tactile sympathy' that clients have for their possessions," in order to prompt a more "rational assessment" of the item.[19]
The organizers I worked with tended to agree that touching an object
can make one feel connected to it, which in turn makes it harder to
part with.

To keep up the pace, and to prevent the client from deliberating too
long about any individual item, organizers usually employ a sort of
binary shorthand—"keep or give," "yes or no," "stay or go," or something to that effect. When sorting this way, organizer and client tend
to develop a staccato rhythm I rather enjoyed overhearing: Keep, give,
keep, keep, give. When this approach works, the pen you used to help
your child correct their homework decades ago is reframed as just
another pen that is out of ink and needs to be discarded. Sometimes,
though, clients want to touch every single pen themselves, as you read
in the organizing story preceding this chapter. This often involves not
just touching the item, but talking about it. Some organizers might
interpret this as a problem, obstructing the swift process of parting
with items. Others, though, see these conversations as a key part of
the discarding process, rather than an impediment to it.

Tell Me the Story

In contrast to the strategy outlined above, some organizers employ a
different approach, one that actually encourages the client to linger
on the emotional connection they have to a given object. One organizer told me that when a client "picks up something [an item] that's
really emotional," he will sit with them and say, "Tell me the story.
Tell me the story. That's what you want to get out, get it out." Once the
story has been shared, he and other organizers explained, the client
is often more willing to part with the item itself. Marie Kondo, who
employs a similar approach, writes that "by handling each sentimental item and deciding what to discard, you process your past."[20] Here,
clients' "tactile sympathy" for their possessions is understood not as
something to be avoided or minimized, but as part of the process of
letting go. For clients still not quite ready to let the item go entirely,

organizers often recommend taking a photograph, which can serve as a reminder of the object and its story while allowing the item itself to be discarded.

Beyond its instrumental value, some organizers also place value on the exchanging of stories itself. As organizer Tess explained, "A lot of stories come up . . . all their stuff has stories. I love hearing about them." Through their stories, she explained, she gets to know her clients better. She also saw value in the act of listening itself, witnessing the things that matter to people and how they feel about them. (See the following chapter for an extended discussion of the role of empathetic listening in organizers' work.)

What Does the Sock Want?

Another approach, one central to the KonMari method but used only occasionally by the organizers I worked with, is to reorient the client's focus from their own feelings to the feelings of the object in question. In addition to asking whether an item "sparks joy" for the client, Kondo imbues inanimate objects with emotions and preferences, such as when she insists that socks "cannot rest" when balled up and prefer to be folded into "a simple rectangle."[21] (I don't follow this approach, preferring to ball my socks, but after reading Kondo's book I feel a twinge of guilt whenever I do so, thinking of those poor, restless socks.) Kilroy-Marac describes a similar approach among the Canadian organizers she interviewed, one of whom describes asking a client, "What does this toy want? Where would it be happiest, most fulfilled? Is it happy at the bottom of a pile, not being used, collecting dust?"[22] Organizers describe this approach as especially effective for people who hoard or are chronically disorganized, who tend to personify things anyway.[23]

I did see a variation of this approach among the organizers I worked alongside, especially when dealing with items that had been gifted or inherited. Often, clients struggled to part with objects that had belonged to or been given to them by beloved friends or family, even when they did not like or had no use for those objects. In such instances, like at the organizing boot camp described in the story following this chapter, what clients seemed to want from organizers was permission to get rid of an object while also affirming that the client was a good person who valued their relationships and obligations to others. In such cases, organizers often asked if the giver would have wanted to burden the client with the object. "Would Grandma have wanted you to schlep a box of china you can't stand around with you for the rest of your life?" Similarly, organizers encouraged clients not to conflate an object their family member had given them with their *relationship* to that family member, which would remain meaningful whether they kept the item or not. Often, this strategy was employed in tandem with the next one, so that clients were asked to imagine both the feelings of the person the item came *from* and the feelings of the person they envisaged it going *to*.

Imagine the Recipient

When struggling to part with an item, clients sometimes suggest a middle route, such as setting it aside to sell later or gifting it to a friend or family member.[24] In general, organizers discourage these "solutions." Unless another person has expressed a clear interest in an item, organizers explain to their clients, gifting just foists the decision of what to do with an object onto someone else. Organizers often describe clutter as the product of delayed decision-making; here, the decision-making is delayed by way of forced delegation, as when a parent "cleans out" their memorabilia by packing it up and shipping it to their adult children, who then have to store it or dispose of it themselves. In such situations, organizers encourage the client to think not about the item or how much it means to them, but to think of the recipient and the burden this would create for them to have to be the one who decides what to do with Grandma's quilt collection.

In term of putting something aside to sell later, for the most part, objects are rarely worth as much as people think. Organizers who specialize in estate sales can often quickly assess what an item will—or, more often, will not—sell for; many have a strong network of contacts in antique and other resale businesses who can help them with this. In most cases, though, organizers have to gently disabuse clients of their false sense of an object's financial value or desirability. I attended a presentation by organizer Sara on clutter and its causes at the Los Angeles Gay & Lesbian Senior Center. During the Q&A following the talk, numerous attendees asked Sara about items they believed they could sell, from "retro" 1980s desktop computers, to full sets of Encyclopedia Britannica, to Beanie Babies (at that last one, the organizer just gave a sympathetic frown and shook her head slowly, dramatically, side to side). "Just because it's old," Sara clarified, "doesn't mean it's worth something." Even when something *is* potentially valuable, she warned, "be careful of [thinking] 'I'm gonna sell it one day.' It sitting in the corner for four years is not selling it." Most of the time, she added, the time and energy it would take to find a buyer is worth more than the purchase price would merit. "Often," she said, "you'll make more money if you write it off [as a donation]. Maybe there's somebody who would really like it, someone who could really use it."

Here, Sara employed a strategy I saw many organizers use often and to great effect, invoking the person or people who would make use of the item if the client opted to "let it go." Clients are often reluctant to part with things, even items with little emotional value, because it feels wasteful or because they envision a future in which they might need or want to use the item. In the opening story about Lauren's frames, for example, Lauren was holding on to dozens of empty frames that she hoped would be useful in the more social and creative future she imagined for herself. In other cases, it was books they might one day read, clothes that might one day fit, or pine cones they might one day use for a Thanksgiving centerpiece. Sometimes, organizers approached this sort of reluctance with teasing skepticism. At the Senior Center talk, for instance, Sara said, "The human imagination is wild and crazy. It can come up with a possible scenario to use anything." She gave the example of a set of old Dutch language cassette tapes that filled an entire bookshelf at one client's house. When she suggested donating them, the client hesitated, saying, "If I need to learn to speak Dutch, I'll have all the cassettes here. If I got hired by a multinational company based in Holland and I get transferred there, and I learn Dutch before I go, I'll be way ahead of everyone." As Sara told her audience, this was *a lot* of "ifs," especially for a client who was already retired.

Instead of imagining what one's future self might need, Sara and other organizers asked clients to consider whether the item was serving them *right now*—was it useful, was it beautiful, was it meaningful to them? If not, then let it go. To lubricate that process of letting go, especially when clients were reluctant, organizers often refocused from the self-centered question of whether the client might one day need the item to the outwardly focusing question of who else might be able to make use of it right now.

Sara, for example, often told clients about a local shelter for unhoused and runaway youth she volunteered for. To a client with a dozen brand-new journals sitting in a shopping bag at the bottom of a closet, she might say, "If you're willing to part with these, I know the girls at [the shelter] would love them!" Similarly, an organizer might point out that teachers at a local school would make great use of any board games or puzzles a client decided to donate. Here, organizers' detailed knowledge of local charities—who accepts what, which organizations are acutely in need of certain items— comes in handy, as does their understanding of their clients. A dog lover, for instance, might be more moved by the idea of donating surplus sheet sets to an animal shelter than to Goodwill. Other clients might be motivated to know that most of the proceeds from clothing they donate to Out of the Closet, a chain of thrift stores, will go to HIV care and services. One organizer told me about a client who donated an entire storage unit of "baby stuff" her children had outgrown to a shelter for families fleeing domestic violence. The client was thrilled, she said, to no longer have to pay the monthly storage fee *and* to feel she was helping other mothers and their children. By helping them envision items' potential recipients, organizers encourage clients to part with items they might otherwise have kept *and* to feel good about doing so.[25]

Organizers themselves often find this part of the job, facilitating donations to various causes, especially satisfying. Organizer Tess told me: "I love filling up my car with donations and giving them to people who need them more, where they're not just stuff being ignored." Sara, the organizer who tried to help Lauren part with her many frames, loves seeing teens walking around Hollywood, where the youth shelter she works with is located, wearing clothing donated by her clients, and sometimes by herself. At one speaking engagement I attended, Sara told the audience about a pair of "breathtakingly expensive" pants she no longer wore but was reluctant to part with simply because they'd cost so much. "Sometimes," she said, "we just have to accept that we made a mistake. We spent too much money on something, it was a bad purchase." She donated them to the shelter and one day saw a girl who worked at her neighborhood yogurt shop wearing them. "And they looked great on her. They'd been in my closet for six years!"

In this way, organizers see their work as not just about helping people manage their belongings, but also working to redistribute unused, often forgotten goods to those who need and can use them. They also urge clients to shift their focus from their own relationship to their belongings to the potentially more immediately useful relationships that others—particularly others in greater need than the client themselves (homeless teens, abused women and children, stray animals)—might foster with these objects if given the opportunity. Here, the goal is not so much to sever the emotional relationship between people and their objects as it is to invigorate clients' sense of their relationships to others through the act of donating material goods.

In a related strategy, sometimes the "recipient" that organizers encourage clients to consider is the planet itself, as extending an item's life utility by finding it a new "home" arguably leads to fewer new items being purchased or produced.[26] "Green organizers" even specialize in helping clients lead more environmentally friendly lives, teaching them local recycling laws, helping them transition to paperless homes and offices, and making them more aware of the environmental costs of their consumer choices. One green organizer I interviewed, who drives a nearly twenty-year-old Mazda, relished the many occasions when clients tell her, "You are green! You should get a Prius!" Turning the query into a teachable moment, she explains, "No, my car is fine. I'm not putting it in a landfill." Buying brand-new, environmentally friendly products, she tells them, isn't always the greenest option.[27] "If you take care of your stuff, it will last you a long time. So many people don't value what they buy or what they own." Here, too, organizers push clients to think in different ways about the items they buy, keep, and discard. As I'll return to at the close of this chapter, this represents a fundamentally different sort of orientation to things, people, and the planet than is typical under consumer capitalism.

Putting It Back

In the course of encouraging clients to part with objects, organizers also encourage them to imagine what their space will *feel* like at the end of the process. They ask clients how it will feel to be able to walk through the guest room without having to navigate stacks of boxes, how it will feel to park a car in the garage, how it will feel to be able to find their keys every single morning without having to search for them. More often than not, these visions concern how a client will use the space and the things in it, rather than the space's appearance alone. As organizer Sara told me, "I'm not the organizer that comes in and makes things look pretty, in pretty colored bins." I heard nearly identical disclaimers from at least half a dozen organizers, hence the title of this book. Like the dabbler, the organizer who just puts things "in pretty colored bins" functions as a common foil for organizers trying to convey their focus on function and organization, rather than aesthetics alone. Thus, unlike in media representations of organizing, which tend to play up the visual contrasts between what a space looks like "before" and "after" it gets organized, in real life it's less important to organizers how a space looks than how well it functions in the long term for the person or people using it.

Organizers often point out that just because a space appears unattractive or disorganized to an outsider doesn't mean that it necessarily needs to be changed. One business organizer told me about going into a client's garage workspace. "I walk in," she told me, "and he's got rows of file cabinets but there's nothing in them." Instead, all of his paperwork was stored in clear plastic pockets attached to the wall. "He would use the plastic overlay sheets, the kind with different colors that you put papers in." Items in the red pocket were urgent; the clear pocket held receipts that needed to be kept. While she looked over his unorthodox system, the client said, "You probably don't like these pockets on the wall." She replied, "No, I think it's genius. It's probably one of the most ingenious filing systems I ever saw! If it works for you, that's great!" The client was a very visual person, she explained. He simply wouldn't remember paperwork stored away in file folders; as it was, within a minute he could locate any piece of paper he needed. Thus, a space that might appear disorganized or unsightly to an observer could in fact be perfectly designed for the person using it.[28]

This is one reason, organizers say, that the most organized people sometimes make the worst organizers. I should mention that organizers are quick to poke fun at their own preference for order. At one NAPO Annual Conference, multiple organizers joked with me that at an event full of organizers, sessions had *better* start on time. Addressing readers looking to start a home-based organizing business, one author wrote, "Okay, who am I kidding. I'm talking to a professional organizer, right? You want a list and you want to be able to check it twice."[29] But while a few organizers embrace the label "neat freak," most organizers balk at such descriptions.[30] Longtime organizer Estelle Gee told a reporter from the *Toronto Star*: "The image is of these self-righteous, rigid, anal-retentive people walking around the planet telling everyone what to do. . . . But we're not like that at all."[31] Gee is right about the prevailing image of organizers as joyless control freaks. The professional organizer in T. Coraghessan Boyle's short story "Filthy with Things," for example, is described as "a tall, pale, hovering presence, a woman stripped to the essentials—the hair torn back from her scalp and strangled in a bun, no cheeks, no lips, no makeup or jewelry, the dress black, the shoes black, the briefcase black as a dead black coal dug out of the bottom of the bag."[32] The realm of nonfiction offers similarly unflattering stereotypes. An article about the 1999 NAPO conference described the audience as consisting "almost entirely of brisk no-nonsense women with spit-polished shoes, understated lipstick, and complimentary canvas sacks for their seminar notes."[33] Many years later, a *New York Times* journalist offered a similar assessment, describing the Black and White Ball at NAPO's 2016 conference as a place where "the NAPO women would cut loose as much as their personalities would allow them. . . ."[34] Yet, these images don't align with my own experiences of organizers, who are both warmer and more diverse in style and temperament than such descriptions suggest.

In fact, organizers often say, if you can't tolerate disorder, this isn't the occupation for you. "It's one thing to be passionate about organizing; it's another to do it for a living," proclaims one book for would-be organizers, before offering a quiz to help readers determine which category they fit into.[35] Another book puts it similarly: "Many people come to me saying they've been organized all their lives, but that doesn't always translate into being a fantastic professional organizer. It's one thing to organize for yourself. It's another to transfer your skills to other people based on their needs, lifestyles, and learning styles."[36] As one speaker at a NAPO meeting put it, "Your clients don't want to be you. They just want to be more organized than they are." Experienced organizers often found themselves breaking this news to would-be organizers. One organizer told me about a call she'd received from a woman interested in entering the field: "And she goes, 'Oh, whenever I go into a department store, I always organize the t-shirts.'" The experienced organizer told her, "This is not the field for you. You will go crazy. If all the t-shirts in a department store have to be in order, this is not the field for you." As organizers regularly remind people, this job means being surrounded by other people's messes all day, every day, and you have to be okay with that.

In order to tackle "other people's messes," organizers thus need to know many different systems—different ways to go about "putting things back"—in order to select the approach, or, more often, combination of approaches, that will work for a given client. As one organizer put it, "In the real world when you're with clients, the reality is you want to find something that works for them. You actually need to have a method that is flexible depending on who your client is." As another organizer explained, "There's no one way to file. No one way to label things. There's no one way to organize stuff. It just depends on how you think, what your learning style is, what your priorities are, what you're willing to do." She says some clients have difficulty accepting this, especially if they are looking for the *one right way* to get organized. "Someone can come in and totally organize your house," she explains to clients, "but then you have to keep it up. You've got to maintain that." If the system someone else devised is "not really working for you, if it doesn't work the way *you* think, it's going to get back the way it was. It's just a matter of time."[37]

As organizers' emphasis on creating a system that "works" for the client suggests, the end goal of organizing is not a pretty, one-time fix but a sustainable system. After a long day of organizing, once everything is put back, a room might look clean, spacious, and beautiful, but that's not the test of whether it's well organized. For an organizing system to work, the person using it has to be both willing and able to keep it up. This is an important difference between real-life organizing and organizing shows and magazine spreads, which usually produce impressive "after" shots but, with few exceptions, rarely follow up over time to see if a system "stuck" or a space stayed organized.

Teachers, Not Doers

The best way to ensure a positive long-term outcome, then, is to organize a space or system from the start in collaboration with the end user. For this reason, as I've mentioned, organizers rarely do a job without the client present, as it's difficult to design an effective system without the input of the person who will be using it. Because the goal is to create spaces and systems designed to continue to work *after* the organizer has gone home, and ideally well into the future, most organizers therefore aim to *teach* the client how to be organized, not to do it for them, which organizers say is rarely sustainable and not nearly as satisfying.[38] As one organizer explained, "If they're not there doing it with me, then what's the point? They're just gonna go back to their old way. But if they see what I'm doing and how I'm doing it, they will understand why and how we've put systems into place and how to be able to maintain them." In addition to setting up maintainable systems, organizing therefore also involves teaching clients the skills they need to *stay* organized.

For example, a common adage among organizers is "a place for everything and everything in its place." If your keys always "live" on the hook by the door, you'll always know where to put them and, more importantly, where to find them. But where it makes sense to store something depends on the logic of the user themselves. For example, I have a set of travel adapters for electrical outlets in various countries. I use them once a year, if that. Inevitably, when I'm packing for a trip where I *do* need them, I can't remember where I stored them after the last trip. Then, years ago, I heard an organizer advise a client to store things together with other items they'd need at the same time, even if the items themselves are very different. I went home, moved the adapters to the garage next to the suitcases, which of course I also use when I go abroad, and I've never lost them since. That system wouldn't work for everyone—maybe you'd keep the adapters with the chargers or your passport—but it works for me because it's logical *to me*. And it didn't just work that one time, for that one type of item. Whenever I'm looking for something, I head first to where I store items I'd likely use along with it. It's not a foolproof system. I still lose things, as my family will happily attest. But it works more often than not. And that's because I didn't learn where to put an adapter, I learned a system for storing things that I could apply again and again.

As organizer Vanessa explained it, organizing is a process, not an event. "It's not something like 'I got organized this week and that's it and I'll never do anything about it again.' It is a skill and you can learn it, and you have to work at it all the time." Vanessa then drew a parallel I heard from other organizers, too, between getting organized and losing weight.[39] She said, "You can't just lose a bunch of weight and then go back to not eating well and not exercising. You have to keep doing it." The same, she said, is true of organizing. "So, you get organized and you have to maintain it. It's just the way it is. You can't let things go back the way it was. And it is not something that you just do it once and it's over." The fact that organizers draw parallels between getting organized and losing weight is significant on multiple fronts. In American culture today, accumulating too much and weighing too much both tend to be classified as both medical disorders and moral failings, although as I note in the next chapter, organizers tend to reject moralistic condemnations of disorder.[40] This parallel is also significant in the way it positions the people who help people achieve these outcomes. If you hire a dietitian or personal trainer to help you lose weight, they don't lose the weight for you, they help you do it and, in the process, aim to teach you a set of practices or perspectives that help you maintain it over time. The same is true of organizers, who aim to *teach* rather than *do*, with the ultimate goal of transforming the client themselves, and not just the space in which they live or work. In this sense, organizing has more in common with professions like personal training and life coaching—both of which usually require the client's presence (in person or virtually) and aim to achieve some form of personal transformation—than with personal concierges, household managers, or other service professionals whose work is performed *for* clients, but less often *with* clients.

As this chapter illustrates, in a variety of ways, organizing involves what Josh Seim calls "people-changing work."[41] Clients themselves, and not their stuff or their spaces, are the real focus of organizers' labor. Organizers aim to help clients see the value of workable spaces, ones designed to accommodate clients' current lives, not the needs of their imaginary future selves. By invoking an item's potential recipient, and the social and environmental benefits of extending objects' utility, organizers help clients envision other ways of living and relating to one another and to the objects we possess. This represents a dramatic shift from consumer capitalism's endless cycle of buying and discarding. Organizers also teach us to treat things with more care and attention, and to be accountable for the objects we accumulate and ultimately abandon.[42] In doing so, organizers also nudge clients to be more attuned to other people, to imagine who might make better use of, or have greater need for, our possessions than we currently do.[43] This ethic of responsible stewardship and mutual concern distinguishes organizers' ethos from the instrumental, impersonal relationships that typically characterize life under market capitalism.

As the stories above suggest, the emotional connections clients have to their possessions are embedded within a sticky web of personal and cultural beliefs and ideals. Untangling those webs in order to help a client achieve, or even envision, a different way of living requires that organizers forge and navigate relationships with the people they serve, relationships that are intimate but not equal, genuine but temporary, nonjudgmental but in service to specific outcomes. Rather than simply a means to an organized end, in the next chapter I argue that these relationships are core to the work organizers do with clients, and to our understanding of the challenges facing so many American households today.

I parked my car in the tiny lot behind a Korean church in Los Feliz, a neighborhood in Central Los Angeles, and walked down the cement steps to the church basement. At the door to the large downstairs rec room, a tall, quiet man with tousled hair sat at a small folding table, checking people in for today's four-hour Organizing Boot Camp, which cost $25 per attendee.

There were four large tables set up in the center of the room, each topped with two cardboard file boxes. I sat down at a folding chair in front of one of the boxes. While upbeat music played in the background, Jessica, the professional organizer leading the event that day, walked between the tables, greeting and chitchatting with each attendee as they arrived.

Once everyone was checked in—there were six attendees in total, all white women in our thirties to fifties—Jessica stepped to the front of the room. Slim and stylish with long dark hair, pale skin, funky glasses, and a nautical striped t-shirt, Jessica was in her early thirties and had been running her organizing business for about five years. She introduced herself and, gesturing with a smile to the man seated at the check-in table, David, "my assistant-slash-boyfriend-slash-mascot."

Our goal for the day, she said, was to make organizing easy. As she spoke, she clicked through a set of cute, colorful slides. The slide titled "dive into organizing," for instance, featured a photo of David diving onto a bed. There would be no paper handouts, she told us—just more clutter—but she'd email us the presentation if we'd like.

Today's boot camp would focus on organizing our files, which was why each of us had been instructed to bring a batch of paperwork in need of organizing. I'd grabbed a stack of personal files from home and brought them in a paper shopping bag. They weren't disorganized, exactly, but I figured they could use some updating.

Jessica walked us through her tips for organizing files. Eighty percent of what we file, Jessica told us, we never retrieve, so the first step in organizing your files is purging what you don't need. As well, she said, "we think we need all these products to keep us organized, but really the opposite is true." She recommended choosing one type of file folder—manila or hanging, not both—and keeping our system as simple as possible. She talked about creating general color-coded categories, and reminded us to keep our categories broad so we didn't need to change labels often. For instance, you might make all financial files green, then create subcategories like bills, credit cards, and bank statements.

After reviewing the general principles we should keep in mind and offering tips for purging paper (scan it then toss it), setting up a simple filing system (use straight-line tabs, so "your eyes don't need to follow a zig-zag line"), and maintaining it ("Set a monthly Google reminder to check your files and get rid of what you no longer need"), it was time for each of us to tackle the paperwork we'd brought with us.

The attendees, who had been quiet and focused during her presentation, jumped right in. Jessica had provided us with cardboard file boxes, letter openers, label makers, staple removers, digital scanners, and other tools, as well as manila file folders. I was sharing a table with Brooke. This was her second boot camp. She'd met Jessica at a business networking event and hired her to organize her office. She'd loved the experience, and used the boot camps to keep things from getting out of hand. "I could do this at home alone," she told me, "but I know I'll do it here."

While David read quietly at a table on the other side of the room, Jessica walked between the tables, answering questions, nodding in agreement at the categories people were coming up with, asking clarifying questions. She detailed for one attendee how long you need to keep certain tax records, and advised another on local spots for bulk shredding or recycling. Mary, a blonde woman at the table behind me, was stuck on whether to toss a personal note from a friend. "I think," Jessica said gently, "you're needing someone to say it's okay [to throw it away]." Mary nodded briskly, and tossed the card in the recycling bin next to her table.

Similar scenes repeated over the next few hours, as the basement room darkened into the afternoon. One woman was holding on to a receipt for the catering for her daughter's wedding so she'd be able to remember "in case someone asked how much the catering cost." Another had a sheet of her son's adorable elementary school photos with a few cut out. She'd long ago framed one of the larger photos and sent a few of the smaller ones to relatives, but hadn't been able to bring herself to toss the remaining images. People had brought old maps, sheets for practicing multiplication tables (her kids were now adults), unopened account statements from years previous. The pattern seemed to be that if they were uncertain enough to ask Jessica's opinion about it, they were probably going to end up tossing it. The stuff they definitely wanted to keep, they didn't feel the need to discuss. More often than not, after describing out loud what it was she was holding on to and why, a woman opted to toss it. Sometimes they kept it—one woman didn't feel comfortable letting go of the carbon copies of her checks—in which case they tucked it away into the appropriate section of their new filing system.

I went through my files, tossing old statements and out-of-date paperwork. I rejiggered my files a bit and created a new "To Read" file to store the myriad articles I print out or tear from magazines and journals. When that was done, I outlined in my notebook a filing system for storing the records I'd need when I went up for tenure the next year. (It worked!)

When our four hours were up, Jessica congratulated everyone on their progress. She invited us to sign up for her digital newsletter and daily blog, and briefly described the organizing services she offers. When she finished, we attendees chatted as we ascended the stairs, holding our newly organized and decidedly lighter file boxes in front of us.

5

Where It Hurts

Connective Labor and the Feminist
Work of Professional Organizing

As much as organizers deal with stuff, what they *really* deal with is people. As NAPO founder Stephanie Culp explained to me, "Organizing is not really rocket science. What *is* rocket science is dealing with the clients. That is the part that's tricky." The nonjudgmental, supportive connections organizers work to establish with clients are often the most challenging, and rewarding, aspects of organizers' work. Organizing can be an intimate process; to do it well, organizers need to build trust, empathy, and rapport with clients before they can even begin to deploy the approaches to "letting things go" outlined in the previous chapter. Sociologist Allison Pugh has coined the term "connective labor" to refer to this work of establishing personal, emotional connections between practitioners and recipients, an often invisible form of labor crucial to success in a range of occupations, from healthcare to hairstyling, teaching to therapy, sex work to policing, and, I argue, professional organizing.[1] Connective labor is also most commonly expected of and performed by woman, harkening back to previous chapters' discussions of the gendered nature of both the work organizers do and why they do it.

In this chapter, I explore the relationships organizers forge with clients and how they manage those relationships when conflict or other challenges arise. This can require navigating tricky expectations around "real" relationships versus those we pay for, as well as class differences and other asymmetries between practitioners of service work and their clients. Despite the work such relationships require, when they describe the rewards of getting organized, organizers rarely talk about the money they made, snazzy systems they implemented, or number of dumpsters they filled with discarded items. They talk instead about the ways in which clients felt better, about themselves, their homes, and their lives, after working with an organizer. These results were also gratifying for organizers themselves, who see organizing as a "helping" profession, one that helps not just with clutter, but with other challenges facing American households, and the women who often lead them.

While others have accused organizers of enforcing impossible standards and rigid aesthetic norms on their clients, here I argue they often do the opposite. Through connective labor, organizers aim to convince clients to stop chasing aesthetic and organizational ideals that are unnecessary, even impossible, for most households to achieve. They also encourage clients, especially women, to see that the responsibilities placed on them—at home, in their jobs, or both—are untenable; no one, not even the most organized and efficient among us, can do it all. In this way, I understand organizing as feminist work. In small, everyday ways, organizers work to lighten the load society has placed upon women, and that women in turn enforce upon themselves. This chapter thus reveals both the extent of the burdens under which American women are laboring as well as the connective labor organizers perform to help ease those burdens.

• • •

One morning over tea, before we headed to an organizing job, organizer Sara told me about a consultation she'd had with a potential client the week before. A couple in their forties had called her for help getting their home organized. When Sara arrived, Ana and her husband Joel escorted her through the house while their young twins watched TV in another room. Sara prides herself on "going deep," getting to the heart of the problem *causing* the organizational issue, but in this case, she was having trouble figuring out what exactly the problem *was*. The home looked pretty organized to her—there was the regular clutter and disarray of daily family life with young kids, but no area stood out as in dire need of help.

As Joel led Sara into different rooms of the house, Ana followed behind them, calling out directions. "Show her the closets!" The closets in the master bedroom and guest room were both full of adult clothing. A lot of clothing, Sara told me, but "not bad." Some closets she sees are so jam-packed that it can be difficult to see or remove individual items; others were being used to store items that couldn't fit in other rooms of the house, such as boxes of kids' toys or spare packs of paper towels. None of Joel and Ana's closets were overstuffed or especially messy. "Show her the garage!" Ana directed. Again, Sara thought to herself, "Not that bad." There were clothing racks full of women's clothing set up in a part of the garage, but the garage was spacious and seemed pretty well organized, if too full to store a car. Still unclear as to the exact problem for which the couple was seeking help, Sara asked Joel about the clothing in the garage, and why they'd chosen to store it there. This was when Joel explained that he enjoys dressing in women's clothing at home from time to time; the clothes in the garage, and in some of the closets inside the house, were his for that purpose. Ana knew about Joel's "hobby," as he described it, and they planned to explain it to the kids when they were older. But for now, as the twin toddlers became more mobile, they didn't want them to stumble across Joel's clothing, preferring to tell them "more purposefully" later. This was why they'd called an organizer. Ana and Joel were thinking of storing his clothing offsite in a storage unit until then, but before doing so they wanted to see if Sara might be able to come up with a less costly solution. She suggested a few different ways they might go about dedicating a discreet space within the home for Joel's women's clothing, and the couple hired her on the spot.

I'm sharing this particular job here, even though I didn't assist on it, because it illustrates the intimate nature of the organizing process. The challenge Ana and Joel faced was not every couple's—what to do with the women's clothing Joel likes to occasionally wear until they were ready to explain its presence to their children. In most respects, though, the job was like any other. The couple contacted an organizer because there were belongings in their home that needed to be sorted or stored in a different way than they currently were. The challenge was both logistic and emotional; it had to do with stuff, but the stuff was connected to other issues, specifically the tension around how to make room for Joel's cross-dressing in their home while also wanting to keep that activity concealed from their children for the time being. Sara's job would be to help them figure out where and how to store certain items. In order to do so effectively, she would need to understand different household members' relationships to those items and to where and how they were stored, while also reassuring her clients that her goal was to help solve their organizing challenges, not judge the source or nature of those challenges. This would require building trust with both Joel and Ana, and managing any complicated feelings that arose throughout the process. At core, most organizing jobs involve the same thing.

"This Is Very Personal"

Organizing often involves witnessing and touching parts of people's lives that are usually private—sorting through tax returns and divorce papers, organizing prescription bottles in a medicine cabinet, finding a place to store love letters from an ex. As one organizer put it, "Organizers are people who work intimately with their clients. I mean, you're touching their underwear, you're touching the dish that their grandmother gave them, you know, this is very personal." This requires discretion on the part of organizers, as well as an ability to never be shocked—or at least never appear shocked—by anything they encounter on the job.[2] Numerous organizers told me that often, the first thing a client says when the organizer walks through their front door is "Is this the worst you've seen?" It rarely is, of course; even when it is, organizers assure them it's not. Organizers also employ preventive measures to avoid surprising or embarrassing situations when working in clients' homes. Before she begins working in a new room, one organizer told me, she'll casually tell the client something like "I think we'll work on the bedroom next. If there's anything in there you'd rather keep private, this would be a great time to move it elsewhere." Nevertheless, organizers regularly come across potentially sensitive items, such as weapons, illegal drugs, and sex toys; when they do, organizers told me they might opt not to touch the items themselves, but otherwise they treat them like any other object encountered on a job.

On most jobs, though, the sensitive parts have less to do with the objects themselves than with a client's feelings about them. As I note in the previous chapter, part of what organizers do is adjust clients' relationships to objects in order to help them make decisions about what to keep and what to let go. The other part of what organizers do, the part I focus on in this chapter, is manage the emotions that arise over the course of an organizing session. Often, when a client is struggling to decide what to do with an object, it's because that object brings up difficult or complicated emotions for them. Organizers try to figure out what those feelings are and how they might be managed or resolved in order to keep the organizing process moving forward.

Many organizers explained to me that when working with a new client, the first thing they do is figure out "where it hurts"—what part of the home or workspace, or what type of belonging, is bothering the client most.[3] Because ultimately, organizers told me, clients contact an organizer when their clutter or disorganization has reached a point where it bothers them enough to do something about it. As one organizer put it when talking about clients with severe clutter, "I think the pain of living like they're living finally gets worse than the prospective pain of dealing with it." That's when the organizer comes in. That said, what, exactly, is causing the pain isn't always obvious.

In the example of Ana and Joel, whose story opens this chapter, their house appeared generally uncluttered; the sensitive spot was the husband's clothing, which was not especially copious or disorganized, but still wasn't working for the family in its current locations. For Lauren, the client profiled in the book's first organizing story, what hurt most was a home office too cluttered to be used for the business she wanted to start. For the clothing designer in another story, it was her basement workspace. For the organizing story you'll read next, it was memorabilia from an especially painful time of the client's childhood. I heard other stories from organizers about items that were especially painful for clients to deal with—medical paperwork related to a miscarriage, a glass figurine given them by an abusive family member, the clothing of a recently deceased spouse. It wasn't always immediately apparent, even to the client themselves, why they were having such trouble with a specific item or category of item. In such cases, figuring out what hurts, and why, requires sensitivity and empathy on the part of the organizer, and trust and candor from the client.

Connective Labor in the Organizing Process

This is where connective labor comes in. Sociologist Allison Pugh argues that some forms of work rely "on intimate knowledge, on an emotional understanding between the worker and other people, for its success."[4] Connective labor is the work it takes to achieve this intimate understanding. It involves listening empathetically, managing one's own emotions and reactions in order to facilitate the other person's sharing, and bearing witness to the other person's truth and reflecting that truth back to them.[5] Although the organizers I spoke with did not use the term "connective labor" themselves, their descriptions of the organizing process convey how central it is to their work.

Organizers spoke often of how important it is to connect with and listen to clients. Organizer Hilda says organizing "is about connection and being heard." Organizer Yazmin told me that, as an organizer, "you have to be really in tune in listening to what they're saying, because folks come to you, sometimes they're embarrassed by their situation. And it is important to have a lot of empathy. Empathy is key. Because they're coming to you, they already know they're disorganized, they already know they're in a bind, or most likely they wouldn't be there." In this way, Yazmin and other organizers position their clients—rich or poor, mildly disorganized or awash in clutter—as inherently deserving of empathy, kindness, and care.[6] Thus, even as organizers worked *for* clients, on whom their livelihood depended, they still saw themselves as the one in the position of offering solace to someone in need.

Organizers were equally committed to never judging their clients or the nature of clients' challenges. One young actor-turned-organizer told me the first thing he says to his clients is "I'm here to help you, not to judge you." This emphasis on withholding judgment came up again and again in my conversations with organizers. An organizer who'd had ten full-time employees before the pandemic hit (as of 2022 she was down to three) said the hardest part of hiring was finding people who aren't "judgy," whether on the job or after the fact. As she saw it, the organizer's job is to help the client, "and if we're judging them about it, even after you leave their house, it's not helping." This is especially true for more vulnerable clients, including those with brain-based conditions that contribute to their disorganization. An organizer who often works with people who hoard said her clients frequently feel no one is listening to their perspectives and preferences. "The rest of the family," the organizer explained, is saying of the client's home and possessions, "Hey, if I just had a match, I'd burn it down. If I had a dump truck, I'd back it up to the house." In contrast, she assures her clients, "'I'm not here to throw things out. I'm here to ask you what's most valuable to you.' Suddenly the barrier drops and then I'm able to talk to them." In such cases, where a client might be less than enthusiastic about the process, organizers' insistence on listening conveys both compassion and respect. Connecting with clients is thus a means to achieving an organized end, although as I'll detail later, organizers also see it as an end in itself.

Even organizers who don't see themselves as especially empathetic recognize that many jobs require this skill. Organizer Lara, for example, was a rare exception to organizers' insistence on how crucial being nonjudgmental is to organizing. "You know how we [organizers] all say you can't be judgmental?" she asked me. "You know what? I'm judgmental!" "I'm a New Yorker. I'm just right in your face. I'm hard core. I'm impatient." She clarified that she wouldn't tell a client, "You're a fucking idiot," but she would say to a client waffling over a decision, "Enough already. Make a decision." Occasionally, Lara explained, she might tell a client she's worked with for a number of years, "It's time to let it go. There's nothing to talk about." Because she tends to be "hard core," when she knows a client is going to need a gentler approach, she sends one of her organizing team, rather than doing the job herself. In this way, Lara ensures clients get what they need from their organizer, while she isn't forced to relate to clients in a way that feels unnatural to her.

Lara might have been alone among the organizers I met in describing herself as judgmental, but she wasn't alone in recognizing that sometimes a client and an organizer aren't temperamentally suited to work together. As we all do, organizers differ in their styles and personalities—some fall more naturally into the role of supportive friend, nurturing maternal figure, or tough-love taskmaster. Sometimes clients prefer one style over another. Organizer Eileen described it this way: "Somebody who really wants to be pushed around is never going to hire me. I have a very gentle, nonjudgmental approach. [If] you really like a drill sergeant, I'm just not your person, and some people really need that, want that, and jibe with that." In those cases, she tries to connect the client with an organizer who might better match the client's wants and needs. "I've told people," Eileen said, "that in a funny way it's a little like dating because it's so intimate. So you have to like a person, and you have to think that you're going to be comfortable with them because you're going to be standing right next to them for hours and days and weeks, so if you're uncomfortable or feel judged or whatever, it may not work." Even when she likes a client and wants to work with them, she says, "If I'm the only person that they've called, I'll encourage them to call around and see what it's like, see how different people work, so they get a good feel." That way, she says, both she and the client can feel confident that they ended up working together by choice, not default. Yet even as organizers emphasize the importance of fit, they also describe regularly adapting themselves, not just their organizing methods, to the demands of specific jobs.

Longtime organizer Vanessa, for example, recalled that in her first year in business she worked with a woman in her late thirties whose husband had passed away suddenly. They had three young children, and the husband had always handled the bills and other paperwork. A friend of the couple hired Vanessa to help the woman go through the family's paperwork and the husband's belongings. It was, Vanessa said, "intensely emotional. It was like the saddest thing that could ever happen." Because the woman and the family and friends closest to her were all dealing with their own grief at the man's loss, Vanessa felt she "had to sort of be the brightness." Her job, as she saw it, wasn't just to help with the stuff; it was to help the woman herself by bringing brightness into an otherwise dark time. "I remember," Vanessa told me, "I made her laugh one day, and her mother happened to be there and she said, 'Thank you so much. We haven't heard her laugh in I don't know how long.' That just made me feel so good." Together, Vanessa and the client organized the many condolence cards she had received into binders, one for cards from friends and another for cards from family. "She loved that we did that," Vanessa recalled, but the process of putting them together was, at times, "absolutely horrific" for the young widow, despite her wanting very much to create these keepsakes for her children. "I had to be the strong one," Vanessa said, "to help her get through that incredibly delicate and sensitive time, to respect the feelings that she's going through and honor him [the client's husband] and cherish him in a way so that she felt good about it."

This job was an especially demanding one, emotionally speaking, but that's also part of what made it so rewarding and memorable for Vanessa. The young widow seems to have benefited emotionally from the process, finding some lightness and laughter in a difficult time while also crafting tangible memorials of her husband intended to bring comfort to her and, one day, her children. Helping her client benefited Vanessa as well, not just in the sense that she was paid for her work, but also that it made her "feel so good" about what she'd done for her client.

Many organizing jobs require similar emotional maneuvering on the part of organizers. As Vanessa put it, organizers "have to be teachers, we have to be cheerleaders, we have to be whatever they need us to be. Be quiet if they don't want to talk . . . dance around to the music if that's what they want. We have to really become sort of chameleons and be whatever is going to help them move forward. Because it's not about how I work necessarily or what I want to do. It has to be what's going to make it good for them." Organizers don't just manage their own emotions, becoming what they believe the client needs them to be; they also have to actively manage clients' emotions, especially when the organizing process becomes especially stressful or upsetting. When clients become especially emotional during a session, Vanessa tells them, "'It's alright. Here's a tissue,' and I wait until they're okay. . . . There's a whole different range of emotions I've been able to pick up on," she says, that need to be "either diffused or whatever needs to be done so that it doesn't get crazy." She sometimes asks distressed clients if they'd prefer to take a break and return to the task later, "and they never want to, they just need to get it out of their system but they don't want to stop whatever it is they're doing." As an organizer, the trick is to notice or even predict these moments and to manage them as, or before, they arise. "You have to be certainly sensitive to so many different things and learn what a trigger is," Vanessa said, offering the example of a client getting "angry or pissed off" every time they came across an item that belonged to an ex-spouse. "You have to be positive and help them get through it as you can," she said, "but I don't ever stop anybody from having a breakdown. You have got to get it all out."

I witnessed many similar instances in which organizers gently managed clients' emotional distress. In the organizing story you'll read next, for example, which involves cleaning out storage units filled with inherited goods, the client specifically mentions she prefers her current organizer over a previous one because this one is better at "managing my emotions," such as when she uses humor to help the client push through a challenging box of memorabilia, or when she empathizes with the client's frustrations with her family members. In the organizing story with which I opened the book, organizer Sara sensed when her client Lauren was growing frustrated after a long day of organizing; after acknowledging Lauren's feelings ("It's okay if you're angry with me"), Sara decided to stop for the day and return to the tasks at hand after a night's rest.

This sort of work—sussing out clients' emotional needs and presenting oneself in a way that accommodates those needs in order to achieve a desired result—is often called "emotional labor" or, more broadly, "emotional work," and it's a key component of jobs involving connective labor, including organizing.[7] Since Arlie Hochschild first coined the term "emotional labor" to describe the work of flight attendants expected to, among other things, smile "genuinely" at even the most difficult passengers, emotional labor has typically been understood as harmful to those expected to perform it.[8] And while this sort of labor is performed by a range of practitioners across different occupations, it aligns quite closely with the sort of work—paid and unpaid—that tends to be expected of women.[9] As one sociologist put it, "Westerners expect women as a category to be empathy specialists," and women are often judged more harshly when they are perceived as lacking empathy.[10] Women also predominate in the kinds of paid and unpaid service and caregiving roles that require such labor. In this way, the work of organizing is doubly gendered, requiring both the domestic skills *and* the emotional skills associated with, expected of, and performed by women, both of which are regularly overlooked and devalued in contemporary America.

Friend for Hire

Emotional connection is often understood as a two-way street. As a spouse, sister, or friend, I am supposed to be emotionally attuned to you and your needs and, in return, you are supposed to do the same for me. In personal service work like organizing (as well as many other settings), empathy and emotional caretaking tend to flow in only one direction, compensated with pay rather than mutual concern. To borrow sociologist Candace Clark's terms, organizers are supposed to be the sympathizers, not the sympathizees.[11] This aligns with how organizers describe their work; they offer empathy, listen without judgment, become "whatever they need us to be." Organizers neither expect nor receive the same in return from their clients. Mostly, this works fine. Clients get empathy and care alongside the organizer's organizing expertise; organizers get paid and, as I'll turn to in a moment, also reap other, nonmaterial rewards.

One of the challenges associated with connective labor, however, is the perceived tension between "genuinely" caring for and connecting with someone and caring for and connecting with someone because they're paying you to. If we understand the organizer-client relationship as merely a means to an organized end, then an organizer who expresses empathy or affection for their client is likely faking it, and the client is a dupe if they think otherwise. But this way of thinking assumes there is a clear boundary between relationships that are authentic and those embedded within an exchange of services for money, and that simply isn't true. Many scholars have persuasively argued that intimate life and economic life have always been intertwined, despite economic and social models that prefer to think of these as entirely separate spheres.[12] Nevertheless, the idea that true care should be untainted by financial concerns still pervades American society, as we see, for instance, when teachers and nurses who ask for raises are accused of not loving their students or patients. (It's of course not a coincidence that teaching and nursing are also female-dominated occupations involving care work.)

In contrast, some argue that paid care is actually superior to the sort you get for free from friends and family. As Vanessa saw it, the fact that she *wasn't* personally connected to the young widow and her family, that she was hired help, as it were, wasn't a liability, it was what allowed her to play the important role that she did. "I don't know that anybody in her family could have helped her as I could have," Vanessa explained, because "[I didn't] have my own memories wrapped up into what we were putting away." Not having known the man who died, she was better able to manage her own emotions in order to "be the brightness" for her client.

Other organizers expressed a similar perspective, as do many workers who provide these sorts of personal services.[13] Organizer Lara, for example, described clients trying to care for aging family members while also working full-time and raising young children. When it comes time to help their elderly parents or grandparents move, or to clear out their homes after they pass away, clients "can call me and I'll do it, probably better than you, because I don't have the emotions behind it, I don't have the attachments behind it." Thus, while some argue that hiring this sort of one-sided care may "sap self-confidence in our own capacities and those of friends and family," Lara sees it as a logical response to an existing need, especially for people managing other, equally challenging burdens.[14] From this perspective, not having emotional attachments to the client and their belongings was an advantage, one that made hiring an organizer preferable to seeking help from unpaid amateurs you happen to be related to.

Nevertheless, work that involves both money *and* care, where one is a paid friend, of sorts, can create unique challenges for practitioners like organizers. In the previous example, Vanessa wasn't hired to help her client process her grief at her husband's death, but that was nevertheless part of what the job required of her. As happy as Vanessa was to have been able to support her client this way, being the brightness for another human being is hard work. It requires carefully curating how you present yourself to the client based on your perception of what the client needs and wants. It also requires navigating the tension between being a hired expert and a supportive, empathetic friend. Vanessa, for instance, believes that sharing parts of her own life with her clients is an important part of the organizing process. "If somebody is opening up their world to me, I'm not going to sit there and not share with them. I'm not going to sit there and talk about myself the whole time, but it's a give and take." At the same time, Vanessa believes it's also important to keep certain boundaries in place when working with clients. "You kind of become their friend," Vanessa said, "and you have to be careful about that." She told me that one client suggested they go to the movies together instead of organizing. "I'm like 'No, we can't go to the movies. We're here to work.'" She continued, "You just have to be careful to find a line between 'Okay, I'm friendly and I'm your friend as an organizer, but we're not best friends.'" In one instance, she was concerned that the client was becoming too close to her; she told the client, "I like you but we can't be best friends," and "gently" transitioned the client to working with another organizer.[15] Other organizers described similar, or perhaps more extensive, efforts to keep a certain professional distance in place.

Organizer Sara, for instance, echoed the organizers above about the importance of connection to the organizing process, but she believes it is important to place clear boundaries around the forms that connection takes. Clients "want to connect," she says, but she also advises her organizing assistants not to share private information about themselves with clients. Of her clients, she says, "Nobody knows where I live. Nobody knows how old I am." Clients rarely ask, she says, and when they do, she deflects with a vague answer (saying she lives "in Hollywood," for example, rather than a specific street). Typically, "people are fine [with that] because people don't really want to know about me." In this way, Sara keeps what she sees as a comfortable professional distance between herself and her clients.

It's important to note that in both of these instances, Vanessa and Sara felt empowered to draw boundaries that would prevent the client from demanding more of them emotionally than they were comfortable with. That they did so speaks to a significant difference between organizers and many other practitioners of emotional work. Unlike most service workers, those who ring up your purchase, handle your complaint call, or clean your home, expert service workers like organizers tend to be self-employed, earn high hourly wages, and have similar class backgrounds to the clients they serve.[16] As "lifestyle workers," they are also positioned as experts, which gives them power relative to their clients.[17] Together, these factors make them less vulnerable to the sorts of exploitation and abuse faced by less advantaged workers—I'm thinking especially here of nannies and other domestic workers—who are often expected to perform emotional work in the context of less equitable employment relationships.[18]

When considering how organizers feel about their relationships with clients and the emotional demands of their work, it is key to remember that most organizers are self-employed; they work for themselves, and often by themselves, without managerial supervision or control. This model, in which organizers exercise full control over their own connective labor, is decidedly different from connective labor performed in other contexts, such as by a call center worker following a prepared script while her manager listens in, or a physician trying to build a relationship with a patient while simultaneously documenting the details of their conversation in an electronic health record, all within the fifteen minutes before the next appointment is supposed to begin.[19] When organizers perform connective labor—or any other labor, for that matter—it is usually at their own volition, in a time and manner of their own choosing. They choose which clients to work with and how to interact with them, as well as how to approach the tasks at hand. As Vanessa did with the client who asked her to go to the movies, they may even choose to end a job when the physical or emotional work required moves outside their level of comfort, preference, or ability. This isn't equally true of all organizers, of course. Those who are new to the field, have smaller and less wealthy networks, or face other obstacles in establishing their business may have to take—and stay on in—any job that comes their way, no matter how unpleasant. As I described in chapter 2, this is more often the case for organizers of color, who often struggle to build their businesses and may face racial discrimination from clients atop the other challenges of their work.

And yet, when I read studies of other sorts of service workers and their frustration and resentment at clients' unreasonable demands, I am struck by how rare it was to hear organizers frame their clients as entitled or overly demanding, especially in terms of the emotional work that was expected of them.[20] Organizers had their complaints, of course, but they seemed to perceive their clients, even the wealthiest and most privileged among them, as deserving of support and assistance due to the many demands placed on clients' time and energy.

As business owners with various forms of class and social capital, organizers are usually buffered from some of the uglier aspects emotional work can take on in different careers and work settings. What challenges they do face in managing difficult emotions or establishing boundaries with clients are also compensated for by the gratification they find in their work and the value they see in what they do for clients. Because while connective labor has the potential to be burdensome and exploitative, it can also be deeply rewarding for those who perform it. As Allison Pugh argues in her own research on practitioners of connective labor, this sort of work "often creates profound emotional meaning" for those who perform it, "including a sense of purpose in their own work."[21] This is undoubtedly true for professional organizers. As I have described throughout this book, organizers see the chance to connect with and support clients not as a necessary chore but as one of the most meaningful and rewarding parts of their job. As one organizer told me, "There's a relationship between the organizer and the client that's sacred, that's wonderful, that's beautiful, that's magical, that's combative, that is needle-pushing, that is everything." As this description suggests, the nature of organizers' work with clients extends far beyond organizing people's things, just as the rewards they find in this work exceed the payment they receive when a job ends.

"A Ministry to Help Other Women"

When people imagine the helping professions, they often picture those who care for the most vulnerable among us, people who look after children, tend injured bodies, or feed the hungry.[22] But organizers, too, see helping and caring for others as a core part of what they do and why they do it. Many organizers say the reason they chose this career in the first place was because they wanted to help people. Hilda, who turned to organizing after working in a bank, said that with organizing she had finally regained a part of herself that she'd been missing in her previous job. "There's a serving, helping element to it [organizing]. I love seeing the fruits of what the order, so to speak, and what the organization does for a person." If you do it for the right reasons, she says, rather than just to make money, organizing offers an opportunity "to help your fellow neighbor, regardless of income, regardless of celebrity status, regardless if they're poor or whatever."

More than one organizer described their organizing work as a "ministry," of sorts. One told me, "I always feel like I have a ministry to help other women, just to help other women bring order to their home." In these statements, organizing is framed as a philanthropic endeavor, albeit one done for pay, a job that allows one to feel they've been of service to others while also making a living.

Sometimes, organizers' desire to help others actually trumps their need to make a profit. We see this both in jobs organizers opt to do for free and in their tendency to offer reduced rates to certain types of clients. Organizer Starla, for example, rallied a team of organizers to volunteer to help a mother of two fleeing domestic violence get settled in her new apartment. She even secured donations to help furnish the place, including new toys for the children, who'd left behind most of their belongings when they fled to a temporary shelter. Similarly, at meetings of the Orange County Task Force on Hoarding—a volunteer group that meets to review residential hoarding situations and includes city officials, police officers, social workers, organizers, and others—organizers are often asked to donate their services to help tackle large jobs for individuals facing eviction due to health and safety violations related to their hoarding.

I lost count of the number of organizers who confessed to me that they lower their rates dramatically for particular clients. This was often said in confidence, for fear that such soft-heartedness might reflect poorly on them among other, more "professional" organizers. One Brooklyn-based organizer who usually charges $75 per hour told me she sometimes offers deeply discounted rates to her elderly clients: "I'm soft on them. Don't tell anyone." Some organizers told me they couldn't bring themselves to raise their rates for longtime clients who'd helped them build their businesses. Orange County organizer Dianne, for example, a married mother of six, started organizing in the early 1980s. Now in her mid-seventies, she still does at least five organizing jobs per week, each lasting three to four hours. The going rate for organizers where she lives is $50–$100 per hour, but Dianne charges just $25 an hour. For her, she says, organizing "was never about the money." She was fortunate, she explains, that her husband made enough to support their large family. "It wasn't that I didn't want to make money," she told me, "I just wanted to go where the need was, so it wasn't really about the money." When the Great Recession hit in 2007, for example, she decided not to raise her prices, "because they [clients] won't be able to afford it and I'd rather help them than not help them."

As Dianne notes, she was able to charge well below market value for her services because profit was never her end goal, nor did her family depend on it. Yet even organizers who were entirely self-supporting offered similar discounts when they perceived a client as especially in need of help. I interviewed one team of organizers, both single women, who started a business together after they met in interior design school. One described to me her initial consultation with a client who had a "hoarding situation." When she arrived at the client's home, the client explained that due to her hoarding problem, her boyfriend had moved out and "I think I just lost my chance of true love." The client started crying, then the organizer started crying. "I was so emotionally affected," she told me. "I just felt so bad," she continued, because "I know she can't afford to do what she needs to do to clean out her house." She called her business partner on the way home from the consultation and described the situation, telling her, "I don't know about you, but I am more than willing to offer [to work for free] for her just to help." Her partner agreed. It was neither the first nor the last time they agreed to do a job for free because, she said, "I think we have bleeding hearts for some people." Here, clients that organizers perceive as especially deserving are given preferential treatment, usually in the form of reduced (or no) cost.[23] Despite organizers' consistent emphasis on "treating their business like a business," that mandate is clearly less important to many organizers than their desire to give help to people they believe need it but can't necessarily afford it.

In a female-dominated field like organizing, this emphasis on serving and ministering to others, even against one's own financial interests, is hardly surprising. Women in particular say it is important to them that their work is meaningful and, ideally, makes the world and other people's lives better in significant ways.[24] Women are also generally less willing than men to take morally unattractive jobs, and more likely than men to say that having "a job that helps society" is "extremely important" to them.[25] This is especially true of women undergoing career transitions, who often choose to leave male-dominated or mixed-gender corporate jobs in favor of female-dominated occupations and helping professions.[26] Scholars have also found that the degree to which workers embrace the identity implied by a particular job is "determined in part by the degree to which they can interpret the job as expressing their gender in a satisfying way."[27] In a culture that frames helping and caring for others as women's work, gravitating to a helping profession makes sense for women (although of course there are men who pursue these jobs as well). When that work is performed in domestic spaces, it invokes an additional level of gendered expectations around housework and the home. Female organizers helping female clients get more organized doesn't do much to dislodge the idea that, paid or free, organizing is women's work. And yet, if we look more closely at what organizers aim to help women *with*, their work's relationship to broader gender norms and cultural expectations becomes more complicated.

On the most basic level, organizers enjoy helping people with stuff. One organizer told me that after a long day of organizing, "I go home and even at night when I'm in bed I'm thinking about what it looked like when I got there and all the things we did and how great that looks." The physical impact organizing can make on a space is perhaps most dramatic in instances involving hoarding. Organizer Lara described a particularly intense job where three sisters, after years of hoarding possessions, were sleeping in the same bed because every other room in their house had become uninhabitable. "So, three grown women, sleeping in the same bed," she said. "There was no way to eat, and there was no way to do laundry, and there was no hot water." She worked the job alongside a team of other organizers. "It was a lot of very hard work," she recalled. "It was a hundred degrees and we were working outside and inside with no air conditioning. It was hot and oppressive." By the time the organizing team left, however, "we made quite a difference." Lara said she loves leaving a job and thinking, "Wow, that's huge. This person can now sleep in their own bed, this person can find their important documents, and this person is relieved. This is not rocket science, but we do make a difference. We really do."

As in these examples, organizers regularly articulate the concrete benefits of organizing—how great a space looks, that someone can live more comfortably in their own home, find the things they need, or invite friends over after years of being too ashamed to do so.[28] They talk about saving time looking for your keys or saving money on storage units, late fees for unpaid bills, and purchases to replace things you own but can't find. As they do so, however, organizers move quite naturally from describing how they made a space look and work and how the process and its outcome made the client *feel*. In the previous quotation, for example, the organizer describes clients feeling "relieved" at the end of a job. Another organizer said of her work, "It's the best feeling to have done something complex, something that made them feel good." Other organizers offered more detail on the sorts of feelings they aim to inspire in clients.

One young organizer, Tess, described for me two recent jobs she'd done. In one, she'd been hired to organize a large walk-in closet for a client who'd just relocated to LA. When she arrived, she found the closet was already clean and tidy. "I was like 'What do you need me here for?'" It turned out the client wanted her closet reorganized to look like a boutique shop floor. Tess did as the client asked and was paid generously for it. Soon after, she organized another closet, this one for a woman who'd recently emigrated from Russia and had purchased a discounted organizing package through an online deal Tess had offered. That client's closet was much smaller and "just really kind of filthy. . . . Everything was on the floor in piles. We pulled it all out and sorted and put it all in together and dusted." It was a much messier, more challenging job than arranging a glamorous boutique closet, but Tess enjoyed it far more. "When I go somewhere and it already looks organized and they just want me to fine-tune it, I don't find that as fun or fascinating or challenging. I like to go where it's messy or dirty." For Tess, the second job was harder work, and, discounted as it was, paid her less, but she preferred it anyway because it allowed her to feel she was making a difference for someone who needed it.

Tess's favorite part of organizing, she explains, is "seeing people's reaction and the hope in their eyes that they can have a beautiful place to call home and they are not being judged. Seeing them at the end of a session, it's a 180 sometimes. Like, I'll go in and they're overwhelmed and stressed out and can't find anything. They feel like there's a sense of lack—lack of space and time and energy. . . . I just love to see their relief when we're done." For Tess, the end goal of organizing is not the neatness of the space, number of items purged, or nifty organizing strategies employed. It's the human outcome, the chance to help clients feel hopeful, seen, happy, and relieved. Thus, while organizing is the means by which organizers accomplish these emotional outcomes, the rewards organizers reap from their work stem not from the organization itself—the pretty after picture or alphabetized bookshelf—but from how being more organized helps clients feel.

Other organizers describe working to relieve clients of similar feelings of overwhelm and self-criticism. Organizer Vanessa, for example, said that with every job she does, "I always try and put some sort of optimistic spirit on things if at all possible, or to let people know that they're strong and sort of give people power that you can get through this. Yes, this is hard. Yes, this sucks. . . . But you're smart, you work hard. Let's figure out how we can get through this together." Often, organizing entails reframing clients' sense of themselves as somehow flawed with a different, less judgmental perspective. In the course of organizing, Vanessa said, clients will often come across a paper or item that reminds them of "something that they had to do, didn't do, or [were] late in doing that reminds them they're no good and [they think] 'I can't do anything on time.' It becomes this whole self-defeating, beat-up-on-themselves kind of thing." Rather than encouraging this line of thought, Vanessa suggests immediate action. "Okay," she might tell a client, "so the property taxes are late. Let's just go online and we're going to pay the bill and there might be this extra charge but then you can be done with them. We'll do it right now." Just that one concrete step can make a huge difference in the client's mindset, she says. "It usually makes people feel good. People can be very hard on themselves. I try to point it out because they don't realize how hard they are." As Vanessa explains, the "concrete" steps they accomplish in an organizing session are intended to further the larger goals of helping clients feel better and think differently about their situation.

Organizer Dianne believes the opportunity to help people in this way is what distinguishes organizing from other, less rewarding occupations. "It's a different kind of job than I work somewhere and I get a paycheck and I just do a job. It's this human contact and helping these people believe in themselves, that they're okay." Her clients, she says, "have great hang-ups about themselves," but by the end of a session they feel "like everything is under control. It's not perfect, but it's under control. And that is the real payoff for me because they are so grateful and so happy." "It's a win-win," she says. "I do what I love and I get paid for it, and I get a hug at the door. That's my goal—the hug at the door." Here again, the human relationships in the organizing process, and the opportunity to shift a client's emotional state, are experienced not as burdens or demands but as the most rewarding part of organizers' work.

As we consider these organizers' descriptions of the work they do with clients and how they feel about it, it's worth remembering that most organizing clients are women, so organizers aren't just helping people, they're often helping other *women*, specifically. Organizers are well aware of this, as in the example of the organizer above who described her work as a "ministry to help other women." Because women tend to be responsible for much of the cleaning, consuming, and organizing that goes on in American households, the assistance organizers provide often goes, by default, to women. Just as the work of organizing tends to fall disproportionately on women, so do the costs of disorganization. It's usually women whose time is saved when the keys (or toys or pillowcases) are easy to find, women whose energy is preserved when all the clothes fit in the drawer, all the fixings for school lunches are in the same place. As I mentioned in the introduction, women's stress levels, not men's, rise when they move through cluttered spaces in their home, so it's also women who stand to benefit the most emotionally from the organizing process.[29] And yet, when organizers work with clients, they don't just aim to help women better manage the many responsibilities placed upon them. Often, they encourage women to reconsider whether they—or anyone—should be carrying all those burdens in the first place.

Organizing as a Feminist Act

In one of my very first interviews for this project, organizer Regina Lark told me she sees organizing as "a feminist act."[30] At the time, I found her comment surprising. I'd been imagining the organizing industry as almost anti-feminist, in that it convinced people, especially women, to add having a perfectly organized home to their already teetering tower of gendered responsibilities at home and work. In the years since, I've come to agree with Lark's point. Despite the problematic contexts that have fueled organizing's growth, in the work they do with clients, organizers actually work to relieve clients of some of the burdens that have been placed upon them—as women, workers, and consumers—and to offer different, gentler standards by which they might measure their success.

Escaping the "Feminine Acquire-a-Tron"

As Lark told me at our first meeting, "I've been on the soapbox for years about the feminine acquire-a-tron of life and what it means to be female in our society." Women, she says, "are raised to believe that from the top of our head to the tip of our toes there is something wrong with us and we need to buy something that will fix it, heal it, tame it, create it." When she works with clients who have hundreds of pairs of shoes or drawer after drawer full of makeup, she tries to convey to them that the solution is not just about organization, or curtailing one's buying, but also about rejecting the idea that we, as women, need to buy things to fix our inherently flawed faces, bodies, selves, and homes.

No other organizer I spoke with used the term "feminist" to describe their work, nor are all organizers as explicitly anti-consumerist as Lark. Nevertheless, most organizers I spoke with were quite critical of America's consumerist tendencies.[31] One organizer told me, "All we do is work, work, work so we can buy, buy, buy and then we don't have any time to enjoy the things that we have. And then you have to get a storage unit because we constantly buy, buy. We think it's happiness and it's really not making you happy. I truly believe the more stuff you have, the more problems and more responsibility you have." She and others saw organizing as a means to ultimately help people buy less, if that was something the client was open to. This might entail raising clients' awareness of the costs of all this stuff—not just an item's purchase price but the time, energy, and space committed to storing it. Other times, organizers described buying less not so much as an ideological shift as the natural outcome of becoming more organized, as clients got a more accurate sense of what they already owned and therefore did not need to repurchase.[32] As Kondo writes, "After tidying, many clients tell me that their worldly desires have decreased. Whereas in the past, no matter how many clothes they had, they were never satisfied and always wanted something new to wear, once they selected and kept those things that they really loved, they felt that they had everything they needed."[33] The goal here, then, is not to convince people to buy less, but to create conditions that allow them to buy less without necessarily making a conscious decision to do so.[34]

Organizers' anti-consumerist tendencies complicate their relationship to other sectors of the organizing industry. As I've mentioned, when I began this study, I assumed peddling products was part of what organizers did, an objective that allied them with stores and magazines that advertise and sell organizing products.[35] My preconception was nicely summed up in a *New Yorker* cartoon where a woman sitting in front of a computer in a living room says to the man standing across the desk from her, "It's an entire Web site of things you can buy to con-sume less."[36] As a rule, however, organizers discourage clients from buying organizing products.[37] For one thing, organizers told me, most people who decide to hire an organizer already own more organiz-ing products than they need. As organizer Eileen explained, "Buying things is what gets my clients into trouble in the first place. . . . Unless these products are used, they're just more clutter. So most of my cli-ents have a lot of organizing books and a lot of organizing tools and a lot of shelves and bins and boxes, but they don't use them." Thus, while most organizers keep a trunkful of basic organizing products handy, they encourage clients to use what they already have, which in most cases is all they need.[38] On the first episodes of the Netflix show *Tidying Up with Marie Kondo*, for example, Kondo shows up to each job with an armful of small cardboard boxes, the sort that once held jewelry or stationery or iPhones, which she uses to subdivide drawers and shelves to keep small items from getting jumbled together. (To see how persuaded I am by this perspective, one need only peek into my son's sock drawer, where his socks sit corralled in a series of rectangu-lar cardboard boxes rescued from the recycling bin.)

This disinclination to purchase organizing products sits at odds with other aspects of organizers' work. Some organizers earn a per-centage on the products they sell to clients; a few even have their own product lines, which they promote to clients, retailers, and other organizers.[39] NAPO meetings and conferences regularly feature pre-sentations and displays by companies promoting their products or services to organizers.[40] Some who equate organizing with minimal-ism find organizers selling products antithetical to their vision, even hypocritical. When Marie Kondo launched her first line of products in 2019, for instance, many were critical of "the downsizing expert's pivot to consumption."[41] And yet, in the years I spent with organiz-ers, I never saw an organizer push a product on a client. When orga-nizers did suggest products, it was usually in response to a specific need that emerged over the course of organizing, such as a shelf to hold items formerly stored, unseen and unused, in cardboard boxes in the garage. Occasionally, a job requires purchasing a full set of new products, for example if a client wants to redo their home office in a specific color scheme, but unless it was a priority for the client, organizers preferred to repurpose items the client already owned and to focus more on function than aesthetics.[42] Organizers' work thus generally entails less shopping and less "taste work" than that of interior designers and personal concierges, who often play a role in shaping clients' aesthetic and purchasing decisions to match certain cultural and class ideals.[43] In contrast, organizers often encourage clients to reject such aesthetic standards, claiming they are both unrealistic and unnecessary.

Debunking House Porn

As I mentioned in the previous chapter, organizers tend to be harsh critics of the picture-perfect homes displayed in magazines and on television and social media. One organizer I interviewed described these images as "house porn" and was actively working against such impossible ideals of domestic order. When her own home was profiled on a lifestyle blog, she insisted the photographers capture evidence of her family's real life—an unmade bed, dog toys on the floor, a dish towel on the counter—so as not to replicate the pristine, minimalist interiors usually held up as aesthetic ideals.[44] Another organizer told me she believes the before-and-after pictures in magazines and TV shows contribute to feelings of "compare and despair" among her clients, as they contrast their homes to the carefully staged images they see on TV and in magazines. When they work with clients, then, organizers strive to mediate "the stringent and often unrealistic goals set by most organization-related cultural texts."[45]

One way organizers go about doing this is by clarifying to clients exactly how much work goes into the images people see in popular culture.[46] Organizer Sara, for example, often tells clients that yes, she can give them "the perfect pantry" they've seen on Pinterest. "I can one hundred percent give you that, but you need to understand how much work that is. The people who really have those [pantries] have full-time staff. No joke, that's what they have. If you want to take that on in your life, if that's important to you, I'll help you get there." Really, she says, it's a matter of where you want to spend your time. For most people, she says, that level of organization and aesthetic perfection simply isn't sustainable, or especially important. By revealing the labor that goes into those images and the impracticality, even impossibility, of recreating them in real life, organizers work to align clients' expectations with the realities of their budgets and lifestyles.

Another approach organizers use to shift clients' unrealistic expectations of their spaces and themselves is by offering themselves as examples of organizational imperfection. In contrast to stereotypes of organizers as rigid perfectionists with perfect homes, many organizers I spoke with are candid with clients about their own organizational struggles. Organizer Marianne attributes her organizing abilities to growing up in a chaotic home. "I found that being organized was a way of having control over something in the environment." As a result, she says, "I'm not the organizer that says, 'I was born organized, I just came out this way.' That is not me at all, and I still have to work at it regularly." When she works with clients who struggle to become and stay organized, she tells them, "I'm just like you and I have to work at it." This is especially important, she says, because clients tend to assume that organizers' own homes must be immaculate. "Clients always think," Marianne said, "your place must be perfect and nothing ever goes wrong for you, and they build up those false ideals and I never want to be known that way. I want them to know that 'hey, we are exactly the same here. I might be a little further along in the process than you, but I had to learn it as well.'" By emphasizing that she both understands and shares her clients' struggles and concerns, Marianne aims to reduce some of their anxiety and self-criticism around the state of their own homes and belongings.

Two of the most experienced organizers I met—with a combined sixty-plus years' organizing experience—sometimes invite potential clients to tour their homes, not just to demonstrate their own organizing strategies but also as evidence that "my house gets messy, too." Similarly, San Francisco organizer Michelle tells clients, "I am not coming to you as someone who's perfect and someone you should try to emulate. I'm coming to you as someone who can help you figure out what's realistic for you and how you can get there." Michelle sees this as important not just as a selling point for her services, but as an antidote to clients' insecurities and overly high standards for themselves. It's important, she says, "to be human and be normal and not hold yourself up as a model of an unrealistic perfection that clients already see everywhere else on TV and magazines."[47] "We can benefit so much," Michelle told me, "from that kind of radical honesty."[48]

By emphasizing their own normalcy and fallibility when it comes to organization, organizers work to lower clients' expectations of themselves and their homes. In this way, organizers make themselves vulnerable to clients, in the sense that they are exposing their own limitations in the very field in which they're hired for their expertise. At the same time, because they are *already* positioned as experts in organization, organizers' critiques of what constitutes "unrealistic perfection" tend to carry more weight. If even an *organizer* can't achieve that ideal, it must be okay for clients to fall short as well. Rather than just deferring to the client's perspective, organizers aim to shift clients' ways of thinking—about themselves, their spaces, and their belongings—in order to reduce their feelings of stress and self-blame. Organizers did something similar when they worked to adjust female clients' equally elevated expectations of themselves as mothers, wives, and homemakers.

"You Cannot Do It All"

When organizers share with clients that they, too, struggle to get and stay organized, they're effectively saying, "It's not just you, it's me, too." There is sometimes an awareness in such exchanges that women are usually the ones expected to achieve that perfect home, but the "bad guy" organizers point to in such moments is typically unrealistic media representations, rather than unequal gender roles. At other moments, however, organizers were more explicitly critical of the impossible and unjust expectations placed on women today, and not just in terms of home organization. In these instances, organizers' core message was "It's not you *or* me, it's society."

As the brief history of clutter in chapter 1 demonstrates, organization has long been seen as both a gendered skill and a gendered responsibility, as women are perceived as more responsible than men for the state of their homes. Failure to keep a clean, uncluttered, organized home is thus cast as a specifically feminine failure. Organizers regularly describe female clients who've internalized such expectations to their own detriment. As organizer Regina Lark explains, many of her clients feel that they are "not fulfilling the goals of womanhood," that they are "just a loser wife and mother, because look at this house." Lark is explicit with her clients that the problem is not with the women themselves, or with their homes, but with the unbalanced and gendered expectations we have of homes and the often invisible and unpaid work it takes to keep them functional and attractive. She has in fact authored an entire book on the subject, in which she argues for a more equitable distribution of such work within households and across society.

Many organizers share Lark's view that the burdens most women bear on the home front are untenable, and that part of organizers' job is to help women see that. In their belief that women today are uniquely burdened with tasks and responsibilities, organizers echo scholars who study the impact of "insecurity culture" on American families. Men and women have both been negatively impacted by the rise of insecure work and economic uncertainty, but across socioeconomic classes, the burdens for managing that insecurity—and the labor and anxiety it generates—tend to fall more heavily on the shoulders of women.[49] Vanessa, for example, specifically mentions working with "moms who are doing so much and have all this stuff and think they're supposed to be able to handle everything." Vanessa explains to them, "You cannot do it all. You can't. So it's okay." Although Vanessa doesn't name sexism as the cause of the untenable amount of work allotted to women, she does recognize that women, "moms" specifically, are the ones who "are doing so much" and expect themselves to handle it all. She encourages women to accept that they cannot "do it all" and that that's okay, working to remove the guilt and self-recrimination weighing women down.

Like most organizers, Vanessa's response in such moments is to focus on individual solutions. After urging women not to be so hard on themselves for failing to do the impossible, for example, Vanessa helps put systems in place to reduce the number of things and tasks her clients are responsible for, such as setting the bills to autopay or going paperless so they no longer have to decide whether and how to file paper bills and statements. "Let's not worry about that anymore," she tells them. "Let's focus on what we can [do] and let's not be so hard on ourselves and let's be happy. And what would make you happy right now? Let's have a couple of M&M's. Let's do—I don't know. What do you want to do for just two minutes to make you feel better?" The goal, then, is to help the client get more organized, but also to make the client feel less bad about not being perfectly organized in the first place, and to set in place systems and strategies that lessen the feelings of overwhelm, inadequacy, and self-blame that so many women succumb to. Achieving this goal means consciously working to move clients from a negative emotional state ("I'm no good") to a positive one ("let's be happy").

Giving clients an M&M and sorting their mail isn't the stuff of revolution. Lark is rare among organizers in calling out and working to combat the sexism behind cultural expectations of women's domestic labor. But she and many other organizers do use the empathetic relationships they form with clients to push back against cultural ideals that devalue the work of organizing and caring for a household while expecting that labor be performed for free, usually by women, to impossible standards. After compassionately witnessing female clients' anxiety, overwhelm, and self-blame, organizers offer a different way of thinking about disorganization and the work of eradicating it. They urge clients to not see clutter as evidence of moral or personal failure, but to accept that this is hard, ongoing work that isn't easy for anybody. Just as organizers give clients permission to part with belongings, they give them permission to let go of the unyielding expectations they and others have placed upon them. This might mean putting in place systems that lessen their workload, insisting that others perform their fair share of such labor, or, when resources allow, outsourcing that work to paid helpers. It might also mean making peace with simply not doing it all, living with lower, gentler expectations of ourselves and our homes. It's worth remembering that organizers were making these sorts of arguments *before* the Covid-19 pandemic drew fresh, intensified attention to the untenable nature of what America asks of its working mothers, and what solutions we—as individuals, families, employers, and society—should be doing about it.[50] Organizers were ahead of this curve, as they'd long been witnessing up close the emotional and material fallout of life under market capitalism.

Therapists of Capitalism

Organizing has been compared to therapy since the occupation's earliest days, yet the organizers I met insisted with great regularity that they are *not* therapists, emphasizing that therapy requires a different sort of training and expertise than organizing. When they are concerned about a client's psychological state, or when the client's thoughts and feelings around their home or belongings are so intense that the organizing process becomes difficult or impossible, organizers will gently recommend the client see a therapist before or while they work with an organizer. This occurred in the organizing story that opened this book, when organizer Sara considered gently nudging client Lauren to think about returning to therapy. Sometimes, especially around instances of hoarding, an organizer and therapist work in tandem to address a client's needs. Organizers are thus generally well informed about what therapy is and what it intends to do, and they see a clear difference between that and organizing.

Despite these disclaimers, organizers and clients alike regularly discussed the ways in which organizing is *like* therapy.[51] I heard and read countless testimonials from satisfied customers that described the organizing process as "therapeutic" or claimed that working with an organizer benefited them more than years of therapy. One organizer I interviewed said she "looks at organizing as a form of counseling." Others referred to themselves as "clutter therapists" or "the paper therapist."[52] A pair of organizers who specialize in organization and design told me they sometimes refer to what they do as "interior therapy." One organizer even trademarked the name "The Organizational Therapist."[53] These parallels make sense for a number of reasons. First, as I discussed in chapter 1, therapists, like doctors, are the type of professionals organizers can liken themselves to in order to distance their work from that of lower-status occupations like housekeeping. Second, the increased popularity of therapy is part of what made possible organizing's rise in the first place.

The "therapeutic turn" of the 1960s brought psychological concepts and language into everyday American life.[54] Therapy culture took new shape in the expanding self-help and makeover industries, in which the self is a constant project, one best advanced by hiring experts to help manage even the most personal aspects of one's life.[55] In this context, many Americans find themselves increasingly comfortable outsourcing even the most intimate tasks to paid professionals, from life coaches to love coaches, party planners to dog walkers, even moms, grandmas, and husbands for hire.[56] Longtime organizers witnessed this shift firsthand. One organizer with more than thirty years' experience told me clients used to insist, "Don't tell anybody that I worked with you." When it came to hiring an organizer, she said, "there was a lot of shame in the game." One organizer remembered a client in the 1990s asking her to hide in her car until the client's husband left the house because she didn't want him to know she needed help organizing their home. Now, that same organizer said, "people love saying, 'Oh, my organizer's here!' 'Cause everyone knows about organizers." Just as seeing a therapist has evolved over time from a stigma to a status symbol, so, too, has hiring an organizer.

Another parallel between therapy and organizing has to do with the connective labor at the heart of both professions. When clients tell her she's like a therapist to them, organizer Hilda said, she thinks what they're noticing is that, like therapists, organizers "have the capacity to just listen to them and not judge." Therapy and organizing may differ in many respects, but the act of empathetic listening is a core component of both, as practitioners work to connect with clients in order to achieve a desired outcome. This is likely what clients mean when they say working with an organizer feels like therapy; both involve intimate, empathetic connections experienced within the framework of a commercial exchange and intended to improve clients' lives.

When organizers clarified for me, again and again, that organizing isn't really about "the stuff," this is what they were getting at. The relational labor organizers perform is not just a side course to the main work of getting organized. In fact, I'd argue, the reverse is sometimes true. My inside look at the organizing process has led me to believe that what many people are looking for when they hire organizers, whether they're conscious of it or not, is for someone to help them manage the unmanageable lives they find themselves living. The stuff is just a symptom of the larger feelings of overwhelm brought on by a culture of overwork, constant consumption, and rising uncertainty. In this context, organizers provide a particular kind of therapeutic relationship suited to people trying to manage their copious belongings while also working through their feelings around their stuff *and* the labor it demands of them. They are, as it were, therapists of capitalism.[57]

Over the last half century, rising insecurity and eroding social supports have created new financial, emotional, and administrative burdens for Americans. This is the trick of neoliberalism—it celebrates individual responsibility and agency (not terrible things unto themselves) and, in doing so, removes accountability for Americans' well-being from governments, employers, and communities. Individuals and households are thus left to their own devices to safeguard their professional and personal futures while managing an increasingly tenuous present. And yes, the pressure to be organized, to have an orderly, uncluttered home or workplace, is one more atop this growing pile of expectations. We are supposed to work hard, look good, eat well and exercise, parent attentively, *and* be able to find that file folder in less than five minutes.

In her book *Cannibal Capitalism*, Nancy Fraser argues that the feelings of overwhelm these overlapping demands produce are "not a coincidence but rather a baked-in consequence of twenty-first century global capitalist society."[58] Capitalism, Fraser writes, is a "guzzler of care," relying on women's unpaid labor of caregiving, maintaining households, and building social relationships even as it denies that work has any monetary value and expects it even from women who also perform paid work outside the home.[59] Those with the resources to do so often hire other women, often poorer women of color, to perform this work on their behalf.[60] This is the context in which the demand for organizing services has grown.[61]

The state of overwhelm so many Americans exist in—short on time, long on responsibilities, anxious, lonely, uncertain, awash in consumer goods yet feeling they're always falling short—these are the conditions that propel people to hire organizers (and therapists, personal trainers, life coaches, cleaning services, nannies, caregivers, tutors, financial advisors, doulas, the list goes on). Organizers reassure anxious, self-blaming clients that there is nothing wrong with them, that they feel overwhelmed because what they're being expected to do is, in fact, overwhelming, not just for them, but for everyone. In doing so, they give clients a gentle nudge in the direction of "it's not you," encouraging them to cast off some of the harshest edges of society's expectations of them, as well as their own. For women especially, this message, and the compassion and empathy that accompany it, can be a real gift, albeit one they paid for themselves. This work—what Beckman and Mazmanian call "the scaffolding" that helps people and households keep going in difficult times—deserves to be valued and recognized, as do those who perform it.[62]

A key shortcoming of this sort of purchasable care and support is that the people who need it the most are the ones least likely to receive it. Organizing may not be the luxury service some dismiss it as, but it's safe to say most organizing clients are better off financially than the typical American household. Those on whom the demands of contemporary life weigh most heavily generally lack the resources to hire or access help, whether from a therapist, an organizer, or both.

Organizers themselves are aware of this conundrum. Organizer Tess, for instance, believes organizers need to get organizing "more into the hands of people who wouldn't traditionally afford that luxury because it's a need. They're not able to do it themselves and they need help." She and other organizers told me they look forward to a day when all communities have equal awareness of and access to organizing services. Some envisioned that organizing might be "provided as a service from the government or from some kind of nonprofit" to ensure it reaches those who would most benefit from it. Other organizers suggested organizing skills should be taught to high school students who, in turn, could use those skills to help people who can't afford to pay an organizer. As I've mentioned, many organizers already offer free or low-cost organizing workshops and courses through schools, libraries, colleges, community centers, and programs for people with disabilities.[63]

And yet, even if they were equally available to all, services like organizing are not a solution to overwhelm, nor will they fix the yawning insecurity and inequality that underlie it. They are fleeting fixes for endemic social problems. Recognizing this doesn't diminish the value of what organizers do, but it does reveal the extent to which organizers, and other providers of personal services, are a Band-Aid, not a cure, to life in a culture steeped in anxiety, uncertainty, and material excess. Organizers offer care and connection aimed to ease the pain of whatever is hurting most in that moment, but their work doesn't alter—and rarely even names—the underlying social structures that encourage consumption, undervalue women's work of caring for others and for households, and drain families of the time and energy they need to sustain themselves and their communities. These sorts of systemic problems require bigger, broader interventions, ones that organizing arguably has the potential to further, and to thwart.

The day was swelteringly hot, and the parking lot of the North Hollywood storage facility where I was meeting organizer Lila and her client had no shade. I cracked the car door to allow in a breeze, of which there really wasn't any. Lila had told me to bring a lot of water, as we'd be working in a stuffy storage unit all day, but I drank most of it before they even arrived.

Lila, a single organizer in her mid-forties, arrived a few minutes early. Pale and freckled, Lila wore yoga pants and an army green t-shirt reading "Be Happy." Despite having worked seven straight days in a row, she seemed cheerful and brimming with energy.

Her client Denise arrived soon after, holding her infant son on her chest in one of those carriers that looks like an elaborately wrapped scarf. In her early thirties with bright green eyes and shoulder-length brown hair, Denise typed in the code that allowed us through the facility's rolling metal gate. We entered an enormous, poorly lit warehouse full of rows of identical corrugated-iron roll-down doors. Once we arrived at the correct unit, Denise unlocked the door and Lila pushed the button that turned on the lights. The lights were on a thirty-minute timer, so every half hour the lights would turn off and one of us had to get up to reset the timer. The session was scheduled to last three hours. "When we've done this six times," Lila joked, "we'll know it's time to go."

Denise's mother had passed away a year earlier, leaving Denise not one or two, but four storage units packed to the ceiling with furniture, home decor, and shelves filled with box after box of books, paperwork, and memorabilia. Some of the items belonged to Denise's grandmother, who had died not long before Denise's mother. At the time of her death, Denise's mother had been spending $1,000 a month on storage units, some of which she'd had for a decade.

(Monthly storage rates tend to start quite low, but the longer you keep the units, the higher the monthly rates.) Rats had gotten into some of the boxes; during a previous organizing session, Lila had made sure they were gone and "cleaned up the evidence." As Lila put it, Denise had inherited the "delayed decision-making" of her grandmother and mother, along with other family members, none of whom had been willing to part with the items Denise was now tasked with either getting rid of or finding a place to store.

Lila and Denise had already been working together twice a week for four months. They'd initially planned to meet more than twice a week, but "more than two days and I start to lose my will to live," Denise told me. "Less and we'll never get anywhere." Together, they'd emptied two of the four storage units so far. One had housed Denise's grandmother's furniture. Denise and her husband, who lived in a small rented house nearby, kept one piece and sold the rest to a furniture reseller. Lila had helped Denise condense the second unit, selling and giving away most of the large items and squeezing the smaller stuff into the remaining two units, which were being paid for out of her mother's estate, as was Lila's $75-an-hour fee.

The unit we were working in that day was about two-thirds full. Lila had set up a small kitchen table at the front of the unit along with two chairs. She'd thought-fully brought an additional camping chair for me to use on the day I assisted. While Denise sat at the table holding the baby, Lila went box by box, holding up items for Denise to see. Denise told her whether to keep, donate, toss, or set aside for another family member to look through, and Lila put the item in an appropriately labeled box or pile. "It's not my job to make the decisions," Lila explained to me. Smiling, Denise added, "It's her job to sit here and make me make the decisions." Because the job was such a big one, Lila had implemented a color-coded labeling system, with a corresponding key taped on the wall listing which color meant what (yellow for "Denise keep," green for donations, pink for Denise's sister to look through on her next visit to town, etc.).

Lila kept the mood light and playful as they worked. Denise is one of Lila's favorite clients, both because the two enjoy each other's company and because Denise is good at getting rid of stuff; Lila estimated that about nine of every ten items they went through headed to the trash or donation piles. The two clearly knew each other well after so many hours working together. Lila listened to the stories Denise told about the items she sorted. By this point, Lila was intimately familiar with the details of Denise's childhood and family dynamics. When Denise told a story about her younger sister, whom Lila has met only once but clearly heard a lot about, Lila smiled and rolled her eyes. "That's so Jasmine." Occasionally, Denise expressed her understandable frustration at being the one charged with sorting through everyone else's stuff. In those moments, Lila took on the role of emotional cheerleader, sympathizing with Denise's situation and complimenting her on how much progress she's made already. Denise's mother had actually employed her own organizer, who Denise had initially hired to work alongside Lila. But Lila, Denise explained, does a better job "managing my emotions," moving her to an easier, less emotionally laden task when she feels overwhelmed.

At one point, Lila held up a large bouquet of artificial flowers that had belonged to Denise's mother. "Ugh," Denise said. "I don't want to keep them, but I can't stand to see them thrown away." Lila nodded. "Then maybe," she said wryly, "they'll just disappear one day when you're not here?" Denise didn't object. Lila turned to me with a smile. "Did you hear that? That's why we work well together."

While I held the baby (best job ever), the two made quick work of a box of books, with Denise keeping some of the children's books and donating the rest. As she does every time Denise finishes a box, Lila praised her. "Very nicely done. Good job."

Lila brought over another box, warning Denise, "This might be a little scary." "Bring it on," Denise replied, "we've got to do it sometime." This particular box held a number of items reflecting Denise's childhood love of the boy band New Kids on the Block. She opted to keep a baseball cap with the band's logo and a small stack of unsent letters to her favorite band member (Joey, obviously). She read parts of the letters aloud to us. Along with her love for the band, they detailed how lonely Denise felt at her school, how mean the other kids were to her. Pausing to fill in details for us, Denise recalled with intensity childhood slights and crushes, the names of her childhood aggressors. It was painful to listen to, both because she'd had such a difficult time and because those experiences, and the feelings they prompted, were clearly still very much alive for Denise.

That single box felt endless, like a clown car with absurdly large capacity. Lila noted that their pace had slowed, blaming the box rather than Denise. "This box is a killer," she said. "This is the weirdest box, all sorts of random things, that's why it's taking so long." To speed the process, Lila started sorting the contents into piles, which she then handed to Denise, rather than having Denise take out each item one at a time. "School work?" Lila asked, holding up a stack for Denise to see. "Toss," Denise declared. Other stacks Denise kept to sort through, making her own keep and toss piles, which Lila regularly relocated to the appropriate box or recycling bin.

At the end of the three-hour session, they'd gone through about ten boxes. Lila loaded up the back of her SUV with two boxes of paper to take to the shredder. Dropping off loads of paper to be shredded, Lila said, "That's organizer porn." She loaded another few boxes of donations. She used to leave donations labeled at the end of a job for the client to drop off, but she often found the boxes still sitting there on her next visit. She started offering to drop them off herself, for a fee, and clients love it. Because Denise is such a good client and because it's hard to manage all this stuff with a baby in hand, Lila drops her stuff off for free.

Denise's eventual goal, Lila told me, was to take home just six boxes to sort through, one a week for six weeks. Looking around the unit, I noted at least ten boxes already labeled "Denise Sort." Lila suspects Denise will be surprised at the end of the process how much she has actually earmarked to take home. They will likely do a second round of sorting, Lila said, to pare what remains to a more manageable size. At that point, Lila said, she might push Denise a little harder to let go of some things. Denise, for her part, is eager for the process to be over. "I'm tired," she told us, "of having my mother's affairs be my whole life apart from my baby."

Conclusion

As I write this conclusion, it's late August and I'm living what I've been writing about. My university starts classes on Monday, my son begins fourth grade two days later. Book revisions are due at the end of the month, I have a new course to prep, and my to-do list just reached a second page. Meanwhile, I'm being peppered by emails from my son's school with forms to complete, school supplies to buy, events to volunteer for. My usually tidy desk is cluttered with papers, bills, and Post-it note reminders. I have twenty-seven open browser windows on my phone (I counted), each a reminder of something I need to do, buy, or read.[1] I feel guilty that I'm not working enough and simultaneously guilty that I'm working too much when I should be spending these last precious days of summer with my family. And I'm a healthy, securely employed professional with a rewarding job that comes with great benefits, living in a nice home in a safe neighborhood just down the street from the award-winning public school my son attends. My husband and I share the work of cooking and cleaning, we're able to pay wonderful people to help tend our home and yard twice a month, and I have family, friends, and neighbors who've come through for me time and time again whenever I needed them. These are rare privileges, and I'm grateful for them. Nevertheless, I feel anxious and overwhelmed, short on time and pulled in so many directions it's difficult to complete any one task successfully. I can't begin to imagine what these pressures feel like for people living paycheck to paycheck, or without a paycheck at all; working longer hours at more physically and emotionally exhausting jobs; managing their own and loved ones' health and other crises; and whose personal and communal support networks are nonexistent or themselves struggling to stay afloat. We're all at sea, but at least I have a boat.

The way we live and work today is not working, especially not for women. There is a palpable "too-muchness" to everyday life that demands an unsustainable level of work and worry. Organizers aren't the answer to this crisis, but through their career choices *and* their work with clients, organizers *can* help us better understand both the nature of the problem and the sorts of solace, support, and solutions that might help ease it.

It strikes me as ironic that I spent so much time clarifying that the organizers I studied *weren't* labor organizers, and I've ended up making the case that professional organizers can, in fact, help us imagine better ways to organize our labor. The women who founded and joined this profession did so because there was a fundamental mismatch between the work they'd been doing (whether as unpaid homemakers or in paid jobs), what their family needed (whether more time, more care, or more income), and what they wanted for themselves (meaning, autonomy, self-determination, human connection). In organizing, they found both an escape from some of the worst aspects of standard employment and an opportunity to do meaningful work that meshed better, though by no means perfectly, with their other values and responsibilities. With the professional community they have established, organizers also demonstrate that people who are ostensibly competitors can nevertheless support, assist, and educate one another. As collaborative competitors, organizers work to make money from their individual businesses, but they also model a way of operating that privileges mutual respect, ethical engagement (with one another and with clients), and shared values over profit at any cost. This praise isn't intended to minimize problems within the organizing profession, especially the ways in which it has ignored or replicated social and economic inequalities around gender, race, and class. Organizers need to focus more attention on the unequal barriers to success in their field and work, collaboratively, to make their profession more equal and inclusive. They should also consider how old, inherited ideas about professionalism—especially around blending paid work with caregiving—have created unnecessary divisions and hierarchies in their ranks.

Despite these shortcomings, I continue to be moved by organizers' descriptions of what they do and the meaning, connection, and validation they receive from their work. This is especially impactful in an era when so few Americans, even the wealthiest and most professionally successful among them, feel that way about their jobs. In organizing, we might find clues to how we might go about creating forms of work that—with better, fuller supports—offer a viable, satisfying alternative to the way most Americans currently work. This seems an especially ripe time for such innovations, as the pandemic has revealed the many ways traditional employment is no longer working, if it ever has, mobilizing renewed interest in unions and other forms of collective action. During the pandemic, some Americans discovered the benefits of working from home, on more flexible schedules, for fewer hours. For others, Covid brought home exactly how few protections they have at work, whether from sudden job loss, unsafe working conditions, or unreasonable demands. In the first months of the pandemic, the US unemployment rate (which consistently underestimates job losses) reached a height not seen since the Great Depression.[2] The combination of enforced time at home and temporary financial security (provided through unemployment benefits and other forms of Covid-related relief) allowed others an opportunity to reflect on the work they'd been doing and imagine other, more lucrative and fulfilling careers they might pursue instead. Workers laid off or furloughed during the pandemic were more likely than those who remained securely employed to say their attitudes toward work had changed, and that they now placed greater import on doing work they felt passionate about.[3] After an initial dip, the pandemic also prompted new interest in self-employment, "as people look to bring in extra income, explore ways to continue to work from home and reevaluate their personal and professional priorities."[4] Compared to previous years, people starting new businesses post-pandemic were much more likely to be Black, Hispanic, or Latinx, and nearly half of them were women (compared to less than a third in recent years).[5]

Amid this ongoing tumult lies the potential to reimagine—and actively lobby for—better, fairer, more sustainable ways of working and living.[6] In the female-led world of organizing, we might find a model, albeit an imperfect one, of what such careers might look like.

In addition to the way they've structured their occupation and professional community, organizers' work itself can help us envision other ways of living and relating, to one another and to the objects we possess. They encourage us to think harder about what we own—where it comes from, where it ends up, and what it costs us, not just in purchase price, but in the time and energy spent buying, storing, cleaning, and discarding, and the lost opportunity to share our resources with those who may need them more. Organizers question our culture's tendency to devalue the work of organizing a household while also expecting that work to be performed for free, usually by women, to impossible standards. They point out the untenable nature of the work required of us in these neoliberal times, at our jobs and in our households, and they help women navigate the many burdens and stresses contemporary society has placed upon them. In their work with clients, organizers also model how care and connection can lessen, and perhaps even defy, the too-muchness of contemporary life, with its dwindling supports and rising demands. In this way, they reveal, even in shadowy form, other, more humane ways of living and working under capitalism.

Clearly, I like organizers, and I think their work has the potential to help people, sometimes a little, often a lot. At the same time, the cynical social critic in me can't help but ask, so what? So a few people feel better because they were able to hire an organizer who helped tame, at least temporarily, their belongings and the feelings of guilt, anxiety, and overwhelm those belongings prompt. On a broader scale, in terms of the insurmountable pressures facing American households and the deeply dysfunctional nature of contemporary American work life, how much of an impact can that really make?

Organizers' decision to pursue this line of work as an alternative to standard employment shows us what's not working in a world of work that feels constricting, meaningless, and uncertain while also demanding long hours and clashing with familial responsibilities. But, of course, not everyone can or wants to be an organizer, and organizing itself replicates many of the problems of standard employment. Organizers, too, often work long hours and face uncertain financial and professional futures. And the same groups that face discrimination and marginalization in standard employment do so in organizing, too. It's harder to make a business work when you lack certain gender, racial, and class privileges. The meaning organizers find in organizing is a wonderful thing, especially when so many people feel trapped in miserable, meaningless jobs, but we also know that making a career out of doing what you love can replicate occupational segregation and workforce inequalities, as meaningful work becomes yet another thing only the most privileged can obtain.[7] Fleeing standard employment for the greener pastures of self-employment also distracts attention from collective efforts to hold employers accountable. In this way, organizers' flight from standard employment might be understood as releasing just enough pressure to allow the unequal, untenable nature of how Americans work today continue uninterrupted, further disadvantaging the most vulnerable and marginalized among us.[8]

The second thread of this argument concerns the work organizers do with clients. Most Americans are awash in consumer goods, and they lack the time, energy, and knowledge to sort and corral their myriad things. Organizers help with these material challenges, aiming to minimize or eliminate clutter and the work it demands of those held responsible for it. They also validate clients' perceptions that life has become unmanageable, as has the amount and nature of the work expected of women, both at home and in their jobs. Here again, though, these are individual-level changes, focused more on self-help than on social transformation. Many have in fact criticized the self-improvement industry for focusing people inward, on changing their individual selves and surroundings, while distracting them from broader, more collective efforts and concerns.[9] Organizing, with its focus on individual- and household-level changes, is vulnerable to the same critique. Perhaps each automated bill or easily located set of car keys releases just enough steam to allow households to go on functioning, rather than grinding to a halt or exploding in frustration. In helping women manage the unmanageable, organizers might inadvertently be forestalling collective efforts to demand more from our partners, employers, communities, and government.

It seems a bit much to claim that the rise of organizing is going to either help thwart a revolution or incite one. Either way, that would be a lot to ask of one small occupation. Instead, as one of my colleagues regularly tells her students, if someone offers you a choice between A and B, pick C. In this case, option C might be the possibility that in organizing—the career it provides to its practitioners and the support they in turn provide to their clients—we might find seeds of the sort that, in the right conditions and with the right encouragements, could grow into broader social changes. For, as some scholars have persuasively argued, helping oneself and helping one's society are not necessarily mutually exclusive.[10]

In her book *True Wealth*, Juliet Schor argues that our economic system is broken and in need of deep transformations. Rather than criticizing changes at the individual level as inconsequential or distracting, Schor suggests the most effective way to combat some of the major challenges of our day—climate destabilization, economic meltdown, and rising food and energy costs—is for people to "work and spend less, create and connect more."[11] Like organizers, Schor encourages people to consume less and think more carefully about what and how much they purchase and to tend more carefully to what they own. Also like organizers, she and others contend that Americans are overworked and need to reclaim their time for more meaningful, gratifying purposes.[12] Those who embrace these principles, Schor contends, "are not merely adopting a private response to what is perforce a collective problem. Rather, they are pioneers of the micro (individual-level) activity that is necessary to create the macro (system-wide) equilibrium, to correct an economy that is badly out of balance."[13] In other words, efforts to improve oneself and one's life—such as hiring a professional organizer, or becoming one, for that matter—may have the potential to help foster large-scale social change.[14]

I'd like to think organizing can at least point us, individually and collectively, in some productive directions. In chapter 3, I note specific changes that could improve organizers' work lives and level the playing field for those whose class or race put them at a disadvantage in the industry. Self-employment would be less stressful and more accessible if Americans were provided with more robust and flexible benefits that aren't dependent on a single employer, such as universal healthcare, subsidized childcare and parental leave, unemployment and disability insurance, and a minimum guaranteed income, all delinked from a single job or employer. Together, innovations like this would reduce the emotional and financial tolls of precarious work by establishing a financial floor beneath which American households cannot fall, a safety net that actually helps people feel safe.

Interestingly, many of the same changes that would help organizers build and maintain their businesses might also reduce the demand for their services. As I've argued, one of the main reasons people contact organizers is that they feel overwhelmed by the many demands on their time and attention. Similarly, many people buy the things they do because they don't know what they already have, don't have the time to find it, or use shopping to ease anxiety or to buy quick fixes to problems that, with more time and attention, could be solved by other means. If all Americans knew they were protected in case of a health crisis, job loss, or slow business month; if they had a predictable income; if they had the educational and financial resources to train for a new career or start a new business; if their work hours were shorter and more flexible; if they knew their kids were in safe, high-quality schools or daycares while they worked or managed household tasks; any and all of these things would lessen those feelings of anxiety and overwhelm.[15] I don't mean to draw a direct line from universal healthcare to buying less or finding time to sort your mail each day, but I do think that if we give people more time and less uncertainty in their daily lives, they will have more breathing room which, for many, may allow them to tackle the less pressing tasks that keep getting pushed to the end of their burgeoning to-do lists. For example, when the required school supply list arrived from my son's school last year, my first instinct was to buy everything on Amazon in one fell swoop and be done with it. Once I took the time to think about it, though, I realized we already had one item on the list (pencil box, check). I asked for a few other items on my local Buy Nothing Facebook group (where members give items away or ask for things they're looking for, all for free); that saved me buying a six-pack of dry erase clipboards on Amazon when I only needed one. Had I been more rushed, though, that initial instinct to just buy it all would have won out, costing me money and missing out on the opportunity to reuse rather than buying new. For those who continue to need or want help, organizers and other service providers would still be there, to offer compassion, encouragement, and organizational expertise.

Organizers themselves aren't afraid of this outcome. In seeing themselves as teachers, imparters of lifelong skills, organizers already run the risk of making themselves obsolete. If clients fully internalize the lessons organizers aim to impart, if they buy less, keep only what they need or love, share the excess with others, and learn to maintain the systems organizers help them put into place, eventually there won't be any need for organizers at all.[16] Indeed, many organizers told me their goal was to put themselves out of business by teaching their clients how to get and stay organized without their help. As I noted in the previous chapter, many hoped organizing classes would one day be taught in schools or provided free as a public service, even though they expected these scenarios might decrease demand for their services.[17]

As much as I enjoy imagining the broader social changes organizers and the work they do have the potential to promote, change doesn't have to be radical or systemic to matter. There is something to be celebrated in people finding work they enjoy that feels meaningful and fulfills their desire to help others. Organizers can't cure people's feelings of anxiety, overwhelm, and inadequacy, or the structural, cultural, and economic forces behind them. What they can do is teach strategies for minimizing and managing that anxiety and its manifestations, for pushing back, however gently, against whatever it is that currently hurts the most. For now, if not forever, that might have to be enough.

Acknowledgments

Over the years I researched and wrote this book, I married, moved, had a child, was promoted to full professor, experienced a pandemic, and nearly lost my husband to a blood infection. Atop my everyday work of teaching, advising, and (so much) emailing, it was sometimes difficult to find the energy and motivation to work on this book. What brought me back to it, time and again, were the organizers I had met, interviewed, and worked with. They'd shared so much of their time with me, been so welcoming and helpful and candid, that I felt I owed it to them to see the project to fruition. And so, it is to the many professional organizers who contributed to this project that I owe my greatest thanks. This book would not exist without you. The same is true of the organizations that allowed me to attend events and meetings in the course of this research, including the National Association of Productivity and Organizing Professionals, especially the Los Angeles chapter, and the Orange County Hoarding Task Force.

I had the pleasure of presenting on this research in a variety of forums, including meetings of the American Anthropological Association, American Studies Association, Global Carework Summit, American Ethnological Society, Work and Family Researchers Network, CSUF Osher Lifelong Learning Institute, Yale Ethnography and Oral History Reading Group, CSUF Department of American Studies Graduate-Faculty Colloquia, CSUF Women's History Month Lecture Series, and the Los Angeles chapter of the National Association of

Professional Organizers. I offer my thanks to those who shared their questions and insights in response to these presentations.

This research was supported by generous grants and fellowships, including the CSUF Office of Research and Sponsored Projects Grant for Faculty Support on Scholarly or Creative Productivity; CSUF Junior and Senior Intramural Research Awards; CSUF Sabbatical Leaves; and State Special Fund Summer Research Stipends.

Three talented research assistants—Mia Calabretta, Megan Feighery, and Bahar Tahamtani—helped locate historical news coverage of organizing and organizers and shared their own insights into what we were learning. I'm grateful for their contributions to this project.

Agent Lauren Sharp kindly lent her savvy support to this book, finding it a wonderful home with University of Chicago Press. I'm deeply grateful to Lauren, and to the fabulous Allison Pugh, who brought Lauren and me together. Allison's work on connective labor—and the many conversations we've had over the years about our overlapping research interests—helped shape this book in innumerable ways. I'm fortunate to have had her as my friend and collaborator.

Elizabeth Branch Dyson and her exceptional team at University of Chicago Press have been a pleasure to work with from start to finish. Special thanks to Mollie McFee and Adriana Smith for their guidance through the process and to Chicago's outstanding design and marketing folks. I'm grateful for Marianne Tatom's expert copyediting, Jen Burton's careful indexing, and the charming line drawings Charlotte Corden created to head each organizing story.

Sociologist Rachel Sherman and an anonymous reviewer provided insightful and helpful feedback on earlier drafts of this manuscript. Their critiques and suggestions made this a stronger, better book.

I wrote the early chapters of this book tucked away in a study room at the Peninsula Center Library near my home in Rancho Palos Verdes, California. Before the pandemic, the library hosted Tea at the Library every Monday, with complimentary tea and cookies. Those mornings were a wonderful break from the work of writing, and I enjoyed my teatime chats with librarians, especially Monique Sugimoto, and fellow patrons. Public libraries will always be among my favorite spaces, and I'm thankful for all that they provide.

The pandemic ended those weekly teas, but it ushered in a new ritual, weekly Zoom conversations with fellow anthropologists of work Ilana Gershon and Caitrin Lynch and editor Fran Benson, formerly of ILR Press. These conversations—around work, culture, our families, and everything else—transformed our already warm professional relationships into deeper, fuller friendships for which I am enormously grateful. Ilana also provided invaluable feedback on an early draft of this book, and Fran generously reviewed my book proposal and early chapters.

I've dedicated this book to Fran, who has believed in me and my scholarship from the moment we met. It's impossible to convey how much that has meant to me. It's so much easier to believe in your work when you know someone as brilliant and incredible as Fran believes in it, too.

Thank you also to Portia Jackson Preston. Early in the pandemic, Portia and I became accountability coaches for one another, touching base every Friday about what we'd accomplished on our writing projects and exercise goals that week. Those check-ins were a welcome boost in a challenging time.

For nearly two decades, I have had the good fortune of working with an exceptional group of faculty and staff in the CSUF Department of American Studies. Some of these folks built this department from the ground up long before I arrived; others of them will continue it long after I retire. It's an honor to work alongside these amazing people every day.

My students at CSUF are the best part of my job. They challenge and charm me every single semester. They are curious, hilarious, creative, and kind. It's a privilege to learn alongside them.

My family moved to a new city weeks before I gave birth to my son. I would never have survived those amazing, exhausting first years had I not lucked into the best group of moms a person could hope for. Anna Avelino, Jenny Azari, Brenda Martinelli, Kimberly Offenberg, Stephanie Santoro, Megan Tsai, and Sandy Yang. Thank you for being your wonderful selves and for cheering me on every step of the way.

Our new home also brought us the best batch of neighbors a family could hope for. Diane, Rex, and Kyle Holloway; Sandy, Chuck, and

Kris Olinger; Jeanine, Ryan, Mia, and Ziggy Moore; Yuki and Mark Olsen; Terri and Brian Handlen; Gordie Hopkins; Judith Diamond; Kara, James, Juniper, and Maggie Carroll; Jinean, Jack, Kyle, and Finn Luttig. You have looked out for us and cared for us through some exceptionally trying times. You've watched our kid, walked our dog, even done our laundry. It will take a lifetime of baked goods to repay you, but I shall do my best.

To Terri Snyder, thank you for our countless early morning text and phone conversations, and for sharing my love of profanity-laden accessories. I'm so grateful for your friendship and support.

Sweet Sofia Smith. Some family is born, and some is made. Your kindness and strength are a marvel. I'm honored to have you as my daughter and excited to watch as you continue to take this world by storm.

Shannon Kemper, you're the best. Thanks for the phone calls, and for knowing me for so damn long. Now move to California.

Thank you to my sisters, Heather Olson and Tawny Lane. Your love, support, and hilarity have seen me through many a rough patch. Tawny's keen eye for detail also makes her an exceptional proofreader, so thank you for that. Now you both need to move to California.

To my parents, Ginger and Jim Lane. Thank you for being proud of me, and for keeping the public library system afloat, one book sale at a time. Also, thanks for living in California.

To Sparky, our pandemic pup. You're lucky you're cute.

To my husband, Matt. Thank you for fighting, again and again, to stay with us. You've been stronger than anyone should have to be, and we love you for it.

When I started this book, my son Frank wrote a list of chapter numbers on a piece of paper, taped it to the wall above my desk in our home office, and checked each one off as I completed it. The process went slower than he'd have liked, but I took comfort in the gradually accumulating check marks. When I told him I'd finished the conclusion, he added a final check and said, "Let me give you a hug, Mom." Frank, you're the best kid a parent could ask for. I'm so happy you're mine.

Appendix

Methodology

Interviews

I located interviewees in a variety of ways. I interviewed people I met at NAPO meetings and conferences. I reached out to organizers profiled in local or national news stories or whose books or articles I read. I contacted organizers recommended to me by friends or on social networks like Nextdoor or Facebook. A few organizers declined to be interviewed—one told me outright he suspected I intended to open my own competing organizing business using the information he shared—but most agreed to talk and were incredibly generous with their time and insights. I obtained informed consent from all interviewees, and the project was approved by the California State University, Fullerton Institutional Review Board for Human Subjects Research.

One of the benefits of conducting most of my research in Los Angeles, where many home organizing shows are filmed, was that nearly every organizer I interviewed had either appeared on an organizing show, worked for a show off camera as part of an organizing crew, or been invited to appear on a show and declined. Some had even created and hosted their own organizing shows; others aspired to one day. The organizers I interviewed could therefore speak from personal experience about how these shows work, as well as to how organizing programs shape the assumptions and expectations of the clients they work with in real life.

Since I started this project, some of the organizers I interviewed have passed away; a few have left the field for other careers. Those who remained had to navigate their way through a global pandemic—some struggled, some thrived. Although most interviews were conducted between 2012 and 2014, in 2021–2023 I reinterviewed ten organizers and interviewed six new organizers, including founders of the National Association of Black Professional Organizers (NABPO) and #BlackGirlsWhoOrganize, to update my findings and learn about the organizing experience during the Covid-19 pandemic.

Of the 51 organizers I interviewed for this study, 46 (92%) were women (the profession itself is approximately 97% female).[1] Forty-one (80%) were white; seven (14%) were Black or multiracial Black; two (4%) were Asian American; and one (2%) was Hispanic.[2] (For reference, NAPO, organizing's largest professional association, is approximately three-quarters white; 4% Black or multiracial Black; 3% Asian American; and 4% Hispanic or Latino.[3]) Interviewees' ages at the time of interview ranged from early thirties to early eighties, with most between 30 and 60 years of age (average age was 50). Here, too, my sample aligns with NAPO's membership, of whom 65% are between the ages of 29 and 59.[4]

All interviewees had graduated from high school. Just over three-quarters (76%) had earned a bachelor's degree (BS or BA); 22% had earned a master's degree (MA, MSW, MFA, MBA); and two had gone on to earn PhDs, one in the sciences, one in the humanities. Of the 12 interviewees who finished high school but did not complete a four-year degree, three had associate's degrees, four completed secretarial school, and two earned nursing degrees (RN, CNA). Twenty-nine (57%) were married or living with long-term partners when I first interviewed them and 22 (43%) were single and entirely self-supporting, though those percentages shifted a bit over the course of the project as folks got married, divorced, or otherwise changed their household or financial situation. Just over half (54%) had children when I first interviewed them.

It's worth noting that the purpose of this study is not to compare organizers' experiences and perspectives by race, gender, income, age, or other differences, although I mention those patterns and distinctions I observed or heard about. For the most part, though, I do not include detailed demographic information when I describe or quote a particular organizer, unless a specific aspect of their identity is relevant to the topic at hand, such as when I discuss the founding of #BlackGirlsWhoOrganize or describe one Hispanic organizer's dream of bringing organizing services to other Hispanic people. While some readers might find such information illuminating, I fear it might obscure more than it reveals by suggesting that some aspects of an organizer's background or identity—her race, marital status, or years in business, for instance—are more significant than other aspects, such as her political inclinations, sexual orientation, or organizing subspecialty, among others.

In terms of their employment status, every organizer I interviewed ran their own business, although I did speak informally with a handful of organizers who worked solely as assistants to other organizers. Most were "solopreneurs," owners of a business of which they were the sole employee, although a few had full-time employees who did most of the hands-on organizing.[5] Many self-employed organizers also worked as assistants to other organizers because their own client base was still small or work was slow that month, or because they enjoyed working alongside and learning from fellow organizers.

All but one interviewee made the majority of their income through organizing or organizing-related income.[6] This usually meant hands-on organizing in people's homes, workspaces, or storage units, but might also include real estate staging, feng shui consulting, or personal assistant work that included but was not limited to organizing. Some organizers earned additional income teaching classes or giving lectures or workshops on organization and time management, writing organizing blogs and books, hosting or appearing on organizing shows and podcasts, designing and selling organizing products, or acting as a business coach to other organizers. A few organizers had additional income streams unrelated to organizing, such as acting, teaching college courses (on topics other than organizing), or managing properties they owned.

It was difficult to get organizers to talk candidly about their rates and incomes. Among NAPO members, there was a perception that discussing rates with one another—or anyone but clients, presumably—was a form of price fixing and therefore illegal or unethical. In Los Angeles, NAPO leaders regularly suggested a range of $50–$150 per hour, depending on the type of job and the organizer's level of experience (business organizing, for instance, regularly earned higher rates than residential organizing). Among interviewees who were willing to share specific figures, hourly rates ranged from $25 to $200 per hour.[7] Organizing assistants were generally paid about $25 per hour.

Organizers in my study struggled when asked to report their average annual earnings, because their incomes varied so dramatically over different periods. Based on organizers' hourly rates and typical hours worked, I can estimate that most of the organizers I interviewed who had been in business more than a year made between $25,000 and $100,000 annually, with just a few regularly earning in the six figures and at least one reaching the low seven figures.[8]

At the time of my first interview with them, 11 interviewees (22%) had been in business for more than 20 years; 5 (10%) for 15–20 years; 7 (14%) for 10–15 years; 11 (22%) between 5 and 10 years, and 17 (3%) for less than 5 years. As of 2023, to the best of my knowledge, 45 of the 51 interviewees were still working as organizers; 3 longtime organizers had passed away since our interviews, and 3 others had moved on to different careers (one took a full-time job as a household manager for a celebrity couple, another took an administrative position at a local nonprofit, and a third designs and sells handmade jewelry online).

Most interviewees, even those who were not financially independent, managed to work full-time as organizers. Among organizers, "full-time" is generally said to mean 20 hours of hands-on organizing per week, with at least 20 additional hours per week spent on client correspondence, marketing and publicity, networking, billing, social media and website maintenance, and the myriad other tasks involved in running a small business. Some hoped to eventually work full-time but had not yet grown their businesses to the point that this was consistently possible. Others worked part-time by choice, either because they had other responsibilities (often caring for young children) that demanded their time, were semi-retired, or could make the amount of money they desired working less than full-time hours (e.g., because their rates were high, expenses were small, or there were other earners in their household).

Most of the organizing clients I interviewed lived in Southern California. Many of these were acquaintances who, upon hearing about my project, casually mentioned they'd worked with an organizer and were then suckered into an interview. Others were friends of friends who were solicited on my behalf and generously agreed to meet with me.

Between 2012 and 2014, a few interviews were conducted by phone but most took place in interviewees' homes or, more often, local coffee shops and restaurants; all were audio-recorded. Interviews in 2021–2023 during the pandemic were conducted and recorded by Zoom. Most interviews lasted between one to two hours; some went as long as three hours. All interviews were transcribed by me or a paid assistant, other than those conducted in 2021–2023, which were transcribed using Otter.ai software.

Participant Observation

I learned about the organizing-related events I attended at NAPO meetings, online, or through word of mouth (from organizers and from friends and colleagues who knew I was studying the field). At each event I attended, I introduced myself, explained that I was a researcher, and invited people to see me after the meeting if they were open to being interviewed. I was also invited to speak to NAPO's Los Angeles chapter about my preliminary findings. Members responded positively to the talk and offered many questions, comments, and suggestions that guided my future research. I paid the required fee to attend NAPO conferences and meetings and, for a portion of the research, registered as an official NAPO member.

The jobs I assisted on varied immensely, but all took place in homes or storage spaces, rather than in businesses or workplaces (except in cases where people worked from home, of course). The decision to focus on home organizing rather than business organizing was twofold. Many of the organizers I met and interviewed worked exclusively or primarily in business organizing, and I discuss this form of organizing in the book. Ultimately, however, I was most interested in how organizers helped people organize their *personal* spaces and possessions. (Of course, people do have personal connections to their workspaces and work-related possessions, and many keep personal items at work, so this division is somewhat overdrawn.) It was also much easier to gain access to home organizing sessions, in which the organizer simply asked the client or clients whether it was okay for me to attend, than to secure official approval from corporate clients. Thus, while the interviews and media research I conducted concern both home and business organizing, my participant observation of the organizing process focused almost exclusively on domestic spaces or storage units holding personal belongings.

Clients were almost always present on these jobs. At the start of the job, either I or the lead organizer introduced me to the client as a researcher studying professional organizing, explaining that I wanted to see firsthand how the organizing process works. Sometimes I was the only organizing assistant on a job; other times there were multiple assistants, often new organizers seeking on-the-job training, friends or family members of the lead organizer who occasionally helped out (such as an adult son who assisted his seventysomething mother when a job required moving heavy objects), or experienced organizers supplementing their income by assisting other organizers.

Other Research

While preparing for and conducting this research, I read dozens of books on organizing and simple living as well as a few on becoming a professional organizer. I read books written or recommended by the organizers I met, books that were especially popular at the time of my research (such as Marie Kondo's *The Life-Changing Magic of Tidying Up*), books suggested on the websites of NAPO or the Institute for

Challenging Disorganization (ICD), and organizing books my helpful mother came across at her local library book sale. I read organizing blogs and joined Facebook groups related to organizing. I read issues of *Real Simple* and *O(prah) Magazine* (both of which I admittedly subscribed to long before I began this project) and paid close attention to the organizing-related features in both. I was often pleasantly surprised to come across articles penned by the very organizers I had interviewed or worked alongside.

I also studied topics related to professional organizing, such as hoarding disorders, famous hoarders (such as the Collyer brothers), and the psychology of hoarding and collecting. I read histories and ethnographies of home organization, interior design, home economics, and domestic work. Although professional organizers are not necessarily advocates of minimalism or critics of consumerism, I read about those topics, too, as well as about the economic, social, psychological, and environmental consequences of overconsumption and cheap, disposable goods. I read the works of material culture scholars who study the cultural history and meaning of objects themselves. Expanding my previous research on unemployment and job insecurity, I read about precarious work, gig work, overwork, self-employment, solopreneurship, emotional labor, and Americans' growing discontent with traditional forms of work. While these sources may not all appear in the pages of this book, they nevertheless laid an important foundation for thinking through the cultural and economic landscapes in which the organizing profession emerged.

Notes

1 In this book, I follow the practice of capitalizing Black but not white, as the former references a general sense of culture and history, as well as experiences of racial discrimination, that the latter does not. See Bauder, "AP Says."

Introduction

1 For a critique of the idea that Americans should "simplify by shopping," see McGee, *Self-Help, Inc.*, 103.

2 Kelly, "Organizing." Throughout this book, I draw on Kelly's insightful analyses of *Real Simple*, the Container Store, and decluttering books and television shows, as well as her interviews with seven professional organizers in Texas.

3 In 2006, for example, Stanley Bing (a pen name for former executive and "business humorist" Gil Schwartz) included "closet organizer" on his list of "100 Bullshit Jobs," alongside ayurvedic healer, backup dancer, cheese artisan, consultant, dolphin trainer, marriage counselor, and university administrator. Bing rated closet organizing's "bullshit quotient" at 99 out of 100. His list of organizers' roles included "soothe nutty, confused person" and "gain her trust, or his trust if you're dealing with a male homosexual," conveying his disdain for organizers and their clients, as well as his sexism and homophobia (Bing, *100 Bullshit Jobs*, 75–76). See also "Gil Schwartz," *Wikipedia*; Nusca, "Gil Schwartz, a.k.a. Stanley Bing."

4 Ted Lasso, season 2, episode 7, "Headspace," directed by Matt Lipsey, aired September 3, on Apple TV (2021).

5 Other home organizing shows followed soon after—*Clean Sweep* and *Mission: Organization* in 2003, *Hoarders* in 2009, *Hoarding: Buried Alive* in 2010, *Extreme Clutter* and *Enough Already* in 2011, *Master the Mess* in 2018, *Tidying Up with Marie Kondo* in 2019, and *Get Organized with the Home Edit* and *Hot Mess House* in 2020, to name some of the best-known programs. (See Kelly's analysis of home organizing television shows, particularly *Hoarders* and *Clean House*, in "Organizing," 69–118.) Though these shows differ in style, format, and focus, they all fall squarely within the genre of "makeover television" or "life intervention" programs that became popular in the early twenty-first century, where experts of one kind or another purport to help people overcome various struggles in their homes, lives,

and careers. See McGee, *Self-Help, Inc.*, 17–18; Ouelette and Hay, *Better Living*, 63–64; Weber, *Makeover TV*.

6   See, for example: Brodesser-Akner, "Marie Kondo"; Young, "Domestic Purging"; Yourgrau, "Origin Story."

7   One survey found that "quasi-house arrest has made seventy-eight per cent of respondents realize that they have more possessions than they need" (Marx, "A Guide to Getting Rid of Almost Everything"). See also Petersen, "I Don't Feel Like Buying Stuff Anymore." Others dismiss the pandemic-inspired decluttering craze as merely an environmentally irresponsible way to dispose of "burdensome objects without confronting the significant ecological costs" of doing so (Sandlin and Wallin, "Decluttering the Pandemic").

8   Young, "Domestic Purging."

9   Others have suggested this is hardly new advice; Howard describes an 1880 speech advising listeners to "have nothing in your houses that you do not know to be useful or believe to be beautiful" as "a 19th-century precursor of Marie Kondo's 'spark joy' test" (*Clutter*, 100).

10   *The Big Bang Theory*, season 6, episode 19, "The Closet Reconfiguration," directed by Anthony Rich, aired March 14, 2013, on CBS; *Modern Family*, season 7, episode 8, "Clean Out Your Junk Drawer," directed by Steven Levitan, aired December 2, 2015, on ABC; *Modern Family*, season 7, episode 12, "Clean for a Day," directed by Beth McCarthy-Miller, aired February 10, 2016, on ABC.

11   Wood, *Christmas in the Air*.

12   See Mary Jane Maffini's Charlotte Adams Series and Sara Rosett's Mom Zone Mysteries. Leslie Caine's Domestic Bliss Mysteries almost made the list (especially book four, *Killed by Clutter*), but Caine's heroine is technically an interior designer, not a professional organizer.

13   From the start, home organization shows have been as controversial as they are popular. Critics allege such programs are not only exploitative and voyeuristic, as are arguably all reality shows, but also classist, racist, and anti-gay (e.g., Herring, *Hoarders*). Some contend home organizing shows are effective anti-consumerist propaganda, making viewers "anxious and apocalyptic about materialism and junk culture" (Gauld, "Underneath Every Hoarder"). Others suggest these programs "contribute to a cultural discourse on clutter that fuels the need for home organization," while simultaneously serving as "essentially long-format advertisements for products wherein consumers are encouraged to create positive change in their lives and fix their problems through consumption" (Kelly, "Organizing," 83). Some celebrate these programs for raising awareness of and support for people who hoard possessions and animals (e.g., Steketee and Frost, *Stuff*; Paxton, *Secret Lives*). Still others decry organizing shows as part of a "neoliberal theater of suffering" (McCarthy, "Reality Television") that works to transform participants and viewers alike into "self-disciplining, self-sufficient, responsible, and risk-averting individuals" (Ouellette, "Take Responsibility," 232) or rational "agents of order" (Lepselter, "Disorder of Things"). Others object to the "narratives of addiction" on which the shows tend to rely, or say they have "provoked questions about the slippery boundaries around diagnosed illness and the ethical parameters of documenting mental disorder" (Bishop, "The Armoire Is Your Mother"; Kelly, "Organizing," 73).

14   Kelly elaborates on the ways in which professional organizers, while part of the containo-industrial complex, differ from the more "consumption-oriented,

exacting, or perfectionist" images depicted in organizing books, magazines, and television shows ("Organizing," 287–90).

15 For representations of organizers that sustain these stereotypes, see Brodesser-Akner, "Marie Kondo"; Boyle, "Filthy with Things."

16 This is one reason my conclusions differ from those of other scholars who have written about the organizing industry. Most studies of professional organizing are based on analysis of organizing television programs or organizing self-help books. Scholars have valuable insights about how organizing books and shows can reinforce dominant aesthetic and cultural norms, create new forms of labor for homemakers, and exercise social control through discourses of addiction, disease, and morality. These studies are less insightful when it comes to understanding how organizers work in everyday, real-world contexts. See, for example: Bishop, "The Armoire Is Your Mother"; Herring, *Hoarders*; Lepselter, "Disorder of Things." Exceptions to this tendency to focus on media representations of organizers rather than on organizers themselves include Beecher, "A Place for Everything"; Kelly, "Organizing"; and Kilroy-Marac, "Magical Reorientation."

17 See George, "Seeking Legitimacy"; Hochschild, *Outsourced Self*; Sheehan, "Paradox of Self-Help Expertise"; Sherman, "'Time Is Our Commodity.'"

18 Bureau of Labor Statistics, "Personal Care and Service Occupations."

19 Duffy et al., *Caring on the Clock*, 4–5.

20 George, "Seeking Legitimacy."

21 As of the early twenty-first century, Americans were said to be getting "more mail in a month than our grandparents got over the course of their lives" ("Stuffbusters"). In the past, not opening your household's mail on a daily basis wouldn't have amounted to much clutter. Today, a week's worth of unopened mail—not to mention email—constitutes a sizable backlog for most households.

22 Hochschild, *Outsourced Self*, 9. In some respects, this is just an exacerbation and democratization of an earlier shift, noted as early as 1956, from relying on kin for advice and assistance to consuming professional advice (Dizard and Gadlin, *Minimal Family*, 108–9, 131–32).

23 The perception that Americans don't know how to organize their homes and belongings also connects with recent debates over young adults' alleged inability, or unwillingness, to shoulder the daily responsibilities required of American adults. It was in this context that the verb "adulting" was coined to describe "the practice of behaving in a way characteristic of a responsible adult, especially the accomplishment of mundane but necessary tasks" (Hill, "The Waiting Room," 155).

24 Arnold et al., *Life at Home*.

25 Arnold and Lang, "Changing American Home Life," 88.

26 Arnold et al., *Life at Home*, 25. The average size of the American home has grown consistently larger over the last half century, while the average number of household members has declined; and yet, there is still not enough room in most Americans' homes for their accumulated stuff (Pinsker, "Why Are American Homes So Big?"). See Edlund, "40 Years of the American Home," for a video review of changes in American home size over a forty-year period.

27 Arnold and Lang, "Changing American Home Life," 43. This trend is intensified in Los Angeles, where homes tend to lack basements for extra storage (Arnold et al., *Life at Home*, 44–47), but it is hardly unique to the region. Across the United States, approximately one-quarter of households use their garage solely for storage (Gladiator GarageWorks, "Almost 1 in 4 Americans").

28   Harris, "U.S. Self-Storage Industry Statistics."

29   *Self-Storage Industry Statistics.*

30   Saxbe and Repetti, "'No Place Like Home.'"

31   Arnold et al., *Life at Home*, 26; Saxbe and Repetti, "'No Place Like Home,'" 78. Other researchers have found that frustration with clutter seems to increase with age, regardless of gender (Ferrari and Roster, "Delaying Disposing"). As early as 1989, Hochschild and Machung (*Second Shift*) blamed the "speed-up" in work and family life on a combination of more American mothers working outside the home, increasingly long work hours, and inflexible models of work and career designed for male workers with wives overseeing the home. "In two decades," Hochschild argued in a more recent work, "women have gone from being mainly at home to mainly at work," and yet, she continued, "women have undergone this change in a culture that has neither rewired its notion of manhood to facilitate male work-sharing at home, nor restructured the workplace so as to allow more control over and flexibility at work" (*Commercialization of Intimate Life*, 217). The gender revolution, she contended, has stalled, especially for mothers, who now worked a "first shift" for pay before heading home to the "second shift" of housework and caregiving.

32   Despite being around 400 percent more productive than they were in 1950, Americans today work more hours—nearly two weeks' worth—than workers in most other large countries around the world. Although numerous studies confirm that workers are more productive when they work fewer hours, the United States is the only wealthy country that does not limit the maximum hours a person can work, nor does it guarantee workers paid vacation time or parental leave. When these leaves are available, more than half of American workers do not take them. See, for example: Fremstad, "Vacations for All"; Pencavel, "Productivity of Working Hours"; Schor, *Overworked American*; Warren and Tyagi, *Two-Income Trap*; York, "Why It's So Hard for US Workers." Even outside official work hours, many workers are nevertheless available to their coworkers and supervisors by cellphone and social media (see Gregg, *Work's Intimacy*; Perlow, *Sleeping with Your Smartphone*).

33   US parents across races and social classes express similar support for child-centered, time-intensive parenting, which includes things like supervised playtime, frequent conversations with children, and numerous extracurricular activities intended to enrich children's minds, bodies, and social lives (Ishizuka, "Social Class, Gender, and Contemporary Parenting Standards"). In the words of one parenting expert, "our standards have changed. One hundred years ago a parenting win was getting your child to live to adulthood" (Holohan, "Not Your Mother's Motherhood"). Working mothers now spend more time on childcare than stay-at-home mothers did in the 1960s; fathers are spending more time on childcare as well, although still less than mothers. And yet, prior to the pandemic, at least, over a third of mothers and nearly two-thirds of fathers believed they still spent too little time with their children, usually due to work obligations (Pew Research Center, *Modern Parenthood*). Pugh (*Tumbleweed Society*, 165–68) argues that intensive parenting is a direct response to rising insecurity in American life. In *The Cultural Contradictions of Motherhood*, Hayes notes that the expectation that mothering requires intensive interaction with and selfless devotion to one's children has only appeared since married mothers entered the workforce in large numbers.

34   About a quarter of American parents—and more than half of parents in their forties—also care for another adult, usually a parent or grandparent, increasing the hours committed to care work each week (Horowitz, "More Than Half of Americans").

35   Ochs and Kremer-Sadlik, *Fast-Forward Family*, 92.

36   NAPO, *2019 Public Survey*, 10.

37   Despite innumerable technological advances that promised to reduce time spent on domestic chores, employed married women spend almost exactly the same amount of time each week on housework (27 hours) as they did *one hundred years ago* (Ramey, "Time Spent in Home Production"). See also Dolores Hayden, *Redesigning the American Dream*.

38   By 2008, the average American was consuming three times as much as she or he did in 1960 (Schor, *Overspent American*). Feminist critics have pointed out that the suburban nuclear homes that flourished in the post-WWII period were effectively "a box to be filled with commodities" (Hayden, "What Would a Non-Sexist City Be Like?," S174).

39   Schor, *Overspent American*.

40   Lodziak, "On Explaining Consumption," 12; Dizard and Gadlin, *Minimal Family*, 98. Americans' exceptionally long working hours are also blamed for fueling consumption because people lack the time to do things for themselves. Instead, they end up meeting their needs through the purchase of consumer products—ready-made meals, store-bought Halloween costumes, or new goods purchased in lieu of repairing old ones. In these instances, buying things is not about wishful thinking or flashy consumption; it's a strategy for managing shortages of time and energy (Lodziak, "On Explaining Consumption," 127).

41   Kruse, "Wishful Shopping." Organizer Tracy McCubbin refers to these items as "fantasy stuff for my fantasy life" (*Making Space*, 25). When Arlie Hochschild interviewed working families for her book *The Time Bind*, she noticed garages full of brand-new tools, unused skis, cameras, boats, and campers, "even the equipment purchased to harvest maple syrup," all bought with the idea that one day, their owners would be the kind of families who had the time and energy to partake in the activities and outings these items represent (13–14). Some suggest this type of purchasing is unique to individuals with hoarding disorders (e.g., Tolin et al., *Buried in Treasures*, 179), but Hochschild and the organizers with whom I spoke see it as a common behavior.

42   Miller, "Someday Never Comes," quoted in Howard, *Clutter*, 110.

43   Arnold et al., *Life at Home*, 23.

44   Cohen, *Consumers' Republic*.

45   See Cline, *Overdressed*; George, *Ninety Percent of Everything*; Leonard, *The Story of Stuff*; Minter, *Secondhand*; Shell, *Cheap*; Woloson, *Crap*.

46   Some argue that the ease and speed with which people can now buy things have further fueled Americans' consumer tendencies. "Before the advent of the internet," a recent *Atlantic* article stated, "we had to set aside time to go browse the aisles of a physical store, which was only open a certain number of hours a day. Now, we can shop from anywhere, anytime—while we're at work, or exercising, or even sleeping. We can tell Alexa we need new underwear, and in a few days, it will arrive on our doorstep" (Semuels, "We Are All Accumulating"). See also Wong, "What I Learned."

47   Kelly, "Organizing," 52–53.

48 Cooper, *Cut Adrift*; Pugh, *Tumbleweed Society*; Beckman and Mazmanian, *Dreams of the Overworked*. See also Gusterson and Besteman, *Insecure American*; Lipsky, *Age of Overwhelm*; Malesic, *End of Burnout*; Schulte, *Overwhelmed*.

49 Cooper, *Cut Adrift*, 2. Hochschild makes a similar argument: "Private moments of confusion or conflict about care are often directly linked to contradictory social pressures in society at large. Sometimes these pressures originate in one area and show up in another, as in what doctors call 'referred pain.' Just as pain in a leg may originate in a slipped disk in our back, so too a painfully deteriorating bond between parent and child may link back to a company speed-up or government retrenchment. Increasingly we feel in our moments of detachment and neglect the referred pain of unfettered global capitalism itself" (*Commercialization of Intimate Life*, 3).

50 Cooper, *Cut Adrift*, 3.

51 Sharone, *Flawed System/Flawed Self*. Kelly similarly argues that "In its emphasis on personal responsibility in the absence of state and structural support, neoliberalism entails the cultural dissemination of messages about self-improvement rhetoric, often through the lens of personal consumption" ("Organizing," 56).

52 Cooper writes about the "upscaling of insecurity" among wealthy families, who fear their children may not be able to reproduce their privileged class position in light of rising insecurity in a changing economic climate (*Cut Adrift*, 92–126).

53 See Pugh, *Tumbleweed Society*.

54 Dizard and Gadlin, *Minimal Family*, 64–65.

55 As Stack (*All Our Kin*) and others have noted, this has been less true among poor communities of color, for whom discrimination and dire need necessitated close kin and communal ties in order to survive.

56 Beckman and Mazmanian, *Dreams of the Overworked*.

57 Adams, "Unhappy Employees Outnumber Happy Ones." On Americans' discontent with their work and prospects, see also Gallup, *Most Important Problem*; Puerto et al., *Youth and COVID-19*.

58 In this regard, organizers resemble the career waitresses described in Candacy Taylor's *Counter Culture* and the factory workers in Caitrin Lynch's *Retirement on the Line*.

59 These remarks were given on an "Ask an Organizer" panel at the 2012 NAPO National Conference.

60 Schwartz, *Why We Work*, 1–2.

61 Moreton, "The Future of Work."

62 Schwartz, *Why We Work*, 2. Scholars of work are equally invested in the twin questions of what constitutes meaningful work and how we can create more of it. See, for example: Bailey et al., "Five Paradoxes of Meaningful Work"; Laaser and Karlsson, "Towards a Sociology of Meaningful Work."

63 Kalleberg, *Good Jobs, Bad Jobs*.

64 See, for example: Noble, *How to Start a Home-Based Professional Organizing Business*; Pedersen, *Born to Organize*; Tiani, *Organizing for a Living*; and NAPO's educational resources (https://www.napo.net/page/Education).

65 Shi, *Simple Life*; Chayka, *The Longing for Less*.

66 Beecher, "A Place for Everything"; Hayden, *Grand Domestic Revolution*; Howard, *Clutter*; Isenstadt, *Modern American House*; Kelly, "Organizing."

67 The decluttering memoir is a growing genre. Representative works include: Bruno, *100 Thing Challenge*; Howard, *Clutter*; Schaub, *The Year of No Clutter*; Yourgrau, *Mess*.

68   Autoethnography is a form of research that uses personal experience and self-reflection as a means to understanding broader cultural meanings and experiences.

69   Ethnographies of work, such as this one, are especially well positioned to identify emerging trends around work and to better understand puzzling patterns around labor and employment. See Anteby and Bechky, "Workplace Ethnographies"; Anteby et al., "Three Lenses."

70   There is no official tally of people working as professional organizers. The Bureau of Labor Statistics declined in 2010 to add "professional organizer" as a Standard Occupational Classification ("Response to Comment on 2010 SOC: Docket Number 08-0314," https://www.bls.gov/soc/2010_responses/response_08-0314 .htm). The largest professional association for organizers, the National Association of Productivity and Organizing Professionals (NAPO), has approximately 3,500 members (https://www.napo.net/page/joinNAPO#). Other professional associations for organizers include the Institute for Challenging Disorganization (challengingdisorganization.org), the National Association of Black Professional Organizers (nabpo.org), the Photo Managers (https://thephotomanagers.com/; formerly the Association of Professional Photo Organizers), and the American Society of Professional Organizers (https://www.amspo.org/), among others.

71   All my assistant jobs were unpaid, except one where, as I describe later in this book, the lead organizer refused *not* to pay me. Clients were informed that I was a researcher studying the organizing profession. I use pseudonyms for clients and have changed some minor details of the jobs I worked on in order to obscure clients' identities and protect their privacy.

72   I asked the organizers depicted in each story to review them to ensure they were accurate and effectively obscured the identities of both the organizers and their clients. Happily, their feedback was uniformly positive—one loved her pseudonym, and another told me she got emotional reading her story, which brought her back to that particular moment in her life and career. I went through the same process with most organizers who were featured prominently in specific chapters to ensure they felt their experiences and perspectives were accurately represented. I received a few minor suggestions, which I incorporated.

Chapter One

1   Although I generally employ pseudonyms for the organizers I interviewed, I use real names when relating stories that have already been shared publicly. For example, one organizer told me a story during our interview that she'd spoken about on a panel at a NAPO conference the previous year. When I retell that story in this book, I attribute that story to her real name, since others who attended that meeting would immediately know who I'm quoting. For other quotations from my interview with her, however, I use a pseudonym or avoid using a name altogether in order to protect her anonymity. This is especially true for my interviews with NAPO's founders, whose names and backstories are well known in the organizing community. I refer to the founders by names in most instances, except when sharing details or opinions from personal interviews that, as far as I am aware, have not been previously shared elsewhere.

2   This continued to happen well into the 2010s, when many new organizers still believed they were the first of their kind to make a living from organizing until

someone referred them to NAPO, mentioned someone else doing similar work, or told them about the new spate of organizing TV shows.

3   Online Etymology Dictionary, "Clutter."

4   For fuller histories of clutter, see Kelly, "Organizing"; Howard, *Clutter*.

5   A news article published one year after the Great Recession reported that "A craving for a simpler, slower, more centered life, one less consumed by the soul-emptying crush of getting and spending, runs deep within our culture right now" (Walker, "Exclusivity for All," 20). One post-recession survey found that 83 percent of respondents believed they had made permanent changes to how they spend and save; 76 percent said they had come to a deeper understanding of how buying shapes their self-image; and 61 percent had decluttered their homes or taken items to consignment shops over the past year (Context-Based Research Group, *Coming of Age in the Great Recession*). In 2010, Dave Bruno's *100 Thing Challenge* dared Americans to winnow their belongings down to just 100 items, and a father-daughter team published a best-selling book (Salwen and Salwen, *The Power of Half*) about their family's decision to sell their mansion and donate half the sale price to charity. The tiny house movement (see Wilkinson, "Let's Get Small") took off around the same time, touting the financial, spiritual, and environmental bene-fits of downsizing into homes as small as 100 square feet. See Allison Formanack's incisive critique of the tiny house movement in light of persistent negative stereo-types around mobile homes ("Mobile Home on the Range").

6   Claims of widespread cultural shifts, such as those celebrating Americans' embrace of simplicity and frugality, also tend to overgeneralize the scope of such changes, mistaking trends among certain influential social groups for broad-based movement (Humphrey, *Excess*, 65–68).

7   Shi, *The Simple Life*, 275.

8   Elgin, *Voluntary Simplicity*.

9   Glock, "Back to Basics."

10   Rose, "Real Simple's High-Concept." When the first issue did arrive, advertisers complained that the magazine's aesthetic was so austere as to be anti-consumerist (Kelly, "Organizing," 225).

11   Kelly, "Organizing," 24.

12   Taylor, *Principles of Scientific Management*; Gilbreth and Gilbreth Carey, *Cheaper by the Dozen*.

13   See Des Jardins, *Lillian Gilbreth*.

14   Dreilinger, *Secret History of Home Economics*.

15   Gilman, *Women and Economics*, 257.

16   Herring (*Hoarders*) and Kelly ("Organizing") persuasively trace organizers' lineage back to the scientific housekeeping movement, which brought concerns with efficiency, hygiene, and productivity into the domestic sphere at the turn of the twentieth century.

17   "Rid the House of 'Clutter' to Cheer It."

18   On the gendered nature of early office work, see Davis, *Company Men*; Kwolek-Folland, *Engendering Business*; Robertson, *Filing Cabinet*.

19   "Business Women Praised."

20   "Business Women Praised."

21   Wiles, "Unhappy? Clean House," 10.

22   Kelly, "Organizing," 47–48. See Kelly's introduction ("Organizing") for a detailed overview of modernism and its influence on ideals of home organization.

23 Madison, "Less Cluttered Homes," 16.

24 Hartmann, "Prescriptions for Penelope," 228, 230.

25 Manners, "Clutter Deplored," B1.

26 Hurley, "Three Freedoms—and Plenty of Closets," J4.

27 "Simplicity vs. Clutter," H13.

28 Arnold and Lang, "Changing American Home Life," 36; see also Ochs and Kremer-Sadlik, *Fast-Forward Family*, 26.

29 There have always been a few voices pushing back against anti-clutter campaigns. A 1957 *New York Times* article announced the return of clutter, attributing the shift to changing fashions in modern art and interior design: "Slowly but inevitably, resentment against the imprisoning confines of modernism grew until at last householders flared into open rebellion. Determined to reassert their individuality, they grasped at clutter" (Robsjohn-Gibbings, "Revival: Clutter Returns," 241).

30 Rowan, "'Clutter? What Clutter,'" A7.

31 Pither, "Why Some Women Hate Housekeeping," TW28. In a statement that seems ahead of its time, a male educational and vocational counselor quoted in the article stated: "The profession of homemaking, like every other job, requires specific traits, talents and interests. *Woman* is no more synonymous with *housework proficiency* than *man* is with, say, *mechanical skill* or *salesmanship*. Some have it, some don't [italics in original]."

32 Kron, "Second Most Satisfying Thing," 59.

33 Kron, "Second Most Satisfying Thing," 59.

34 Kron, "Second Most Satisfying Thing," 60.

35 Kron, "Second Most Satisfying Thing," 60.

36 White, "Sinking under the Clutter?," B1. Prior to this usage, the term "organizer" was mostly used to describe leaders of military troops; religious, political, professional, and social groups; business departments; and, occasionally, orchestras and expeditions. Like the word "computer," "organizer" was also used to describe objects, such as a partitioned wallet or sectional tray, before becoming the name for the people who might utilize those objects in their work.

37 Nemy, "It's Her Business."

38 White, "Sinking under the Clutter?," B6.

39 White, "Sinking under the Clutter?," B6.

40 White, "Sinking under the Clutter?," B6.

41 On Darwin and Wallace's independent discoveries of the theory of evolution, see "Wallace and Darwin: A Pact for Evolution."

42 Kleiman, "They'll Help Unscramble Your Life," C13.

43 Hemphill's decision to start an organizing business is also described in Lett, "Out with the Old," 10A.

44 A 2006 *Christian Science Monitor* article (Gardner, "Professional Organizers," 14) mistakenly reported that Hemphill had approached the SBA for a loan; she corrected that error in our phone interview.

45 Gardner, "Professional Organizers," 14.

46 Nelsen and Barley argue that the transformation of unpaid work into paid work is "the oldest and least well-studied source of new occupations" ("For Love or Money?," 621–22).

47 When she'd told this story previously at an organizing conference (Vanderkam, "Core Competency Mom Part II"), Robertson had described this man as her guidance counselor, a mistake she corrected in our interview.

48 One organizer capitalized on this perception by naming her business the Occasional Wife: The Modern Solution to Your Busy Life (https://www.theoccasionalwife.com/).

49 Fuller, "At Your Service," H4.

50 Culp's entry into organizing and contributions to NAPO's founding are also detailed in Rose and Ogas, *Dark Horse*, 230–31.

51 This perception remained even decades later. A 2007 book on how to start an organizing business states: "A professional organizer is an educator, trainer, coach, or consultant, *not* a cleaning person" (Pedersen, *Born to Organize*, 7; emphasis in original). Waiting for a panel at the 2012 NAPO conference to begin, I overheard two organizers seated in the row ahead of me. One complained that recently a client had balked at her hourly rate, saying he'd be willing to pay her about what he paid his "cleaning lady," but no more. The other organizer was outraged on her behalf. "You are not a cleaning lady! You need to ask him," he said with intensity, "what would you pay your therapist? What would you pay your massage therapist? *That's* what he should be paying *you*."

52 England, *Comparable Wealth*; Folbre, *Invisible Heart*; Kwolek-Folland, "Gender, the Service Sector, and U.S. Business History"; Zelizer, *Purchase of Intimacy*.

53 "Adam Smith: Father of Capitalism."

54 Folbre, *Invisible Heart*, 9.

55 Sherman, "'Time Is Our Commodity'"; George, "Interactions in Expert Service Work"; George, "Seeking Legitimacy."

56 Nemy, "It's Her Business."

57 See Meyerowitz, *Not June Cleaver*.

58 https://majormom.biz/; https://www.findmyorganizer.com/profile.b.507.r.54137.u.fofb78.html; https://www.theoccasionalwife.com/. Some personal concierges similarly promote their services, especially to male clients, as replacing the unpaid labor of moms, wives, and girlfriends, even naming their businesses "Rent a Mom" or "Rent a Wife" (Sherman, "'Time Is Our Commodity,'" 97).

59 This strategy was often employed by the personal concierges Sherman studied, who typically worked to establish occupational legitimacy by using gender-neutral frames when discussing their work and specifically distancing their work from that of homemakers and housekeepers ("'Time Is Our Commodity'").

60 Fuller, "At Your Service."

61 "Desktop Disasters."

62 Lawrence, "Conquering Clutter"; Soman, "The Paper Chase."

63 There is some debate over who came up with the title "professional organizer." Multiple organizers in Southern California told me Stephanie Culp invented the title in the early 1980s, but, as I note earlier in this chapter, the same term was used to describe Stephanie Winston in a 1978 *New York Times* article (Kleiman, "They'll Help Unscramble Your Life").

Chapter Two

1 Granberry, "Nation's Disorganized."

2 Granberry, "For Hire: An Organization of One."

3 I was unable to locate Shortridge for an interview. She relocated decades ago to Florida, where she continued to work as an organizer until at least 1998. This account is constructed from news articles, an interview with Susan Rich, and the

sometimes conflicting memories of others who attended the early meetings Shortridge and Rich convened.

4   Eyerly, "Organizing the Organizers."

5   "About Founder Ali Lassen," https://leadsclub.com/home/about/about-founder -ali-lassen/.

6   Wielenga, "Organizer Gets Your Act Together."

7   Hornstein, "The Rise of the Realtor"; Lees-Maffei, "Introduction." See also Dreilinger, *Secret History*, on the history of the home economics industry.

8   In 2017, the group was renamed the National Association of Productivity and Organizing Professionals.

9   Jeanne Shorr was the only NAPO founder I was not able to interview for this project. She left the organizing field many decades ago.

10   Harris, "Women's Clubs."

11   Dudley, "How Organized Is Your Life?"

12   Allen, "Organization Is in Their Blood," 5.

13   "Ten Clutter Correctives," 5.

14   "Chuck Your Chores and Have Fun."

15   NAPO organizers' emphasis on collaborative competition reminded me of the networking groups for unemployed tech workers I'd studied for a previous book (Lane, *Company of One*). Those, too, were friendly, communal settings in which people who were ostensibly competitors offered one another advice, encouragement, and validation as they struggled to move forward in their careers. One major difference was that the tech job-seekers I observed were mostly men, while the organizing profession is overwhelmingly female.

16   Akst, "A Tidy Sum."

17   Similarly, organizer Regina Lark writes, "There's more stuff out there that needs clearing than there are those of us with the gift to clear it" (*Before the Big O*, 5).

18   One organizer told me, eyebrow raised, that this man clearly didn't know what the term "cottage industry" means, pointing out that it describes work done in one's own home, not in other people's homes.

19   Kelly writes of one of the Austin organizers she interviewed: "To [the organizer] CM, a professional organizer should join NAPO because it shows they take their business seriously—she related a story about meeting a woman who called herself an organizer but who was not a member of NAPO and therefore showed a lack of dedication to furthering her professional persona through education, meeting attendance or dues paying" ("Organizing," 306).

20   To become a Certified Professional Organizer (CPO), one must: have at least a high school diploma or the equivalent; document at least 1,500 hours of paid organizing experience within the previous five years; agree to adhere to the NAPO Code of Ethics; and pass a standardized CPO exam composed of 125 multiple-choice questions. NAPO's certification program was officially approved for launch in 2007, but as early as 1997 NAPO leaders said "developing a certification program is the most crucial item on our national agenda . . . We have to create a standard by which the public can determine the basic skill of a professional organizer" (Hudgens, "In the Business"). See https://www.napo.net/page/NAPOHistory; https://www.napo.net/page/Certification.

21   Many female organizers, although no male organizers, also said promoting their businesses was their least favorite part of the job. As one organizer told me, "You have to sit there and sell yourself. Why do I have to do that? I don't want to sell

myself." Even after twenty-five years in business, one organizer told me, she still found marketing her business difficult. "You know how you have to really sort of brag about yourself? And I'm not that kind of person. So, marketing was very hard for me to do." In a culture that describes people as "companies of one" and "bundles of skills" to be hired out to the highest bidder, organizers' discomfort with "selling themselves" is noteworthy, as it implicitly resists the reigning discourse of personal branding (see Gershon, *Down and Out in the New Economy*; Vallas and Cummins, "Personal Branding and Identity Norms," 308–10). It should also be noted that women are often viewed more negatively than men when they do promote themselves (Rudman, "Self-Promotion as a Risk Factor").

22   No mention was made of the fact that, unlike men, women who do attempt to negotiate for higher pay tend to be perceived negatively for doing so (Bowles et al., "Social Incentives for Gender Differences").

23   Bourdieu, *Distinction*; Kelly, "Organizing," 340–41.

24   None of the organizers Kelly interviewed had been asked these questions by clients, either ("Organizing," 310). In her book for new organizers, Noble writes that "certification doesn't guarantee quality" (*How to Start*, 4).

25   Sherman, "'Time Is Our Commodity,'" 96.

26   Sociologists refer to this as boundary work, or "the strategies through which social actors negotiate their understanding of categorical differences and mobilize group characteristics" (O'Mahony, "Boundary Work," 34–35).

27   Among Kelly's interviewees, the "girl around the corner" was the derogatory term used for the nonprofessionals among the professional organizers. "The figure of the 'girl around the corner' stands in for an amateur organizer . . . professionalism is pitted against the casual female helper with neither a specifically developed skill-set nor a dedication to long-term career building" ("Organizing," 306).

28   "Pin money" is an old-fashioned and decidedly gendered term for a small amount of money used for non-essentials. It was often used to refer to spending money given by a husband to his wife.

29   As far as I am aware, none of the lesbian organizers I interviewed were married or in a longtime partnership at the time of our interview, so I can't say whether sexual orientation played a part in these stereotypes, although based on long-held American stereotypes of male breadwinners and female dependents, I suspect that it did.

30   Pew Research Center, *Growing Share of U.S. Marriages*.

31   See, for example, women's outraged responses to a 2014 message on the homepage of a small business directory: "This is a serious website for serious men with serious businesses. If you are just a little housewife running a little business from home earning some pin money while your man is out earning a living—please don't register your latest hobby business here" (https://www.prowess.org.uk/small-business-sexism).

32   Noble similarly advises new organizers to "Make sure that wherever the phone is located, any little ones in the house can't accidentally pick it up and answer when potential clients are on the line" (*How to Start*, 24).

33   Davis, *Company Men*.

34   Inspired by William H. Whyte's 1956 book of the same name, in the mid-twentieth century the "organization man" was understood as a conformist (invariably a white, male, middle-class one) who offered his employer loyalty and hard work in return for job security and upward mobility.

35   I found a similarly singular emphasis on hard work in the networking groups for high-tech job-seekers I researched for a similar project (Lane, *Company of One*). Tech job-seekers were regularly instructed to schedule specific hours during which they would look for work and designate a "work space" for their search. They were assured that their own efforts were the key to securing new jobs, despite the brutal job market in which they found themselves following the combined impact of 9/11, the dot-com and telecom busts, and the "jobless recovery" that followed. These similarities demonstrate the ubiquity of neoliberalism's emphasis on individual agency and responsibility, and its dogged refusal to acknowledge barriers and inequalities beyond the individual's control.

36   In 2024, an annual NAPO membership cost $319, with lower rates available for students and retirees. To join a regional chapter (or the virtual chapter for organizers who live in regions without local chapters) ranged from $100 to $175 per year. Regular registration for the NAPO 2024 Annual Summit ranged from $749 for members to $949 for nonmembers.

37   Having financial resources often makes it easier for women to remain at work, rather than easier to leave it (Damaske, *For the Family?*). See also Jurik, "Getting Away and Getting By."

38   For insight into the lives of New York's ultra-rich and their relationship to their wealth, and to the many service providers they employ, see Sherman, *Uneasy Street*.

39   I use Lott's real name here because he has related similar versions of this story in his own podcasts and in media interviews.

40   As I note in chapter 2, some Black organizers described a similar point of view toward hiring organizing help within the Black community.

41   https://nabpo.org/find-your-organizer. On racial matching in worker-client relationships, see Watkins-Hayes, "Race-ing the Bootstrap Climb," and Wingfield, *Flatlining*. These texts do not address the practice of Black clients intentionally hiring service providers based, at least in part, on their shared racial background, a subject that merits closer study.

42   Although I did not hear or see evidence of this in my fieldwork, it is possible that these pre-existing racial inequalities in income and wealth might make it more likely for Black organizers, forced to run their organizing businesses atop other full-time employment, to be lumped into the category of "dabbler," those who do not take their businesses "seriously."

43   Cech, *Trouble with Passion*, 25.

44   Williams, *Still a Man's World*; Wingfield, "Racializing the Glass Escalator."

45   Druckman, "Why Are There No Great Women Chefs?"

46   An organizer in his fifties told me, "I'm headed toward some ages I've never been before." There are times when at the end of a day of organizing he realizes, "Wow, I'm sore today. Wow, my arm hurts." "I'm still young," he said, then paused, smiling. "I'm still *kind* of young. Young enough and spry enough to do stuff," but he feared that may not be the case forever. Another organizer said that as she approaches sixty, "I'm looking at things in a different way, being closer to retirement." As a result, "I guess my focus has been on trying to do things that are less taxing on the body, because nobody's getting any younger." With their potential future physical limitations in mind, she and other older organizers I spoke with are passing more of the hands-on work to their employees and expanding their areas of expertise into less physically intensive tasks, such as public speaking, writing,

offering organizing webinars, or taking household inventories for insurance and estate planning purposes.

47   For an overview of neoliberal ideology, see Harvey, *A Brief History of Neoliberalism*.

48   Cech, *Trouble with Passion*, 183–84.

49   On colorblind racial ideology and its perpetuation of systemic racism, see Delgado and Stefancic, *Critical Race Theory*, 26–28.

50   Ray, "Why So Many Organizations Stay White."

51   This information is drawn from my 2022 interview with Dalys Macon via Zoom. Macon relates many of the same experiences in "Representation in the Organizing Industry."

52   Macon, (@blackgirlswhoorganize), "Hi 🖐, I am Dalys." Similarly, organizer James Lott Jr. said in a Super Organizer Show podcast episode that he'd been an organizer for around twelve years before he met another Black organizer ("NAPO Members").

53   Nelson and Vallas ("Race and Inequality at Work") consider racial barriers to occupational attainment, including the ways in which workers of color might not align with images of the "ideal worker" in a specific occupation.

54   The term "counterspace" was introduced in Solórzano et al., "Critical Race Theory." It is used most often with regard to educational settings to refer to campus spaces intended specifically for marginalized students.

55   Wirtschafter, "George Floyd Changed the Online Conversation."

56   NAPO member demographics (which I detail in the Appendix) support her perception. The organization is 97 percent female; approximately three-quarters of its members are white; and nearly two-thirds are 49 years of age or older. Home economics, another field whose practitioners are "overwhelmingly, older white women," has faced similar challenge in its efforts to diversify (Dreilinger, *Secret History*, 291).

57   Porter et al., "Incorporating an Anti-Racist Mindset."

58   I learned about Professional Organizers Latinas (https://beacons.ai/proorganizerslatinas), a community of Spanish-speaking Latina professional organizers, when this book was already in press. Had I known of them sooner, I would have welcomed the chance to interview the group's founders and members.

Chapter Three

1   Taylor, *Counter Culture*, 106–13.

2   As Sarah Damaske has argued, focusing on the different decisions women make over the course of their lives, their "work pathways," allows us to examine "the multitude of decisions women make that are influenced by personal motivations, structural constraints and opportunities, and competing cultural mandates" (*For the Family?*, 15).

3   Pagis, "Self-Work Romantic Utopia," 41.

4   McCubbin, *Making Space*, 11.

5   In framing their organizing skills as an innate aptitude they are moved to share with others, organizers connect their work to the long history of the concept of the "calling" in American history (see McGee, *Self-Help, Inc.*, 25–48).

6   "Organization Is in Their Blood," 13. Organizers' tendency to connect their childhood habits to their current career aligns with sociologist Erving Goffman's concept of the moral career, in which individuals craft a narrative of their life that makes their current situation seem logical, if not inevitable ("The Moral Career of the Mental Patient").

7   Kondo, *Life-Changing Magic*, 13.

8   Woodards, "'Less Is More.'"

9   Life coaches describe themselves in similar terms, saying they have "always been coaching" (George, "Seeking Legitimacy," 198).

10   When I asked male organizers what drew them to the field, for example, they didn't talk about how much they love organizing, nor did they share stories of organizing their childhood bedrooms. Instead, they all described wanting to start their own business and choosing organizing because it was a growing industry that aligned with their skill sets.

11   Cech, *Trouble with Passion*, 5.

12   Judge et al., "Pay and Job Satisfaction," cited in Schwartz, *Why We Work*, 40.

13   Cech, *Trouble with Passion*; Pagis, "Self-Work Romantic Utopia," 64.

14   DePalma, "Passion Paradigm," 146.

15   See, for example, Cech, *Trouble with Passion*; DePalma, "Passion Paradigm"; Pagis, "Self-Work Romantic Utopia."

16   Cech, *Trouble with Passion*, 9.

17   As Pagis contends, the cultural ideal of "doing what you love" serves to "strengthen the precarious, noncommitted, and individual-oriented structure of this market, resulting in flexible, individualistic solutions that replace workplace responsibility" ("Self-Work Romantic Utopia," 41). And, as Cech argues, "By framing the pursuit of self-fulfilling work as an antidote to these problems of labor force participation and by making it individuals' own responsibility to find a self-expressive place in the labor market, the passion principle may stifle such critiques of the capitalist work structure—critiques that might, under other circumstances, kindle collective demands for shorter work hours, more equitable pay, or better work-life integration" (*Trouble with Passion*, 225).

18   I met just one organizer for whom this was her first job out of college. Her university allowed students to design their own major, so she designed a custom major in professional organizing that included courses on housing and interior design, family systems, psychology, and business management, as well as an internship in the organizing industry. I don't expect organizing majors to begin cropping up on college campuses anytime soon, but experienced organizers tell me they're seeing more young women entering the profession straight out of school. And as more young people who've been exposed to organizing through the media come of age, it's likely that more will choose to pursue organizing as a first, rather than eventual, career.

19   Underwood, "The Magic Touch." For additional narratives of how various organizers came to work in this field, see Lark, *Before the Big O*.

20   Lane, *Company of One*, 136–37.

21   On the decline of leisure among precarious workers, see Standing, "Tertiary Time."

22   Multiple organizers described to me the challenges of receiving Pandemic Unemployment Assistance or Paycheck Protection Program loans (see US Small Business Administration, "Paycheck Protection Program"). One organizer said, "I had applied for the self-employed unemployment, which took forever to get. I was so upset," she told me. "You could never get anybody on the phone. I mean, I literally would try 300 times, no lie, dialing to try to get somebody from EDD [California Employment Development Department] on the phone and it was just not happening. . . . That was like day after day after day that I would try that." When the money finally did arrive, months later, she was thrilled.

"Then the good thing was, when I finally did get it, I want to say in June [2020] or something, I got a big giant chunk of money, because it went back to when I had filed."

23   These, too, are unequally distributed, as Black business owners are turned down for loans at twice the rate of white business owners (Marks, "Black-Owned Firms").

24   For example, during the pandemic, one organizer, drawing on her accounting background, shifted her business's focus from physical organizing to helping clients manage their finances and properties. Another organizer began offering virtual life coaching before the pandemic, integrating organizing with a more holistic approach to clients' physical, spiritual, mental, and emotional wellness. When the pandemic hit, she was forced to lay off all but one of the employees who'd been doing the hands-on organizing and refocused her efforts on growing the coaching side of her business, which she was able to do entirely remotely.

25   Self-employed Americans are hardly alone in their vulnerability to unexpected downturns. The Covid-19 pandemic made it abundantly clear to anyone who had not yet bothered to notice that for most Americans even a minor work disruption, let alone a major one, is enough to unravel their precarious hold on financial stability. See Deevy et al., *Financial Resilience in America*; Edin and Shaefer, *$2 a Day*.

26   As DePalma argues, in a "culture of precarity," individuals must "rise to the challenge of acculturating to risk" ("Passion Paradigm," 146) .

27   It's worth noting that women are more likely than men to say job security is "extremely important" to them (Pew Research Center, *On Pay Gap*, 38–46).

28   Sociologist Molly George has identified a similar trend among life coaches, who she argues "exemplify an emerging trend in the American labor market: college-educated workers pursuing non-standard work as independent contractors in personalized service occupations" ("Seeking Legitimacy," 179).

29   As I write this paragraph, I remember returning to teaching after giving birth to my son. My university offered only six weeks of paid maternity leave, but my son was born at exactly the start of the spring semester—the result of luck, not planning—so I was able to use my accrued medical leave to carry me through to summer, allowing me a full seven months at home with him. When I returned to teaching that fall, one of my students, a young Latinx woman in her early twenties, shared with me that she, too, had just had a baby. Hers was just a month or two old, but she was already back to attending school full-time on top of a part-time job. I remember thinking that I could not have done what she was doing, and she shouldn't have had to, either.

30   https://bipartisanpolicy.org/explainer/paid-family-leave-across-oecd-countries/.

31   Despite long-standing legislation barring workplace discrimination on the basis of gender or parental status, women with children are less likely to be hired than both men with children and women without children. See, for example: Cheung et al., "Beyond the Baby Bump"; Correll et al., "Getting a Job."

32   Lovejoy and Stone, "Opting Back In," 635.

33   https://bipartisanpolicy.org/explainer/paid-family-leave-across-oecd-countries/.

34   PEW Research Center, *Growing Share of U.S. Marriages*.

35   Hillbrecht and Lero, "Self-Employment and Family Life"; Lovejoy and Stone, "Opting Back In"; Osnowitz, *Freelancing Expertise*.

36   See Beckman and Mazmanian, *Dreams of the Overworked*.

37   Beckman and Mazmanian, *Dreams of the Overworked*, 23.

38   Beckman and Mazmanian, *Dreams of the Overworked*, 47.

39   Wilson and Yochim ("Mothering through Precarity") document other forms of "mamapreneurship" that mothers pursue to augment their families' incomes, including couponing, budgeting, working as staff for self-employed husbands, and digitally enabled work-at-home jobs.

40   A desire to "have something of their own" came up repeatedly in my conversations with mothers who had started, or hoped to start, organizing businesses.

41   Pagis argues that, in this regard, "women, who usually inhabit the less privileged positions in the job market, find themselves in a better relational position on their path to [professional] self-fulfillment when compared with men. Being secondary or equal earners, they can choose this relatively risky strategy [of following their passion] as the household is less dependent on their income" ("Self-Work Romantic Utopia," 55). See also Cech, *Problem with Passion*.

42   See Barley and Kunda, *Gurus, Hired Guns, and Warm Bodies*; Rogers, *Temps*.

43   Wood, *Despotism on Demand*.

44   For an overview of the decline of secure employment and the rise of precarious work, see Hyman, *Temp*; Kalleberg, "Precarious Work, Insecure Workers"; Moen and Roehling, *Career Mystique*; Ross, *Nice Work If You Can Get It*; Standing, *The Precariat*.

45   Duhigg, "Wealthy, Successful, and Miserable."

46   As of 2019, more Americans were self-employed than at any time since 1957, when the IRS began collecting that data. Women, and women of color especially, have been at the forefront of this trend. From 2014 to 2019, women-owned businesses increased by 21 percent in the United States; as of 2019, half of those women-owned businesses were headed by women of color (American Express, *2019 State of Women-Owned Businesses Report*).

47   Roswell and Harlan, *2019 Gig Economy and Self-Employment Report*. Self-employed women are even more likely to be highly satisfied with their work than self-employed men or traditionally employed women, although these results vary by race, with lower levels of satisfaction among Black women (Maguire and Winters, "Satisfaction from Self-Employment").

48   Roswell and Harlan, *2019 Gig Economy and Self-Employment Report*, 7.

49   Binkley, *Happiness as Enterprise*; Freeman, *Entrepreneurial Selves*; Gershon, *Down and Out in the New Economy*; Lane, *Company of One*.

50   Rivers, "Iteration of or Escape from Neoliberalism." See also Rivers, "'Meat and Three.'"

51   Rivers, "Iteration of or Escape from Neoliberalism," 29. See also Freeman, *Entrepreneurial Selves*.

52   Rivers, "Iteration of or Escape from Neoliberalism," 30.

53   Rivers, "Iteration of or Escape from Neoliberalism," 30.

54   Pagis, "Self-Work Romantic Utopia," 64.

55   The notion of a UBI smacks against certain long-standing American ideals, namely that waged work is supposed to be how people meet their basic needs; anything else is a handout, whether from the state or a spouse, and a sign of personal and moral failure (see Weeks, *Problem with Work*, 6–7). On a cultural level, these ideas are hard to shake, although if anything can dislodge them it might be a global pandemic and the resulting economic fallout. On a practical level, UBI experiments seem to be working. On the whole, receiving regular payments *at a livable level* decreases poverty levels, increases educational attainment, and improves

recipients' physical and mental health. Contrary to critics' predictions, receiving UBI does not discourage most people from working (single mothers are an exception, for obvious reasons). Some studies actually found that labor force participation increased with UBI; it made people *more* likely to work. Ideally, establishing a stable floor beneath them will allow people to choose better work, rather than choosing not to work at all (although there is something to be said for the freedom to do that, too). See Hasdell, *What We Know*, 16–17.

56   At one point in America's history, it was hotly debated whether social supports like healthcare, pensions, and disability and unemployment insurance should be provided directly to vulnerable Americans (especially women and children) or linked to wage earning (usually the province of men). Ultimately, the United States embraced the latter option, making paid employment a prerequisite to receiving most forms of social security. See Goodwin, *Gender and the Politics of Welfare Reform*; Skocpol, *Protecting Soldiers and Mothers*. Twentieth-century welfare reforms only strengthened this connection of welfare to work (see Edin and Schaefer, *$2 a Day*, chapter 1), at a time when the jobs required to secure these benefits were themselves disappearing and declining in quality. The sudden and devastating economic impact of the Covid-19 pandemic, and the controversies around direct aid programs to struggling Americans, threw the shortcomings of this model into high relief.

57   On the various forms such expanded social safety nets for independent workers might take, see Erikson and Meyer, *Economic Security*; Hill, *New Economy*.

58   See, for example, Kanter, *Men and Women of the Corporation*, chapter 5, which discusses the unpaid labor corporate wives had to perform to help build and maintain their husbands' careers.

59   As George has argued, "the destabilization of familiar work structures . . . have produced opportunities for new types of work" ("Seeking Legitimacy," 179). See also Horowitz, "Freelance Surge."

60   See Moreton's incisive critique of the job as a social contrivance in "The Future of Work." See also Chamberlain, *Undoing Work*; Weeks, *Problem with Work*.

Chapter Four

1   Geertz, *Interpretation of Cultures*, 14.

2   Organizers who specialize in these and related conditions often affiliate themselves with the Institute for Challenging Disorganization (https://www .challengingdisorganization.org/), a professional association that provides its own research, education, and certifications for organizers. Many NAPO members are also members of the ICD. One organizer who belongs to both associations described ICD as "more academic," or "the research leg" of organizing, while NAPO is the "social and business leg of it."

3   Respectively, Kondo, *Life-Changing Magic*; Morgenstern, *SHED Your Stuff*; Shearer and Teplin, *The Home Edit*.

4   A similar instance came up at a NAPO panel on ethics. A panelist asked whether organizers should advertise their businesses on their vehicles. When an audience member suggested this was a good form of inexpensive advertising, the presenter disagreed. "What if," she asked, "your client doesn't want her neighbors to know she hired an organizer, and there's your car parked in front of her house with your business name on it?" Another audience member disagreed, saying it's the organizer's car so she has a right to do whatever she wants with it. The panelists

unanimously rejected that statement, saying, in essence, that concern for the client comes first.

5   White, "Clutter Threshold."

6   See Isenstadt, *Modern American House*, for a history of American ideas, and ideals, of spaciousness in middle-class homes.

7   Freedman and Abrahamson, *Perfect Mess*; Steketee and Frost, *Stuff*.

8   Bernstein, "Marie Kondo." Bernstein's point is similar to the argument Csikszentmihalyi and Rochberg-Halton make in *The Meaning of Things*.

9   Illouz, *Cold Intimacies*, 60. For histories of hoarding, see Herring, *Hoarders*, and Acocella, "Let It Go." I'll address these arguments in greater length toward the end of this chapter when I consider the role television programs about hoarding have played in raising awareness of professional organizing.

10 Boyle, "Filthy with Things," 86.

11 See also Kelly, "Organizing," 333. This is of course not the case in hoarding situations where government agencies force people to clean out their homes in light of concerns around public safety, fire hazards, or the protection of children, animals, or the elderly. In this respect, the organizers I spoke with did not align with Kilroy-Marac's finding that "POs adhere to a pervasive cultural logic . . . that reads material disorder as evidence, symptom, or potential cause of mental disorder" ("A Magical Reorientation," 451).

12 During my fieldwork, I attended meetings of the Orange County Hoarding Task Force and interviewed a clinical social worker with more than twenty years' experience working with clients who hoard. Hoarding task forces, of which there are now more than seventy-five across the United States, bring together city officials, social workers, firefighters, police officers, junk haulers, organizers, and others for the purpose of educating one another and the public about hoarding and coordinating services to assist people who hoard. See International OCD Federation, "The Role of Hoarding Taskforces." Among taskforce participants, it was an accepted fact that forced clean-outs don't work because they do not address the issues underlying hoarding behavior. In such cases, clients usually refill the home immediately, sometimes with even more belongings than before. Many people experience physical or mental health crises following a clean-out, some even dying by suicide (Steketee and Frost, *Stuff*, 97).

13 Denegri-Knott and Parsons, "Disordering Things," 89.

14 Kilroy-Marac, "A Magical Reorientation," 451.

15 See Kilroy-Marac, "A Magical Reorientation," 451–52; Kelly, "Organizing," chapter 5.

16 Kilroy-Marac, "A Magical Reorientation," 449.

17 In addition to physical fatigue, organizers are also aware of what has been called "decision fatigue," in which people's decision-making abilities decline after having to make decision after decision (Tierney, "Decision Fatigue?").

18 A third option is to craft custom packages for certain types of jobs. For a $1,500 "garage package," for example, one Los Angeles organizer will provide eight hours of organizing by a two-person team; safely remove all trash, household contaminants, and electronic waste; deliver donations and provide a tax receipt; and have three bankers' boxes of paper shredded offsite. For $49, another organizer will review photos of your organizing project, do a thirty-minute phone organizing session, and create "homework" and an action plan for future reference. Here, organizers group certain services together based on their experience of what clients tend to need and how long those jobs tend to take.

19   Kilroy-Marac ("A Magical Reorientation," 449) describes two techniques the Toronto organizers she interviewed use to "intervene in the complex affective attachments their clients have with their things." I touch on both here as well as additional approaches used by the US organizers I interviewed and worked alongside.

20   Kondo, *Life-Changing Magic*, 116.

21   Kondo, *Life-Changing Magic*, 81–82.

22   Kilroy-Marac, "A Magical Reorientation," 450.

23   Kilroy-Marac, "A Magical Reorientation," 450.

24   Sometimes clients try to gift items to the organizer herself. As was discussed at multiple NAPO panels on ethics in organizing, organizers are discouraged from accepting gifts from clients, because it muddies the organizer-client relationship and might be seen as exploitative, especially if the item has high monetary value and/or the client is especially vulnerable. For this reason, numerous organizers told me they refrain from complimenting any specific belongings in case the client interprets this as a wish or request for the item.

25   The study of objects and their meanings is a burgeoning field, one I engage with only cursorily here, as my focus is more on the relationship between organizers and their clients than between clients and their belongings. Readers interested in the latter should see Csikszentmihalyi and Halton, *The Meaning of Things*; Steketee and Frost, *Stuff*; Gosling, *Snoop*; Kilroy-Marac, "An Order of Distinction"; Miller, *The Comfort of Things*; Miller, *Stuff*; Roster, "Letting Go"; Newell, "The Matter of the Unfetish."

26   That said, see Minter's *Secondhand* on the inner workings and environmental costs of the enormous secondhand industry.

27   For similar critiques of "buying green," see Humphrey, *Excess*; Littler, "Good Housekeeping."

28   In her classic organizing book, *Organizing from the Inside Out*, Julie Morgenstern writes, "There are people whose homes and offices appear neat as a pin on the surface. Yet inside their desk drawers and kitchen cabinets, there is no real system and things are terribly out of control. By contrast, there are many people who live or work in a physical mess, yet feel very comfortable in this environment and can always put their hands on whatever they need in a second. Could they be considered organized? Absolutely" (7).

29   Noble, *How to Start*, 22.

30   Organizer Ellen Vitt describes herself as a "neat freak" in Killham, "Clutter Busters."

31   Gordon, "Professional Organizers."

32   Boyle, "Filthy with Things," 77.

33   O'Brien, "Making a Specialty of Order."

34   Brodesser-Akner, "Marie Kondo." Brodesser-Akner's article, which in general took a rather snarky and cynical tone toward organizing, suggested that NAPO members are harshly critical of Kondo, both her specific approach to organizing and her overwhelming popularity compared to organizers who've been in the field for decades. In my fieldwork, which took place when Kondo's book came out but before the corresponding TV show, I heard similar critiques of Kondo, but rarely with the venom Brodesser-Akner attributes to NAPO's organizers.

35   Noble, *How to Start*, 1–2.

36   Pedersen, *Born to Organize*, 6.

37   Even Marie Kondo, whose KonMari organizing method is presented as a strict step-by-step plan to getting organized, writes that "no matter how perfect a storage system I devise I can never put someone else's house in order . . . Order is dependent on the extremely personal values of what a person wants to live with" (Kondo, *Life-Changing Magic*, 6). More recently, Kondo's once-rigid take on tidiness has loosened somewhat, a shift she credits to her own challenges managing a growing family and expanding business (Koncius, "Marie Kondo's Life").

38   Some organizers already teach organizing classes, either independently or within high schools, colleges, and adult schools. One longtime Los Angeles organizer, for example, has been teaching classes on clutter and organizing since the 1980s. More recently, an organizer in Brooklyn told me she was thinking of offering a course she'd jokingly named "Housewifery 101," though it would be for men and women, and teenagers, too. The class would cover "certain things that everybody needs to know to keep their apartment or home kind of in shape." In the past, she said, "it was the mom or the housewife-type or the maid or whomever who did that stuff." Now, she suggested, nobody is learning these skills. Interestingly enough, the same need seems to have existed nearly four decades earlier; in 1979, Orange County, CA, organizer Dee Vance actually offered a similar course for "Sidetracked Home Executives," designed to "teach the homemaker how to organize her day so she can dress well, serve well-balanced meals and still have time for an outside job" ("3 Seminars Set to Begin").

39   Some organizers actually frame organizing as a means to weight loss. See, for instance, organizer Dorothy Breininger's *Stuff Your Face or Face Your Stuff*; and Deborah Gussoff's *Organizing for Weight Loss*.

40   Kilroy-Marac, "A Magical Reorientation," 446–47.

41   Seim, "Connective Labor and Street-Level Bureaucracy."

42   There is evidence that people who make the conscious decision to consume less tend to be civically engaged and are "likely to express their personal values and political orientation through consumer activism such as boycotts and buycotts" (Nelson et al., "Downshifting Consumer = Upshifting Citizen?," 152). ("Buycotts" refer to consciously purchasing products from the competitors of ethically dubious companies.)

43   Such moments of introspection have the potential to foster broader critiques of contemporary life, as overwhelmed Americans become "finally weary and fed up enough to throw off the fantasy of self-sufficiency and to demand, instead, sufficiency for each and all" (McGee, *Self-Help, Inc.*, 191).

Chapter Five

1   Pugh, "Emotions."

2   Wealthy or famous clients sometimes ask organizers to sign a non-disclosure agreement agreeing to keep private anything they see, hear, or do on the job, but most organizers agree that this should be a given on all organizing jobs, whether clients make you sign something or not. Thus, while I did hear a few organizers name-drop the celebrities they'd worked with, more often than not, organizers deliberately obscured famous clients' identities when talking with me.

3   This is in part why some organizers disagree with Kondo's programmatic approach, which has every person progress through specific spaces in a certain order—clothes, books, papers, miscellany, and finally sentimental items. Instead,

many organizers tailor the approach to the client; even Kondo herself does this occasionally, as in an episode of *Tidying Up with Marie Kondo* where Kondo acquiesced to a widow's wish to go through her deceased husband's clothes "out of order" because that felt like the most pressing issue to the client (*Tidying Up with Marie Kondo*, season 1, episode 4, "Sparking Joy After a Loss").

4   Pugh, "Emotions," 1.

5   Pugh, "Emotions," 1.

6   Among the personal concierges she studied, Rachel Sherman identified three different orientations to the emotional work they perform for clients: positive, in that they "saw their emotional work as essentially voluntary, felt their clients' emotional needs were essentially legitimate and enjoyed their relationship with clients"; ambivalent, because they enjoyed relationships with some clients but sometimes found demands unreasonable or overwhelming; and a third group who "enjoyed giving their clients relief but drew strong boundaries against forming close relationships" ("Caring or Catering?," 166). As I detail later in this chapter, while some organizers maintained stronger boundaries than others in their relationships with clients, for the most part organizers fell decidedly in Sherman's first group.

7   Scholars differ on how they define and utilize the concepts of emotional work, emotion work, and emotional labor. The authoritative work on emotional labor is Arlie Hochschild's *The Managed Heart: Commercialization of Human Feeling*. Hochschild's definition concerns emotional performances scripted and demanded by an employer; other scholars have tweaked and blurred that original concept to encompass emotional and mental work performed across a range of contexts (see Beck, "Concept Creep"). I borrow from Rachel Sherman ("Caring or Catering?") in using the more encompassing term "emotional work." See also Bulan et al., "Doing for Others on the Job"; Kang, *The Managed Hand*; Lopez, "Emotional Labor and Organized Emotional Care."

8   For a thoughtful review of and response to these competing schools of thought, see Pugh, "Emotions."

9   Lauren Berlant (*The Female Complaint*) has argued that women's responsibility for performing emotional labor is central to the stereotyped and homogenized "women's culture" propagated by magazines and literature directed at American women over the last two centuries. I argue that the same applies to connective labor, which involves emotional labor as one of its key components. See also Hackman, *Emotional Labor*; Hartley, *Fed Up*.

10   Clark, *Misery and Company*, 42. Similarly, Morini argues that "cognitive capitalism tends to prioritize extracting value from relational and emotional elements, which are more likely to be part of women's experiential baggage" ("Feminization of Labor").

11   Candace Clark writes that "sympathy is an antidote to life's misery and an important form of social interaction," noting that the giving and receiving of sympathy has both patterns and rules (*Misery and Company*, xi).

12   See, for example: Illouz, *Cold Intimacies*; Zelizer, *The Purchase of Intimacy*.

13   Hochschild (*Outsourced Self*, 192–97) details similar examples in which people argue that help from "friends you paid" was preferable to that of "real" friends and family.

14   Hochschild, *Outsourced Self*, 223.

15   These awkward moments are common in economic actions involving both money and care, where one is a paid friend, of sorts. For a helpful overview of sociological

scholarship on this sort of "relational work" undertaken to negotiate the intersections between intimate and economic relations, see Bandeji, "Relational Work." See Hochschild, *Outsourced Self* (188–92), for additional examples of the ambiguity inherent to friendships that emerge in commercial transactions.

16 As such, organizers and other expert service workers complicate the usual dichotomy between "higher-skilled, higher-paid professional work and lower-skilled, lower-wage frontline service work" (George, "Seeking Legitimacy," 180). For instance, organizers are technically part of the "emotional proletariat," required to display both friendliness and deference on the job, but their class advantages relative to frontline service workers, and the status they hold as business owners, rather than employees, set them apart from most other workers in this category (Macdonald and Sirianni, "The Service Society," 2).

17 See Sherman, "Caring or Catering?," 166.

18 See, for example: Hondagneu-Sotelo, *Domestica*; Eisenstein and Gershon, "'Saying No and Staying Flexible."

19 Sherman ("Caring or Catering?") makes a similar point about personal concierges, whose emotional work is neither scripted, systematized, nor controlled by an employer. Like organizers, personal concierges enjoy some—but not all—aspects of their relationships with clients.

20 See, for example: Hondagneu-Sotelo, *Domestica*; Sherman, "Caring or Catering?"

21 Pugh, "Emotions," 7–8.

22 Duffy et al., *Caring on the Clock*, 4–5.

23 There are parallels here to Josh Seim's ("Connective Labor and Street-Level Bureaucracy") findings on welfare workers, who offer additional care and services to clients they perceive as especially deserving.

24 Ward and King, "Work and the Good Life," 74.

25 Folbre, *The Invisible Heart*, 47. See also Pew Research Center, *On Pay Gap*.

26 Lovejoy and Stone, "Opting Back In," 635.

27 Leidner, *Fast Food*, cited in Weeks, *Problem with Work*, 194.

28 See also Koncius, "Clutter Wars."

29 Saxbe et al., "No Place Like Home."

30 Although these quotations are from my interview with her, I use Lark's real name because she has published a book on this exact subject. Regina Lark and Judith Kolberg's *Emotional Labor: Why a Woman's Work Is Never Done* documents the burdens women tend to carry with regard to home and family and advocates for organizers to help clients reframe and reduce that burden. As has become common in recent years, Lark uses the term "emotional labor" to refer to the mental and physical load women tend to carry in the home, rather than in the specific sociological sense coined by sociologist Arlie Hochschild (*The Managed Heart*). See Beck, "The Concept Creep of 'Emotional Labor.'"

31 Kelly, "Organizing," 276.

32 Kelly ("Organizing," 338–39) heard the same things from the Texas organizers she interviewed.

33 Kondo, *Life-Changing Magic*, 195.

34 Kilroy-Marac argues that contemporary "consumption-critical lifestyle movements," such as professional organizing, minimalism, and the tiny house movement, reinforce classist ideals of "appropriate" consumption by advocating "a shift to 'inconspicuous consumption' among the affluent . . . a turn toward spending money on experiences, services, and personal enrichment rather than material

goods. Consumption is still central to the good life, then, but it is a particular form of consumption that is weary of accumulation, critical of disorder, and most visible in the conspicuous display of what is not there" ("A Magical Reorientation," 447).

35 When the Container Store first opened, one longtime organizer told me, the company saw organizers as competition, rebuffing organizers' efforts to collaborate. The Container Store has since changed their tune and now offers an industry discount to NAPO members. Similarly, when the magazine *Real Simple* first launched, "advertisers expressed dismay at an aesthetic deemed too austere, even anti-consumerist" (Kelly, "Organizing," 225).

36 Smaller, "It's an Entire Web Site."

37 I did hear from one friend that the organizer his family hired came for a consultation then had the Container Store deliver "a whole bunch of stuff" to their home, on which she received a discount. Whatever they didn't use, the organizer would return; whatever they kept, she added to their bill.

38 Organizer Lila, for example, opened her hatchback to show me her supplies after I assisted her on an organizing gig. They included: wet wipes, rags, multiple types of tape, trash bags, twist ties, Ziploc bags, disposable gloves, pens, pencils, highlighters, notebook, paper clips, rubber bands, tarp, bungee cords, scissors, box cutters, label maker, furniture sliders, adhesive utility hooks, a first aid kit, and an assortment of folders, binders, and accordion files donated by previous clients that she repurposes for new jobs.

39 One organizer told me she refuses to mark up the cost of items she purchases for her clients, charging them only whatever the item itself cost. "I never want to put them [the client] in the position where I want them to buy something, where I benefit financially from something that's actually harming them."

40 At NAPO Los Angeles meetings I attended, these presentations included vendors of filing products, companies that specialize in installing garage storage solutions, and a company that digitally catalogs clients' wardrobes in a "virtual closet," stores them offsite, and delivers specific items upon request worldwide (https://garderobeonline .com/). NAPO conferences are also awash in products. Attendees are gifted all sorts of organizing goodies—sticky notes, storage bags and bins, labels and label makers, letter openers, staples, calendars, planners—by exhibitors hoping organizers will refer them along to their clients (see Brodesser-Akner, "Marie Kondo").

41 Green, "Marie Kondo." See also Green, "A Tidiness Empire."

42 This differs dramatically from the sort of approach presented on the organizing show *Get Organized with the Home Edit*, in which organizers provide beautiful, usually rainbow-themed storage solutions, often for celebrities, that clearly prioritize aesthetics and involve substantial expense.

43 Sherman, "The Production of Distinctions."

44 See Breaux, "Professional Organizer's Philosophy." One psychologist has proposed the diagnosis "Home Dysmorphic Disorder" to characterize a person having an unrealistic ideal of what their home should look like (Allen, "How Instagram Makes Us Feel").

45 Kelly, "Organizing," 342.

46 As Kilroy-Marac writes of *Real Simple* magazine, "The catch, of course, is that the real portrayed in this magazine is an intricately manufactured and carefully produced image, and the aesthetic of the simple itself takes a huge investment of time, energy, and even (despite the emphasis on frugality and saving that runs throughout the magazine) money" ("A Magical Reorientation," 446).

47   As I described in chapter 5, many organizers share Michelle's goal of disabusing clients of unrealistic and harmful expectations of their homes and themselves, and see doing so as a core part of their organizing work.

48   "Radical honesty," in the sense that Michelle used the term, is not a moral obligation to tell the truth but a means of reducing stress and suffering and deepening connections with others through authentic sharing (e.g., Blanton, *Radical Honesty*).

49   See Cooper, *Cut Adrift*; Pugh, *Tumbleweed Society*.

50   See, for example: Miller, "The Pandemic Created a Child-Care Crisis"; Schaeffer, "Working Moms." Across the workforce, the pandemic disproportionately impacted women, resulting in what some have called a "she-cession" (e.g., Gupta, "Some Women Call This Recession a 'Shecession'"). Job losses were highest in low-wage industries, where female workers of color tend to be concentrated. Many women with young children had to stop working or dramatically reduce their hours due to the increased childcare burden generated by school and daycare closings. In total, nearly 1.8 million women left the US workforce in the first year and a half of the pandemic (Bureau of Labor Statistics, *Employment Situation*). The number of women-owned businesses also fell by a quarter within the first two months of the pandemic (National Women's Business Council, 2020 *Annual Report*, 6).

51   George found a similar pattern among life coaches ("Seeking Legitimacy," 193). Some of the organizers Kelly interviewed in Texas, however, explicitly rejected the notion that organizing is therapeutic ("Organizing," 341). Although there's no evidence that clients opt for organizing *instead of* therapy, the association of the two aligns with Wiles's critique that "Doing something about our surroundings has become a surrogate for therapy" ("Unhappy? Clean House").

52   Lawrence, "Conquering Clutter"; Soman, "The Paper Chase."

53   http://www.anorganizedlife.net/leslie.html.

54   Herman, *Romance of American Psychology*. With therapeutic culture has come an emphasis on personal responsibility, one that reinterprets complex social problems, such as professional and financial insecurity, as individual problems. In this framing, it is not society that needs to change, but the individual, whose needs, attitudes, and behavior must be monitored and readjusted, usually under the guidance of professional expertise. On the rise of therapeutic culture, see Illouz, *Cold Intimacies* and *Saving the Modern Soul*; Foster, "Therapeutic Spirit of Neoliberalism"; Madsen, *Therapeutic Turn*. Some describe therapeutic discourses as part of a neoliberal strategy to contain dissent, while others see that as an overly narrow explanation for wide-ranging social and cultural shifts. See also Aubry and Travis, "Introduction"; Furedi, *Therapy Culture*; McGee, *Self-Help, Inc.*, 22–23.

55   On the rise of the self-help industry and makeover culture, see McGee, *Self-Help, Inc.*; Ouelette and Hay, *Better Living*, 63–64; Weber, *Makeover TV*.

56   Hochschild, *Outsourced Self*. See also Dizard and Gadlin, *Minimal Family*; George, "Seeking Legitimacy"; Sherman, "'Time Is Our Commodity.'" Some lament this shift, fearing the incursion of market forces into once-private and intimate corners of Americans' lives; others argue compellingly that family and marketplace have always been more intertwined than economists liked to admit (Folbre, *Invisible Heart*; Illouz, *Cold Intimacies*; Zelizer, *Purchase of Intimacy*).

57   I wish I could say I came up with this term myself, but the magnificent Ilana Gershon suggested it after reading an early draft of this manuscript.

58   McNally, "Book Review: Cannibal Capitalism."

59   Fraser, *Cannibal Capitalism*, 57–59.

60   Ehrenreich and Hochschild, *Global Women.*

61   As Pugh argues, "Features of contemporary capitalism—insecure production, expansive consumption and rampant inequality—generate both an intensifying need for being 'seen' and the connective labor jobs that provide it" ("Emotions," 3).

62   Beckman and Mazmanian, *Dreams of the Overworked*, 12–13. Hackman (*Emotional Labor*) reaches a similar conclusion about women's emotional labor more generally.

63   Gardner, "Professional Organizers."

Conclusion

1   It will surprise exactly no one to learn that this sort of "browser clutter" leads to feelings of stress, frustration, and overwhelm (Rongjun et al., "When Browsing Gets Cluttered").

2   Center on Budget and Policy Priorities, *Covid-19 Economy's Effects.* On undercounting in US unemployment rates, see, for example, Stropoli, "U.S. Unemployment Is Even Worse."

3   Cech and Hiltner, "Unsettled Employment."

4   Kochhar, "Self-Employed Are Back at Work"; Pofeldt, "Finding Funding," 14.

5   Pardue, "New Business Creation."

6   "Many scholars have highlighted how novel circumstances can create conditions that support transformative rethinking of life plans. Anticipated trajectories that typically feel predetermined can be consciously scrutinized when major disruptions interrupt the flow of ordinary temporal experience" (Ravenelle and Kowalski, "'Not Like Chasing Chanel,'" 6).

7   Cech, *Trouble with Passion*, 31.

8   Here and in the following paragraph I draw on James Scott's theories of everyday resistance (*Weapons of the Weak*; *Domination and the Arts of Resistance*), according to which organizers' work might be seen to function as a safety valve, releasing just enough pressure to allow the system to go on functioning, averting the explosion that pent-up pressure would otherwise create.

9   Lasch, *Culture of Narcissism*; Rose, *Governing the Soul.*

10   McGee contends that "the pursuit of individual self-invention continues to hold radical political possibilities" (*Self-Help, Inc.*, 180).

11   Schor, *True Wealth*, 7.

12   See Weeks, *Problem with Work*, chapter 4.

13   Schor, *True Wealth*, 3.

14   Admittedly, Schor herself might disagree with this contention, as she argues that hiring people like organizers has "undermined the need for community interdependence. When people can afford to purchase services, they ask for favors less often" (*True Wealth*, 140). I'd like to think she might change her mind after reading this book.

15   Here I echo Weeks's call to reduce both waged and unwaged work time and fight "to make visible and contest the gender division of unwaged household and caring labor, as well as the lack of adequate publicly funded services to support this socially necessary labor" (*Problem with Work*, 172).

16   As Sherman ("'Time Is Our Commodity,'" 87) notes in her research among personal concierges, service providers of this sort are essentially competing with their

own customers, who would—at least in theory—perform the work themselves had they not hired someone else to do it for them.

17   Arguments for offering students organizing classes or curriculum dovetail with recent initiatives to bring home economics back into classrooms (Dreilinger, *Secret History*, 287-96).

Appendix

1   As of late 2023, of the NAPO members who opted to report their gender, 97 percent identified as female, 3 percent as male, and 0.2 percent as nonbinary. These figures, and other statistics concerning NAPO members provided in this Appendix, are from NAPO's membership database, which the organization generously shared with me after removing names and other identifying details. NAPO's membership is of course not the same thing as the industry as a whole, but since the BLS does not classify professional organizing as its own occupational category, NAPO's membership is the closest available approximation of the profession's makeup.

2   I did not explicitly ask all interviewees about their racial identities (an omission I now regret), although some volunteered that information; these data therefore rely on my own imperfect determination of organizers' racial identities.

3   These figures should be taken only as approximations, as a large percentage of NAPO members (13 percent) chose not to list their race or ethnicity in the organization's membership database, and the identity categories they did name did not always align exactly with my own.

4   Among those who responded to this question, 0.6 percent of NAPO members were ages 79-93; 7 percent were 69-78; 27 percent were 59-68; 32 percent were 49-58; 23 percent were 39-48; 10 percent were 29-38; and just 0.7 percent were under age 28.

5   In this, organizers are typical of most US business owners, who prefer to "stay small" and are uninterested in organizational growth (Hurst and Pugsley, "What Do Small Businesses Do?"). This seems especially true of women business owners, of whom 90 percent have no employees (National Women's Business Council, *2020 Annual Report*). Toward the end of my research, I did notice that more organizing businesses had grown to include a number of part- and full-time employees. This was in part a product of new California legislation drawing a clearer boundary between contract workers and employees (Kim, "Dynamex Decision"; State of CA Department of Industrial Relations, "Independent Contractor versus Employee"). Under the new rules, many of the assistants organizers had previously employed on a contract business now had to be categorized as employees, with all the rights and benefits protected by law.

6   The sole exception was one Black organizer in her late fifties who started her business more than three years ago but has kept her full-time corporate job. She told me she hoped to eventually leave that job in order to dedicate more time to her organizing business. No other organizer in my study (of any race) had a full-time job apart from organizing, although one interviewee with a leadership role in the National Association of Black Professional Organizers told me she believed Black organizers were more likely than white organizers to work other, often full-time jobs in addition to running their organizing businesses. I discuss this in chapter 2 with regard to the uneven challenges of starting an organizing business,

depending on the socioeconomic status of oneself and one's network of friends and acquaintances.

7   Hourly rate figures are somewhat misleading. Many organizers set their rates by project, rather than by hour. For comparative purposes, a 2019 survey found that 18.3 percent of organizers nationwide charged less than $50 per hour; 41 percent between $50 and $74; 26.6 percent from $75 to $99; 10 percent between $100 and $149; 2.1 percent from $150 to $199; and 2 percent charged $200 or above (NAPO, *Membership Survey Results*).

8   Here again, national NAPO statistics provide helpful context. In 2019, NAPO members reported that in their highest-grossing year ever, 39.8 percent earned under $24,999; 19.5 percent earned $25,000 to $49,000; 18.5 percent earned $50,000 to $99,999; 11.8 percent earned $100,000 to $249,000; and 4.1 percent earned more than $250,000 (NAPO, *Membership Survey Results*). (These figures likely skew higher than for organizers as a whole, as low-income organizers may be unwilling or unable to pay NAPO's $300 annual membership fee.)

Bibliography

"3 Seminars Set to Begin This Week." *Los Angeles Times*, October 18, 1979, OC_C25.

Acocella, Joan. "Let It Go: Are We Becoming a Nation of Hoarders." *The New Yorker*, December 8, 2014. https://www.newyorker.com/magazine/2014/12/15/let-go.

"Adam Smith: Father of Capitalism." BBC News World Service: The Forum, November 21, 2017. https://www.bbc.co.uk/programmes/w3csvsfb.

Adams, Susan. "Unhappy Employees Outnumber Happy Ones by Two to One Worldwide." *Forbes*, October 10, 2013. https://www.forbes.com/sites/susanadams/2013/10/10/unhappy-employees-outnumber-happy-ones-by-two-to-one-worldwide/#7e09722a362a.

Akst, Daniel. "There's a Tidy Sum in Turning Chaos to Order." *Los Angeles Times*, December 1, 1992, OCD3.

Allen, Grace. "This Is How Instagram Makes Us Feel about Our Homes." *Ideal Home*, August 6, 2018. https://www.idealhome.co.uk/news/how-instagram-makes-us-feel-about-homes-208263.

Allen, Leslie. "Organization Is in Their Blood." *St. Louis Post Dispatch*, January 8, 1990, 5.

American Express. *2019 State of Women-Owned Businesses Report*. https://ventureneer.com/wp-content/uploads/2019/10/Final-2019-state-of-women-owned-businesses-report.pdf.

Anteby, Michel, and Beth A. Bechky. "Editorial Essay: How Workplace Ethnographies Can Inform the Study of Work and Employment Relations." *Industrial and Labor Relations Review* 69, no. 2 (2016): 501–5. http://doi.org/10.1177/0019793915621746.

Anteby, Michel, Curtis Chan, and Julia DiBenigno. "Three Lenses on Occupations and Professions in Organizations: Being, Doing, and Relating." *Academy of Management Annals* 10, no. 1 (2016): 183–244. https://doi.org/10.1080/19416520.2016.1120962.

Arnold, Jeanne, Anthony Graesch, Enzo Ragazzini, and Elinor Ochs. *Life at Home in the Twenty-First Century: 32 Families Open Their Doors*. Los Angeles: Cotsen Institute of Archaeology Press, 2012.

Arnold, Jeanne, and Ursula Lang. "Changing American Home Life: Trends in Domestic Leisure and Storage among Middle-Class Families." *Journal of Family and Economic Issues* 28 (2007): 23–48. https://doi.org/10.1007/s10834-006-9052-5.

Aubry, Timothy, and Trysh Travis. "Introduction." In *Rethinking Therapeutic Culture*, ed. Timothy Aubry and Trysh Travis, 1–23. Chicago: University of Chicago Press, 2015.

Bailey, Catherine, Marjolein Lips-Wiersma, Adrian Madden, Ruth Yeoman, Marc Thompson, and Neal Chalofsky. "The Five Paradoxes of Meaningful Work: Introduction to the Special Issue 'Meaningful Work: Prospects for the 21st Century.'" *Journal of Management Studies*, 56, no. 3 (2019): 481–99. https://doi.org/10.1111/joms.12422.

Bandeji, Nina. "Relational Work in the New Economy." *Annual Review of Sociology* 46, no. 1 (2020): 251–72. https://doi.org/10.1146/annurev-soc-121919-054719.

Barley, Stephen R., and Gideon Kunda. *Gurus, Hired Guns, and Warm Bodies: Itinerant Experts in a Knowledge Economy*. Princeton, NJ: Princeton University Press, 2011.

Bauder, David. "AP Says It Will Capitalize Black but Not White." Associated Press. July 20, 2020. https://apnews.com/article/entertainment-cultures-race-and-ethnicity-us-news-ap-top-news-7e36c00c5af0436abc09e051261fff1f.

Beck, Julie. "The Concept Creep of 'Emotional Labor.'" *The Atlantic*, November 26, 2018. https://www.theatlantic.com/family/archive/2018/11/arlie-hochschild-housework-isnt-emotional-labor/576637/.

Beckman, Christine, and Melissa Mazmanian. *Dreams of the Overworked: Living, Working, and Parenting in the Digital Age*. Stanford, CA: Stanford University Press, 2020.

Beecher, Mary Ann. "A Place for Everything: The Influence of Storage Innovations on Modern American Domesticity (1900–1955)." PhD diss., University of Iowa, 2003.

Berlant, Lauren. *The Female Complaint: The Unfinished Business of Sentimentality in American Culture*. Durham, NC: Duke University Press, 2008.

Bernstein, Arielle. "Marie Kondo and the Privilege of Clutter." *The Atlantic*, March 25, 2016.

The Big Bang Theory. 2013. Season 6, episode 19, "The Closet Reconfiguration." Directed by Anthony Rich. Aired March 14, 2013, on CBS.

Bing, Stanley. *100 Bullshit Jobs and How to Get Them*. New York: HarperCollins, 2006.

Binkley, Sam. *Happiness as Enterprise: An Essay on Neoliberal Life*. Albany: State University of New York Press, 2014.

Bishop, Ronald. "It Turns Out the Armoire Is Your Mother: Narratives of Addiction in Two Cable Television Organization Programs." *Addiction Research & Theory* 14, no. 2 (2006): 139–57. https://doi.org/10.1080/16066350500508482.

Blanton, Brad. *Radical Honesty: How to Transform Your Life by Telling the Truth*. Stanley, VA: Sparrowhawk, 1994.

Bourdieu, Pierre. *Distinction: A Social Critique of the Judgment of Taste*. Cambridge, MA: Harvard University Press, 1984.

Bowles, Hannah Riley, Linda Babcock, and Lei Lai. "Social Incentives for Gender Differences in the Propensity to Initiate Negotiations: Sometimes It Does Hurt to Ask." *Organizational Behavior and Human Decision Processes* 103, no. 1 (2007): 84–103. https://doi.org/10.1016/j.obhdp.2006.09.001.

Boyle, T. Coraghessan. "Filthy with Things." *The New Yorker*, February 15, 1993.

Breininger, Dorothy. *Stuff Your Face or Face Your Stuff: Lose Weight by Decluttering Your Life*. Deerfield, FL: Health Communications Inc., 2013.

Breaux, Adrienne. "This Professional Organizer's Philosophy on Tidying AND Home Are Refreshingly Realistic." *Apartment Therapy*, January 27, 2022. https://www.apartmenttherapy.com/nonnahs-driskill-get-organized-already-house-tour-photos-37030625.

Brodesser-Akner, Taffy. "Marie Kondo, Tidying Up, and the Ruthless War on Stuff." *New York Times*, July 6, 2016. https://www.nytimes.com/2016/07/10/magazine/marie-kondo-and-the-ruthless-war-on-stuff.html.

Bruno, Dave. *The 100 Thing Challenge: How I Got Rid of Almost Everything, Remade My Life, and Regained My Soul*. New York: Harper, 2010.

Bulan, Heather, Rebecca Erickson, and Amy Wharton. "Doing for Others on the Job: The Affective Requirements of Service Work, Gender, and Emotional Well-Being." *Social Problems* 44 (1997): 701-23. https://doi.org/10.2307/3096944.

Bureau of Labor Statistics, US Department of Labor. *Economic News Release: Employment Situation*. August 2021. https://www.bls.gov/news.release/empsit.t01.htm.

Bureau of Labor Statistics, US Department of Labor. "Personal Care and Service Occupations." Occupational Outlook Handbook. September 8, 2022, https://www.bls.gov/ooh/personal-care-and-service/home.htm?view_full.

Bureau of Labor Statistics, US Department of Labor. "Response to Comment on 2010 SOC: Docket Number 08-0314." March 12, 2009. https://www.bls.gov/soc/2010_responses/response_08-0314.htm.

"Business Women Praised: San Francisco Club Told How Feminine Hands Have Taken Dirt and Clutter Out of Offices." *Los Angeles Times*, April 17, 1928.

Cech, Erin. *The Trouble with Passion: How Searching for Fulfillment at Work Fosters Inequality*. Berkeley: University of California Press, 2021.

Cech, Erin, and Sofia Hiltner. "Unsettled Employment, Reshuffled Priorities? Career Prioritization among College-Educated Workers Facing Employment Instability during COVID-19." *Socius* 8 (2022). https://doi.org/10.1177/23780231211068660.

Center on Budget and Policy Priorities. *The Covid-19 Economy's Effects on Food, Housing, and Employment Hardships*. February 10, 2022. https://www.cbpp.org/research/poverty-and-inequality/tracking-the-covid-19-economys-effects-on-food-housing-and#:~:text=The%20unemployment%20rate%20jumped%20in,2021%20than%20in%20February%202020.

Chamberlain, James A. *Undoing Work, Rethinking Community: A Critique of the Social Function of Work*. Ithaca, NY: Cornell University Press, 2018.

Chayka, Kyle. *The Longing for Less: Living with Minimalism*. New York: Bloomsbury, 2020.

Cheung, Ho Kwan, Amanda Anderson, Eden King, Bhindai Mahabir, Karyn Warner, and Kristen Jones. "Beyond the Baby Bump: Subtle Discrimination Against Working Mothers in the Hiring Process." *Journal of Business Psychology* 37 (2022): 1181-98. https://doi.org/10.1007/s10869-022-09790-7.

"Chuck Your Chores and Have Fun." *St. Petersburg Times* (Florida), City Edition, *Changing Times Magazine*, August 6, 1989.

Clark, Candace. *Misery and Company: Sympathy in Everyday Life*. Chicago: University of Chicago Press, 1997.

Cline, Elizabeth. *Overdressed: The Shockingly High Cost of Cheap Fashion*. New York: Portfolio, 2012.

Cohen, Lizabeth. *A Consumers' Republic: The Politics of Mass Consumption in Postwar America*. New York: Alfred A. Knopf, 2003.

Context-Based Research Group. *Coming of Age in the Great Recession: The Grounded Consumer*. Baltimore, 2008.

Cooper, Marianne. *Cut Adrift: Families in Insecure Times*. Berkeley: University of California Press, 2014.

Correll, Shelley J., Stephen Benard, and In Paik. "Getting a Job: Is There a Motherhood Penalty?" *American Journal of Sociology* 112, no. 5 (March 2007): 1297-338. https://www.jstor.org/stable/10.1086/511799.

Csikszentmihalyi, Mikhail, and Eugene Halton. *The Meaning of Things: Domestic Symbols and the Self*. Cambridge: Cambridge University Press, 1981.

Damaske, Sarah. *For the Family? How Class and Gender Shape Women's Work*. New York: Oxford, 2011.

Davis, Clark. *Company Men: White-Collar Life and Corporate Cultures in Los Angeles, 1892–1841*. Baltimore: Johns Hopkins University Press, 2001.

Deevy, Martha, Jialu Liu Streeter, Andrea Hasler, and Annamaria Lusardi. *Financial Resilience in America*. Washington, DC: Global Financial Literacy Excellence Center, 2021. https://gflec.org/research/?item=27354.

Delgado, Richard, and Jean Stefancic. *Critical Race Theory: An Introduction*, 3rd ed. New York: New York University Press, 2017.

Denegri-Knott, Janice, and Elizabeth Parsons. "Disordering Things." *Journal of Consumer Behaviour* 13, no. 2 (2014): 89–98. http://dx.doi.org/10.1002/cb.1473.

DePalma, Lindsay. "The Passion Paradigm: Professional Adherence to and Consequences of the Ideology of 'Do What You Love.'" *Sociological Forum* 36, no. 1 (March 2021): 134–58. https://doi.org/10.1111/socf.12665.

Des Jardins, Julie. *Lillian Gilbreth: Redefining Domesticity*. New York: Routledge, 2021.

"Desktop Disasters: 'Neatness Doctor' Calls on Offices." *Merced Sun-Star*. September 22, 1982, 25.

Dizard, Jan, and Howard Gadlin. *The Minimal Family*. Amherst: University of Massachusetts Press, 1990.

Dreilinger, Danielle. *The Secret History of Home Economics: How Trailblazing Women Harnessed the Power of Home and Changed the World*. New York: W. W. Norton, 2021.

Druckman, Lisa. "Why Are There No Great Women Chefs?" *Gastronomica* 10, no. 1 (2010): 24–31. https://doi.org/10.1525/gfc.2010.10.1.24.

Dudley, Linda Susan. "How Organized Is Your Life?" *The Tribune* [San Diego], April 5, 1984, C-1. https://cdn.ymaws.com/www.napo.net/resource/resmgr/docs/napo_timeline.pdf.

Duffy, Mignon, Amy Armenia, and Clare L. Stacey, eds. *Caring on the Clock: The Complexities and Contradictions of Paid Care Work*. New Brunswick, NJ: Rutgers University Press, 2015.

Duhigg, Charles. "Wealthy, Successful, and Miserable." *New York Times Magazine*, February 24, 2019, 26–27, 60.

Edin, Kathryn J., and H. Luke Shaefer. *$2 a Day: Living on Almost Nothing in America*. Boston: Houghton Mifflin Harcourt, 2015.

Edlund, Bart. "40 Years of the American Home." https://vimeo.com/119621018.

Ehrenreich, Barbara, and Arlie Hochschild, eds. *Global Women: Nannies, Maids, and Sex Workers in the New Economy*. New York: Holt, 2004.

Eisenstein, Anna, and Ilana Gershon. "'Saying No and Staying Flexible Can Coexist': Utilizing Connective Labor to Assert Personal Autonomy as a Nanny During the Pandemic." Paper presented at the Annual Meeting of the American Anthropological Association, Seattle, WA, November 2022.

Elgin, Duane. *Voluntary Simplicity: Toward a Way of Life That Is Outwardly Simple, Inwardly Rich*. New York: Morrow, 1981.

England, Paula. *Comparable Wealth: Theories and Evidence*, 1st ed. New York: Routledge, 1992.

Erikson, Althea, and Ilyssa Meyer. *Economic Security for the Gig Economy*. New York: Etsy, 2016. https://extfiles.etsy.com/advocacy/Etsy_EconomicSecurity_2016.pdf.

Eyerly, Alan. "Organizing the Organizers." *The Argonaut* (Marina del Rey, CA). June 13, 1985, 15.

Ferrari, Joseph, and Catherine Roster. "Delaying Disposing: Examining the Relationship between Procrastination and Clutter across Generations." *Current Psychology* 37 (2018): 426–31. https://doi.org/10.1007/s12144-017-9679-4.

Folbre, Nancy. *The Invisible Heart: Economics and Family Values*. New York: The New Press, 2001.

Formanack, Allison. "Mobile Home on the Range: Manufacturing Ruin and Respect in an American Zone of Abandonment." PhD diss., University of Colorado Boulder, 2018. https://scholar.colorado.edu/concern/graduate_thesis_or_dissertations/m613mx627.

Foster, Roger. "The Therapeutic Spirit of Neoliberalism." *Political Theory* 44, no. 1 (2016): 82–105. https://doi.org/10.1177/0090591715594660.

Fraser, Nancy. *Cannibal Capitalism: How Our System Is Devouring Democracy, Care, and the Planet—and What We Can Do About It*. London: Verso, 2022.

Freedman, David, and Eric Abrahamson. *A Perfect Mess: The Hidden Benefits of Disorder*. Phoenix: Orion, 2013.

Freeman, Carla. *Entrepreneurial Selves: Neoliberal Respectability and the Making of a Caribbean Middle Class*. Durham, NC: Duke University Press, 2014.

Fremstad, Sean. "Vacations for All." Center for Economic and Policy Research, July 1, 2020. https://cepr.net/vacations-for-all/.

Fuller, Bonnie. "At Your Service: Want Your Shelves Lined? Your Ironing Done? Whatever It Is You Don't Want to Do Yourself, These People Will Do It For You." *Los Angeles Times*, October 30, 1979, H4.

Furedi, Frank. *Therapy Culture: Cultivating Vulnerability in an Uncertain Age*. London: Routledge, 2004.

Gallup. *Most Important Problem*. September 27, 2022. https://news.gallup.com/poll/1675/most-important-problem.aspx.

Gardner, Marilyn. "Professional Organizers Help Fight 'Battle of the Bulging Files.'" *Christian Science Monitor*, March 29, 2006, 14.

Gauld, Tom. "Underneath Every Hoarder Is a Normal Person Waiting to Be Dug Out." *New York Times Magazine*, June 19, 2011, 52–53. https://www.nytimes.com/2011/06/19/magazine/exploring-the-landscapes-of-other-peoples-trash.html.

Geertz, Clifford. *Interpretation of Cultures*. New York: Basic Books, 1973.

George, Molly. "Interactions in Expert Service Work: Demonstrating Professionalism in Personal Training." *Journal of Contemporary Ethnography* 37, no. 1 (2008): 108–31. https://doi.org/10.1177/0891241607309.

George, Molly. "Seeking Legitimacy: The Professionalization of Life Coaching." *Sociological Inquiry* 83, no. 2 (2013): 179–208. https://doi.org/10.1111/soin.12003.

George, Rose. *Ninety Percent of Everything: Inside Shipping, the Invisible Industry That Puts Clothes on Your Back, Gas in Your Car, and Food on Your Plate*. New York: Holt, 2013.

Gershon, Ilana. *Down and Out in the New Economy: How People Find (or Don't Find) Work Today*. Chicago: University of Chicago Press, 2017.

"Gil Schwartz." *Wikipedia*. https://en.wikipedia.org/wiki/Gil_Schwartz.

Gilbreth, Frank B., and Ernestine Gilbreth Carey. *Cheaper by the Dozen*. New York: T. Y. Crowell Co., 1948.

Gilman, Charlotte Perkins. *Women and Economics: A Study of the Economic Relation Between Men and Women as a Factor in Social Evolution*. Boston: Small, Maynard & Co., [1898] 1905.

Gladiator GarageWorks. "Almost 1 in 4 Americans Say Their Garage Is Too Cluttered to Fit Their Car." Cision PR Newswire, June 9, 2015. https://www.prnewswire.com/news-releases/almost-1-in-4-americans-say-their-garage-is-too-cluttered-to-fit-their-car-300096246.html.

Glock, Allison. "Back to Basics: Living with 'Voluntary Simplicity.'" *Oprah Magazine*, January 2009. https://www.oprah.com/omagazine/meet-followers-of-the-simple-living-philosophy/all.

Goffman, Erving. "The Moral Career of the Mental Patient." *Psychiatry: Journal for the Study of Interpersonal Processes* 22: 123–42.

Goodwin, Joanne. *Gender and the Politics of Welfare Reform: Mother's Pensions in Chicago, 1911–1929.* Chicago: University of Chicago Press, 1997.

Gordon, Andrea. "Professional Organizers Are Getting Organized." *Toronto Star Ontario*, November 13, 2003, J02.

Gosling, Sam. *Snoop: What Your Stuff Says about You.* Philadelphia and New York: Basic Books, 2009.

Granberry, Mike. "For Hire: An Organization of One." *Los Angeles Times*, September 8, 1982, G1.

Granberry, Mike. "The Nation's Disorganized Flock to S.D. Woman." *Los Angeles Times*, October 28, 1982, SD-C1.

Green, Penelope. "Marie Kondo Wants to Sell You Nice Things. What's Wrong with That?" *New York Times*, November 24, 2019, ST11.

Green, Penelope. "A Tidiness Empire Expands, Neatly." *New York Times*, January 17, 2021, BU9.

Gregg, Melissa. *Work's Intimacy.* Cambridge: Polity Press, 2011.

Gupta, Alisha Haridasani. "Why Some Women Call This Recession a 'Shecession.'" *New York Times*, May 9, 2020. https://www.nytimes.com/2020/05/09/us/unemployment -coronavirus-women.html.

Gussoff, Deborah. *Organizing for Weight Loss: A Slim Little Guide to Getting Thinner.* Livingston, NJ: Woodpecker Press, 2022.

Gusterson, Hugh, and Catherine Besteman, eds. *The Insecure American: How We Got Here and What We Should Do about It.* Berkeley: University of California Press, 2010.

Hackman, Rose. *Emotional Labor: The Invisible Work Shaping Our Lives and How to Claim Our Power.* New York: Flatiron Books, 2023.

Harris, Alexander. "U.S. Self-Storage Industry Statistics." January 17, 2021. SpareFoot, https://www.sparefoot.com/self-storage/news/1432-self-storage-industry-statistics/.

Harris, Kathryn. "Women's Clubs: New Force in the Workplace." *Los Angeles Times*, July 25, 1982, E1.

Hartley, Gemma. *Fed Up: Emotional Labor, Women, and the Way Forward.* New York: HarperOne, 2018.

Hartmann, Susan M. "Prescriptions for Penelope: Literature on Women's Obligations to Returning World War II Veterans." *Women's Studies* 5 (1978): 223–39.

Harvey, David. *A Brief History of Neoliberalism.* Oxford: Oxford University Press, 2005.

Hasdell, Rebecca. *What We Know about Universal Basic Income: A Cross-Synthesis of Reviews.* Stanford, CA: Basic Income Lab, July 2020. https://basicincome.stanford .edu/uploads/Umbrella%20Review%20BI_final.pdf.

Hayden, Dolores. *The Grand Domestic Revolution: A History of Feminist Designs for American Homes, Neighborhoods, and Cities.* Cambridge, MA: MIT Press, 1981.

Hayden, Dolores. *Redesigning the American Dream: Gender, Housing, and Family Life, Revised and Expanded.* New York: W. W. Norton, 2002.

Hayden, Dolores. "What Would a Non-Sexist City Be Like? Speculations on Housing, Urban Design, and Human Work." *Signs* 5, no. 3 (1980): S170–87. https://www.jstor .org/stable/3173814.

Hayes, Sharon. *The Cultural Contradictions of Motherhood.* New Haven, CT: Yale University Press, 1996.

Herman, Ellen. *The Romance of American Psychology: Political Culture in the Age of Experts.* Berkeley: University of California Press, 1995.

Herring, Scott. *Hoarders: Material Deviance in Modern American Culture*. Chicago: University of Chicago Press, 2014.

Hill, Steven. *New Economy, New Social Contract*. Washington, DC: New America, 2015. https://static.newamerica.org/attachments/4395-new-economy-new-social-contract/New%20Economy,%20Social%20Contract_UpdatedFinal.34c973248e6946d0af17116fbd6bb79e.pdf.

Hill, Susan. "The Waiting Room: Remaking Adulthood Among America's Underemployed." PhD diss., University of Wisconsin, Milwaukee, 2019.

Hillbrecht, Margo, and Donna Lero. "Self-Employment and Family Life: Negotiating Work-Life Balance When You're 'Always On.'" *Community, Work and Family* 17, no. 1 (2014): 20–42. https://doi.org/10.1080/13668803.2013.862214.

Hochschild, Arlie. *The Commercialization of Intimate Life: Notes from Home and Work*. Berkeley: University of California Press, 2003.

Hochschild, Arlie. *The Managed Heart: Commercialization of Human Feeling*. Berkeley: University of California Press, 1983.

Hochschild, Arlie. *The Outsourced Self: Intimate Life in Market Times*. New York: Metropolitan, 2012.

Hochschild, Arlie. *The Time Bind: When Work Becomes Home and Home Becomes Work*. New York: Metropolitan Books, 1997.

Hochschild, Arlie, and Anne Machung. *The Second Shift: Working Families and the Revolution at Home*. New York: Viking, 1989.

Holohan, Meghan. "Not Your Mother's Motherhood: Moms by The Numbers, Through the Decades." *Today*, May 11, 2014. https://www.today.com/parents/not-your-mothers-motherhood-moms-numbers-through-decades-2D79646659.

Hondagneu-Sotelo, Pierrette. *Domestica: Immigrant Workers Cleaning and Caring in the Shadow of Affluence*. Berkeley: University of California Press, 2007.

Hornstein, Jeffrey. "The Rise of the Realtor: Professionalism, Gender, and Middle-Class Identity, 1908–1950." In *The Middling Sorts: Explorations in the History of the American Middle Class*, ed. Burton Bledstein and Robert Johnston, 217–33. New York: Routledge, 2001.

Horowitz, Juliana Menasce. "More Than Half of Americans in Their 40s Are 'Sandwiched' Between an Aging Parent and Their Own Children." Pew Research Center, April 8, 2022. https://www.pewresearch.org/fact-tank/2022/04/08/more-than-half-of-americans-in-their-40s-are-sandwiched-between-an-aging-parent-and-their-own-children/.

Horowitz, Sara. "The Freelance Surge Is the Industrial Revolution of Our Time." *The Atlantic*, September 1, 2011.

Howard, Jennifer. *Clutter: An Untidy History*. Cleveland: Belt Publishing, 2020.

Hudgens, Dallas. "In the Business of Cleaning Up Clutter." *Washington Post*, April 24, 1997, F10. https://www.napo.net/page/NAPOHistory; https://www.napo.net/page/Certification.

Humphrey, Kim. *Excess: Anti-Consumerism in the West*. Malden, MA: Polity Press, 2010.

Hurley, Murtha. "Three Freedoms—and Plenty of Closets." *Los Angeles Times*, November 4, 1951, J4.

Hurst, Eric, and Benjamin Wild Pugsley. "What Do Small Businesses Do?" Brookings Papers on Economic Activity, Economic Studies Program, The Brookings Institution 43, no. 2 (Fall 2011): 73–142. https://www.nber.org/papers/w17041.

Hyman, Louis. *Temp: How American Work, American Business, and the American Dream Became Temporary*. New York: Viking, 2018.

Illouz, Eva. *Cold Intimacies: The Making of Emotional Capitalism*. Cambridge: Polity Press, 2007.

Illouz, Eva. *Saving the Modern Soul: Therapy, Emotions, and the Culture of Self-Help*. Berkeley: University of California, 2008.

International OCD Federation. "The Role of Hoarding Taskforces." https://hoarding.iocdf.org/for-community-responders/working-with-hoarding-disorder-in-the-community/the-role-of-hoarding-task-forces/.

Isenstadt, Sandy. *The Modern American House: Spaciousness and Middle-Class Identity*. Cambridge, UK: Cambridge University Press, 2006.

Ishizuka, Patrick. "Social Class, Gender, and Contemporary Parenting Standards in the United States: Evidence from a National Survey Experiment." *Social Forces* 98, no. 1 (September 2019): 31–58. https://doi-org.lib-proxy.fullerton.edu/10.1093/sf/soy107.

Judge, Timothy A., Ronald F. Piccolo, Nathan P. Podsakoff, John C. Shaw, and Bruce L. Rich. "The Relationship between Pay and Job Satisfaction: A Meta-Analysis of the Literature." *Journal of Vocational Behavior* 77 (2010): 157–67. https://doi.org/10.1016/j.jvb.2010.04.002.

Jurik, Nancy. "Getting Away and Getting By: The Experiences of Self-Employed Homemakers." *Work and Occupations* 25, no. 1 (February 1998): 7–35.

Kalleberg, Arne. *Good Jobs, Bad Jobs: The Rise of Polarized and Precarious Employment Systems in the United States, 1970s to 2000s*. New York: Russell Sage Foundation, 2013.

Kalleberg, Arne. "Precarious Work, Insecure Workers: Employment Relations in Transition." *American Sociological Review* 74, no. 1 (2009): 1–22. https://doi.org/10.1177/000312240907400101.

Kang, Miliann. *The Managed Hand: Race, Gender, and the Body in Beauty Service Work*. Berkeley: University of California Press, 2010.

Kanter, Rosabeth Moss. *Men and Women of the Corporation*. New York: Basic Books, 1993 [1977].

Kelly, Katherine Feo. "Organizing the American Domestic Interior, 1978–2010." PhD diss., University of Texas at Austin, 2013.

Killham, Nina. "Clutter Busters: When You Can't Even Find the Couch It May Be Time to Call in the Pros." *Washington Post*, May 17, 1990, Home section, T20.

Kilroy-Marac, Katie. "A Magical Reorientation of the Modern: Professional Organizers and Thingly Care in Contemporary North America." *Cultural Anthropology* 31, no. 3 (2016): 439–58. https://doi.org/10.14506/ca31.3.09.

Kilroy-Marac, Katie. "An Order of Distinction (or How to Tell a Collection from a Hoard)." *Journal of Material Culture* 23, no. 1 (2017): 20–38. https://doi.org/10.1177/1359183517729428.

Kim, Timothy. "The Dynamex Decision: California Supreme Court Restricts Use of Independent Contractors." *Labor and Employment Law Blog*, May 1, 2018. https://www.laboremploymentlawblog.com/2018/05/articles/class-actions/dynamex-decision-independent-contractors/.

Kleiman, Dana. "They'll Help Unscramble Your Life." *New York Times*, February 1, 1978, C13.

Kochhar, Rakesh. "The Self-Employed Are Back at Work in Pre-Covid-19 Numbers." Pew Research Center. https://www.pewresearch.org/fact-tank/2021/11/03/the-self-employed-are-back-at-work-in-pre-covid-19-numbers-but-their-businesses-have-smaller-payrolls/#:~:text=Among%20men%2C%20self%2Demployment%20dropped,and%20marking%20a%20full%20recovery.

Koncius, Jura. "Clutter Wars." *The Washington Post Magazine*, June 16, 2021.

Koncius, Jura. "Marie Kondo's Life Is Messier Now, and She's Fine with It." *Washington Post*, January 26, 2023.

Kondo, Marie. *The Life-Changing Magic of Tidying Up*. Berkeley, CA: Ten Speed Press, 2014.

Kron, Joan. "The Second Most Satisfying Thing in the World: Getting Organized." *New York Magazine*, September 29, 1975, 59–65.

Kruse, Michael. "Wishful Shopping." *Tampa Bay Times*, December 6, 2013.

Kwolek-Folland, Angel. *Engendering Business: Men and Women in the Corporate Office, 1870–1930*. Baltimore: Johns Hopkins University Press, 1998.

Kwolek-Folland, Angel. "Gender, the Service Sector, and U.S. Business History." *Business History Review* 81, no. 3 (2007): 429–50. https://www.jstor.org/stable/25097376.

Laaser, Knut, and Jan Ch Karlsson. "Towards a Sociology of Meaningful Work." *Work, Employment and Society* 36, no. 5 (2022): 798–815. https://doi.org/10.1177/09500170211105599.

Lane, Carrie. *A Company of One: Insecurity, Independence, and the New World of White-Collar Unemployment*. Ithaca, NY: Cornell University Press, 2011.

Lark, Regina. *Before the Big O: Professional Organizers Talk about Life Before Organizing*. Oxnard: Purple Distinctions, 2014.

Lark, Regina, and Judith Kolberg. *Emotional Labor: Why a Woman's Work Is Never Done*. Independently published, 2021.

Lasch, Christopher. *The Culture of Narcissism: American Life in the Age of Diminishing Expectations*. New York: Warmer Books, 1979.

Lawrence, Beverly Hall. "Conquering Clutter." *Newsday* (Long Island), January 11, 1990.

Lees-Maffei, Grace. "Introduction: Professionalization as a Focus in Interior Design History." *Journal of Design History* 21, no. 1 (March 20, 2008): 1–18. https://www.jstor.org/stable/25228563.

Leidner, Robin. *Fast Food, Fast Talk: Service Work and the Routinization of Everyday Life*. Berkeley: University of California Press, 1993.

Leonard, Annie. *The Story of Stuff*. New York: Free Press, 2010.

Lepselter, Susan. "The Disorder of Things: Hoarding Narratives in Popular Media." *Anthropological Quarterly* 84, no. 4 (2011): 919–47. https://doi.org/10.1353/anq.2011.0053.

Lett, Alexsandra. "Out with the Old, In with the New." *The Daily Record* (Dunn, NC), January 5, 2018, 10A.

Lipsky, Laura van Dernoot. *The Age of Overwhelm: Strategies for the Long Haul*. Oakland, CA: Berrett-Kohler, 2018.

Littler, Jo. "Good Housekeeping: Green Products and Consumer Activism." In *Commodity Activism: Cultural Resistance in Neoliberal Times*, ed. Roopali Mukherjee and Sarah Banet-Weiser, 76–92. New York: New York University Press, 2012.

Lodziak, Conrad. "On Explaining Consumption." *Capital and Class* 72 (2000): 111–33. https://doi.org/10.1177/030981680007200106.

Lopez, Steven. "Emotional Labor and Organized Emotional Care." *Work and Occupations* 33, no. 2 (2006): 133–60. https://doi.org/10.1177/0730888405284567.

Lott, James Jr. "NAPO Members & Black Girls Who Organize Founder Dalys Macon." *The Super Organizer Show*, podcast audio, September 13, 2021. https://www.youtube.com/watch?v=8P3C-VM53dc.

Lott, James Jr. "The Super Organizer Man in the PO Industry: What's It Like for One Man." *The SOS Show with James Lott Jr.*, October 17, 2019. https://www.youtube.com/watch?v=ZvlXUDnmL20.

Lovejoy, Meg, and Pamela Stone. "Opting Back In: The Influence of Time at Home on Professional Women's Career Redirection after Opting Out." *Gender, Work and Organization* 19, no. 6 (November 2012): 635. https://doi.org/10.1111/j.1468-0432.2010.00550.x.

Lynch, Caitrin. *Retirement on the Line: Age, Work, and Value in an American Factory*. Ithaca, NY: ILR Press, 2012.

Macdonald, Cameron, and Carmen Sirianni. "The Service Society and the Changing Experience of Work." In *Working in the Service Society*, ed. Cameron Macdonald and Carmen Sirianni, 1–28. Philadelphia: Temple University Press, 1996.

Macon, Dalys (@blackgirlswhoorganize). "Hi 👋, I am Dalys and I am a BLACK GIRL WHO ORGANIZES. . . ." Instagram, December 24, 2019. https://www.instagram.com/p/B6dN8Xop-_r/.

Macon, Dalys. "Representation in the Organizing Industry with Dalys Macon." Interview with Melissa Klug, *Pro Organizer Studio*, podcast audio, February 21, 2021. https://www.youtube.com/watch?v=4yPFMjabl8c.

Madison, Mary. "Less Cluttered Homes Are Seen When Men Return from the War." *New York Times*, October 7, 1944, 16.

Madsen, Ole Jacob. *The Therapeutic Turn: How Psychology Altered Western Culture*. London: Routledge, 2014.

Maguire, Karen, and John Winters. "Satisfaction from Self-Employment: Do Men or Women Benefit More from Being Their Own Boss?" *Eastern Economic Journal* 46 (2020): 576–602. https://doi.org/10.1057/s41302-020-00169-1.

Malesic, Jonathan. *The End of Burnout: Why Work Drains Us and How to Build Better Lives*. Berkeley: University of California Press, 2022.

Manners, Marian. "Clutter Deplored: Convenience Is Key to Functional Culinary Workshop." *Los Angeles Times*, January 26, 1949, B1.

Marks, Gene. "Black-Owned Firms Are Twice as Likely to Be Rejected for Loans. Is This Discrimination?" *The Guardian*, January 16, 2020. https://www.theguardian.com/business/2020/jan/16/black-owned-firms-are-twice-as-likely-to-be-rejected-for-loans-is-this-discrimination.

Marx, Patricia. "A Guide to Getting Rid of Almost Everything." *The New Yorker*, February 28, 2022.

McCarthy, Anna. "Reality Television: A Neoliberal Theater of Suffering." *Social Text* 25, no. 4 (Winter 2007): 17–42. https://doi.org/10.1215/01642472-2007-010.

McCubbin, Tracy. *Making Space, Clutter Free*. Naperville, IL: Sourcebooks, 2019.

McGee, Micki. *Self-Help, Inc.* Oxford: Oxford University Press, 2005.

McNally, Katherine. "Book Review: Cannibal Capitalism." *Exertions* (2023). https://saw.americananthro.org/pub/541lv317/release/1.

Meyerowitz, Joanne, ed. *Not June Cleaver: Women and Gender in Postwar America, 1945–1960*. Philadelphia: Temple University Press, 1994.

Miller, Claire Cain. "The Pandemic Created a Child-Care Crisis. Mothers Bore the Burden." *New York Times*, May 17, 2021.

Miller, Daniel. *The Comfort of Things*. Cambridge: Polity, 2008.

Miller, Daniel. *Stuff*. Cambridge: Polity, 2009.

Miller, Laura. "Someday Never Comes: The Death-Embracing Magic of Marie Kondo." *Slate*, January 23, 2016. https://slate.com/culture/2016/01/marie-kondos-life-changing-magic-and-death.html.

Minter, Adam. *Secondhand: Travels in the New Global Garage Sale*. New York: Bloomsbury, 2019.

Modern Family. 2015. Season 7, episode 8, "Clean Out Your Junk Drawer." Directed by Steven Levitan. Aired December 2, 2015, on ABC.

Modern Family. 2016. Season 7, episode 12, "Clean for a Day." Directed by Beth McCarthy-Miller. Aired February 10, 2016, on ABC.

Moen, Phyllis, and Patricia Roehling. *The Career Mystique: Cracks in the American Dream*. Boulder: Rowman & Littlefield, 2005.

Moreton, Bethany. "The Future of Work: The Rise and Fall of the Job." *Pacific Standard*, October 22, 2015.

Morgenstern, Julie. *Organizing from the Inside Out*, 2nd ed. New York: Henry Holt & Company, 2004.

Morgenstern, Julie. *SHED Your Stuff, Change Your Life*. New York: Fireside, 2008.

Morini, Cristina. "The Feminization of Labor in Cognitive Capitalism." *Feminist Review*, no. 87 (2007): 40–59. https://www.jstor.org/stable/30140799.

NAPO. *2019 Public Survey of Residential Organizing Attitudes*. March 2019. https://higherlogicdownload.s3.amazonaws.com/PONETWORK/11e1a1de-5555-4727-bf88-f3d908457b28/UploadedImages/Surveys/March_2019_Public_Survey_Final.pdf.

NAPO. *Membership Survey Results: February 2019*. https://higherlogicdownload.s3.amazonaws.com/PONETWORK/11e1a1de-5555-4727-bf88-f3d908457b28/UploadedImages/Surveys/Feb_2019_Membership_Survey_Final.pdf.

National Women's Business Council. 2020 *National Women in Business Council Annual Report*. December 21, 2020. https://www.nwbc.gov/2020/12/21/2020-annual-report/.

Nelsen, Bonalyn, and Stephen Barley. "For Love or Money? Commodification and the Construction of an Occupational Mandate." *Administrative Science Quarterly* 42 (1997): 619–53. https://doi.org/10.2307/2393652.

Nelson, Jennifer, and Steve Vallas. "Race and Inequality at Work: An Occupational Perspective." *Sociology Compass* 15, no. 10 (2021). https://doi.org/10.1111/soc4.12926.

Nelson, Michelle R., Mark A. Rademacher, and Hye-Jin Paek. "Downshifting Consumer = Upshifting Citizen? An Examination of a Local Freecycle Community." *Annals of the American Academy of Political and Social Science* 611, no. 1 (May 2007): 141–56. https://doi.org/10.1177/000271620629872.

Nemy, Enid. "It's Her Business to Take the Disturbing Disarray Out of People's Lives." *New York Times*, September 2, 1974.

Newell, Sasha. "The Matter of the Unfetish: Hoarding and the Spirit of Possessions." *HAU: Journal of Ethnographic Theory* 4, no. 3 (2014): 185–213. https://doi.org/10.14318/hau4.3.013.

Noble, Dawn. *How to Start a Home-Based Professional Organizing Business*. Guilford, CT: Globe Pequot, 2011.

Nusca, Andrew. "Gil Schwartz, a.k.a. Stanley Bing, 1951–2020." *Fortune*, May 30, 2020. https://www.usatoday.com/story/entertainment/celebrities/2020/05/03/gil-schwartz-humorist-under-pen-name-stanley-bing-died-68/3075462001/.

O'Brien, Ellen. "Making a Specialty of Order: Yes, There Are Professionals to Help You Organize Your Clutter. They Held a Convention in Cherry Hill Last Week." *The Philadelphia Enquirer*, May 7, 1999 (Features Magazine, Home & Design), E01.

Ochs, Elinor, and Tamar Kremer-Sadlik. *Fast-Forward Family: Home, Work, and Relationships in Middle-Class America*. Berkeley: University of California Press, 2013.

O'Mahony, Siobhan. "Boundary Work." In *Sociology of Work: An Encyclopedia*, ed. Vicki Smith, vol. 1, 34–35. Thousand Oaks, CA: SAGE Publications, 2013. https://doi.org/10.4135/9781452276199.n15.

Online Etymology Dictionary. "Clutter." https://www.etymonline.com/word/clutter.

"Organization Is in Their Blood." *St. Louis Post-Dispatch*, Business section, January 8, 1990, 13.

Osnowitz, Debra. *Freelancing Expertise: Contract Professionals in the New Economy*. Ithaca, NY: Cornell University Press, 2005.

Ouellette, Laurie. "Take Responsibility for Yourself: Judge Judy and the Neoliberal Citizen." In *Reality TV: Remaking TV Culture*, ed. Laurie Ouellette and Susan Murray, 231–50. New York: NYU Press, 2004.

Ouelette, Laurie, and James Hay. *Better Living through Reality TV: Television and Post-Welfare Citizenship*. Hoboken, NJ: Wiley-Blackwell, 2008.

Pagis, Michael. "Inhabiting the Self-Work Romantic Utopia: Positive Psychology, Life Coaching, and the Challenge of Self-Fulfillment at Work." *Work and Occupations* 48, no. 1 (2021): 40–69. https://doi.org/10.1177/0730888420911683.

Pardue, Luke. "New Business Creation during COVID-19: A Survey of Pandemic Entrepreneurs." *Gusto Company News*, May 13, 2021. https://gusto.com/company-news/new-business-creation-during-covid-19-a-survey-of-pandemic-entrepreneurs.

Paxton, Matt. *The Secret Lives of Hoarders*. New York: Perigee, 2011.

Pedersen, Sara. *Born to Organize: Everything You Need to Know about How to Become a Professional Organizer*. Time to Organize, 2008.

Pencavel, John. "The Productivity of Working Hours." Institute for the Study of Labor Discussion Paper No. 8129 (2014). http://ftp.iza.org/dp8129.pdf.

Perlow, Leslie. *Sleeping with Your Smartphone: How to Break the 24/7 Habit and Change the Way You Work*. Boston: Harvard Business Review Press, 2012.

Petersen, Anne Helen. "I Don't Feel Like Buying Stuff Anymore." *Buzzfeed News*, May 18, 2020. https://www.buzzfeednews.com/article/annehelenpetersen/recession-unemployment-covid-19-economy-consumer-spending.

Pew Research Center. *In a Growing Share of U.S. Marriages, Husbands and Wives Earn About the Same*. April 2023. https://www.pewresearch.org/social-trends/2023/04/13/in-a-growing-share-of-u-s-marriages-husbands-and-wives-earn-about-the-same/.

Pew Research Center. *Modern Parenthood*. March 13, 2014. https://www.pewsocialtrends.org/2013/03/14/modern-parenthood-roles-of-moms-and-dads-converge-as-they-balance-work-and-family/.

Pew Research Center. *On Pay Gap, Millennial Women Near Parity–For Now*. December 11, 2013, 38–46. https://www.pewsocialtrends.org/2013/12/11/chapter-3-what-men-women-value-in-a-job/.

Pinsker, Joe. "Why Are American Homes So Big?" *The Atlantic*, September 12, 2019. https://www.theatlantic.com/family/archive/2019/09/american-houses-big/597811/.

Pither, Marjorie S. "Why Some Women Hate Housekeeping: Count Your Homemaking Skills." *Los Angeles Times*, December 2, 1962, TW28.

Pofeldt, Elaine. "Finding Funding: Here Are Proven Ways to Finance Your Small Business, with Advice from 6 Female Founders." *Millie.Us* (Fall 2021): 13–19.

Porter, Tanisha, Janine Sarna-Jones, and Barbara Polk. "Incorporating an Anti-Racist Mindset and Practices to Build Your 21st-Century Business." General Session held at the NAPO 2020 Summit. https://www.napo.net/page/Anti-racistMindsetandPracticestoBuildyour21stCenturyBusiness?&hhsearchterms=%22diversity%22.

Puerto, Susanna, Drew Gardiner, Jonas Bausch, Mohammed Danish, Eesha Moitra, and Lena Xinyu Yan. *Youth and COVID-19: Impacts on Jobs, Education, Rights and Mental Well-Being: Survey Report 2020*. Geneva, Switzerland: International Labour

Organization, 2020. https://www.ilo.org/wcmsp5/groups/public/---ed_emp/documents/publication/wcms_753026.pdf.

Pugh, Allison. "Emotions and the Systematization of Connective Labor." *Theory, Culture & Society* 39, no. 5 (2021): 23–42. https://doi.org/10.1177/02632764211049475.

Pugh, Allison. *The Tumbleweed Society: Working and Caring in an Age of Insecurity*. Oxford: Oxford University Press, 2015.

Ramey, Valerie. "Time Spent in Home Production in the 20th Century: New Estimates from Old Data." Working Paper 13985, National Bureau of Economic Research Working Paper Series, May 2008. https://www.nber.org/system/files/working_papers/w13985/w13985.pdf.

Ravenelle, Alexandra J., and Ken Cai Kowalski. "'It's Not Like Chasing Chanel': Spending Time, Investing in the Self, and Pandemic Epiphanies." *Work and Occupations* 50, no. 2 (2022): 284–309. https://doi.org/10.1177/07308884221125246.

Ray, Victor. "Why So Many Organizations Stay White." *Harvard Business Review*, November 19, 2019. https://hbr.org/2019/11/why-so-many-organizations-stay-white.

"Rid the House of 'Clutter' to Cheer It: Have a Destruction Day, Throw Out all Furniture, Pictures and Odds and Ends That Are Unnecessary, and You Will Make Home More Attractive." *New York Times*, August 24, 1913, X7.

Rivers, Dawn. "Iteration of or Escape from Neoliberalism: Self-Employment in the Southeastern U.S." MA thesis, University of North Carolina at Chapel Hill, 2018. https://doi.org/10.17615/1zdm-5214.

Rivers, Dawn. "'Meat and Three': Business Ownership as an Alternative Form of Work." *Anthropology of Work Review* 44, no. 1 (2022): 5–14.

Robertson, Craig. *The Filing Cabinet: A Vertical History of Information*. Minneapolis: University of Minnesota Press, 2021.

Robsjohn-Gibbings, T. H. "Revival: Clutter Returns." *New York Times*, February 24, 1957, 241.

Rogers, Jackie Krasas. *Temps: The Many Faces of the Changing Workforce*. Ithaca, NY: ILR Press, 2000.

Rongjun, Ma, Henrik Lassila, Leysan Nurgalieva, and Janne Lindqvist. "When Browsing Gets Cluttered: Exploring and Modeling Interactions of Browsing Clutter, Browsing Habits, and Coping." *Proceedings of the 2023 CHI Conference on Human Factors in Computing Systems*, Association for Computing Machinery, New York, Article 861 (2023): 1–29. https://doi.org/10.1145/3544548.3580690.

Rose, Matthew. "Real Simple's High-Concept Act May Face a Difficult Reception." *Wall Street Journal*, March 13, 2000, B14.

Rose, Nikolas. *Governing the Soul: The Shaping of the Private Self*. New York: Routledge, 1990.

Rose, Todd, and Ogi Ogas. *Dark Horse: Achieving Success through the Pursuit of Fulfillment*. New York: HarperOne, 2008.

Ross, Andrew. *Nice Work If You Can Get It: Life and Labor in Precarious Times*. Boulder: Rowman & Littlefield, 2004.

Roster, Catherine. "Letting Go: The Process and Meaning of Dispossession in the Lives of Consumers." *Advances in Consumer Research* 28 (2001): 425–30.

Roswell, Jonathan, and Jessica Harlan. *2019 Gig Economy and Self-Employment Report*. Mountain View, CA: Intuit, Inc., 2020.

Rowan, May. "'Clutter? What Clutter' Asks Lighthearted Housekeeper." *Los Angeles Times*, March 24, 1958, A7.

Rudman, Laurie. "Self-Promotion as a Risk Factor for Women: The Costs and Benefits of Counterstereotypical Impression Management." *Journal of Personality and Social Psychology* 74, no. 3 (1998): 629–45. https://doi.org/10.1037/0022-3514.74.3.629.

Salwen, Kevin, and Hannah Salwen. *The Power of Half: One Family's Decision to Stop Taking and Start Giving Back*. Boston: Houghton Mifflin Harcourt, 2010.

Sandlin, Jennifer A., and Jason James Wallin. "Decluttering the Pandemic: Marie Kondo, Minimalism, and the 'Joy' of Waste." *Cultural Studies ↔ Critical Methodologies* 22, no. 1 (2022): 96–102. https://doi.org/10.1177/15327086211049703.

Saxbe, Darby, and Rena Repetti. "'No Place Like Home': Home Tours Correlate with Daily Patterns of Mood and Cortisol." *Personality and Social Psychology Bulletin* 36, no. 1 (January 2010): 71–81. https://doi.org/10.1177/0146167209352864.

Schaeffer, Katherine. "Working Moms in the U.S. Have Faced Challenges on Multiple Fronts during the Pandemic." Pew Research Center, May 6, 2022. https://www.pewresearch.org/short-reads/2022/05/06/working-moms-in-the-u-s-have-faced-challenges-on-multiple-fronts-during-the-pandemic/.

Schaub, Eve. *The Year of No Clutter: A Memoir*. Naperville, IL: Sourcebooks, 2017.

Schor, Juliet. *The Overspent American: Why We Want What We Don't Need*. New York: Harper Perennial, 1999.

Schor, Juliet. *The Overworked American: The Unexpected Decline of Leisure*. New York: Basic Books, 1991.

Schor, Juliet. *True Wealth: How and Why Millions of Americans are Creating a Time-Rich, Ecologically Light, Small-Scale, High-Satisfaction Economy*. New York: Penguin, 2011.

Schulte, Brigid. *Overwhelmed: Work, Love, and Play When No One Has the Time*. New York: Bloomsbury Publishing, 2014.

Schwartz, Barry. *Why We Work*. New York: TED Books, 2015.

Scott, James. *Domination and the Arts of Resistance: Hidden Transcripts*. New Haven, CT: Yale University Press, 1985.

Scott, James. *Weapons of the Weak: Everyday Forms of Peasant Resistance*. New Haven, CT: Yale University Press, 1980.

Seim, Josh. "Connective Labor and Street-Level Bureaucracy." Paper presented at the Annual Meeting of the American Anthropological Association, Seattle, WA, November 2022.

Self-Storage Industry Statistics (2022). May 6, 2022. https://www.neighbor.com/storage-blog/self-storage-industry-statistics/.

Semuels, Alann. "We Are All Accumulating Mountains of Things." *The Atlantic*, August 21, 2018.

Sharone, Ofer. *Flawed System/Flawed Self: Job Searching and Unemployment Experiences*. Chicago: University of Chicago Press, 2013.

Shearer, Clea, and Joanna Teplin. *The Home Edit: A Guide to Organizing and Realizing Your House Goals*. New York: Clarkson Potter, 2019.

Sheehan, Patrick. "The Paradox of Self-Help Expertise: How Unemployed Workers Become Professional Career Coaches." *American Journal of Sociology* 127, no. 4 (January 2022): 1151–82. https://doi.org/10.1086/718471.

Shell, Ellen Ruppell. *Cheap: The High Cost of Discount Culture*. New York: Penguin Press, 2009.

Sherman, Rachel. "Caring or Catering? Emotions, Autonomy, and Subordination in Lifestyle Work." In *Caring on the Clock: The Complexities and Contradictions of Paid Care Work*, ed. Mignon Duffy, Amy Armenia, and Clare L. Stacey, 165–78. New Brunswick, NJ: Rutgers University Press, 2015.

Sherman, Rachel. "The Production of Distinctions: Class, Gender, and Taste Work in the Lifestyle Management Industry." *Qualitative Sociology* 34 (2011): 201–19.

Sherman, Rachel. "'Time Is Our Commodity': Gender and the Struggle for Occupational Legitimacy among Personal Concierges." *Work & Occupations* 37, no. 1 (2010): 81–114. https://doi.org/10.1177/0730888409354270.

Sherman, Rachel. *Uneasy Street: The Anxieties of Affluence*. Princeton, NJ: Princeton University Press, 2017.

Shi, David. *The Simple Life: Plain Living and High Thinking in American Culture*. New York: Oxford University Press, 1985.

"Simplicity vs. Clutter." *Los Angeles Times*, August 3, 1952, H13.

Skocpol, Theda. *Protecting Soldiers and Mothers: The Political Origins of Social Policy in the United States*. Cambridge, MA: Belknap, 1995.

Smaller, Barbara. "It's an Entire Web Site of Things You Can Buy to Consume Less." Cartoon, *The New Yorker*, November 15, 2010.

Solórzano, Daniel, Miguel Ceja, and Tara Yosso. "Critical Race Theory, Racial Microaggressions, and Campus Racial Climate: The Experiences of African American College Students." *Journal of Negro Education* 69, no. 1–2 (Winter/Spring 2000): 60–73.

Soman, Shirley Camper. "The Paper Chase: The Proliferation of Paper Has Propagated a New Set of Problems. But There's Help for Those Drowning in a Sea of Paperwork." *Sun Sentinel* (Fort Lauderdale), May 4, 1988, 3E.

Stack, Carol. *All Our Kin: Strategies for Survival in a Black Community*. New York: Harper & Row, 1975.

Standing, Guy. *The Precariat: The New Dangerous Class*. London: Bloomsbury Academic, 2011.

Standing, Guy. "Tertiary Time: The Precariat's Dilemma." *Public Culture* 25, no. 1 (2013): 5–23. https://doi.org/10.1215/08992363-1890432.

State of California Department of Industrial Relations. "Independent Contractor versus Employee." https://www.dir.ca.gov/dlse/FAQ_IndependentContractor.htm.

Steketee, Gail, and Randy Frost. *Stuff: Compulsive Hoarding and the Meaning of Things*. Boston: Mariner Books, 2011.

Stropoli, Rebecca. "Why U.S. Unemployment Is Even Worse Than the Official Numbers Say." *Chicago Booth Review*, May 13, 2020. https://www.chicagobooth.edu/review/why-us-unemployment-even-worse-official-numbers-say.

"Stuffbusters: Suffering from Severe Environmental Disorder? Professional Organizers Are Ready to Help Clear Your Clutter." *Portland Press Herald* (Maine), July 2, 2000, 1g.

Taylor, Candacy. *Counter Culture: The American Coffee Shop*. Ithaca, NY: ILR Press, 2009.

Taylor, Frederick Winslow. *The Principles of Scientific Management*. New York: Harper & Brothers, 1911.

Ted Lasso. 2021. Season 2, episode 7, "Headspace." Directed by Matt Lipsey. Aired September 3, 2021, on Apple TV.

"Ten Clutter Correctives." *Los Angeles Times*, March 24, 1988, 5.

Tiani, Jackie. *Organizing for a Living: How to Build a Profitable Career as a Professional Organizer*. Aspiration Books, 2008.

Tidying Up with Marie Kondo. 2019. Season 1, episode 4, "Sparking Joy After a Loss." Directed by Jade Sandberg Wallis. Aired January 1, 2019, on Netflix.

Tierney, John. "Do You Suffer from Decision Fatigue?" *New York Times,* August 17, 2011. https://www.nytimes.com/2011/08/21/magazine/do-you-suffer-from-decision-fatigue.html.

Tolin, David, Randy Frost, and Gail Steketee. *Buried in Treasures: Help for Compulsive Acquiring, Saving, and Hoarding.* Oxford: Oxford University Press, 2014.

Underwood, Karen. "The Magic Touch: Professional Organizer Helps You Make the Best Use of Your Space." *High Point Enterprise* (NC), Lifestyle section, November 24, 2008.

US Small Business Administration. "Paycheck Protection Program." https://www.sba.gov/funding-programs/loans/covid-19-relief-options/paycheck-protection-program.

Vallas, Steve, and Emily Cummins. "Personal Branding and Identity Norms in the Popular Business Press: Enterprise Culture in an Age of Precarity." *Organization Studies* 36, no. 3 (2015): 308–10.

Vanderkam, Laura. "Core Competency Mom Part II: Life, Uncluttered." *Huffington Post*, May 29, 2008. https://www.huffpost.com/entry/core-competency-mom-part_n_104001.

Walker, Rob. "Exclusivity for All." *New York Times Magazine*, October 4, 2009.

"Wallace and Darwin: A Pact for Evolution." OpenMind BBVA, July 1, 2015. https://www.bbvaopenmind.com/en/science/leading-figures/wallace-and-darwin-a-pact-for-evolution/.

Ward, Sarah, and Laura King. "Work and the Good Life: How Work Contributes to Meaning in Life." *Research in Organizational Behavior* 37 (2017): 59–82. https://doi.org/10.1016/j.riob.2017.10.001.

Warren, Elizabeth, and Amelia Warren Tyagi. *The Two-Income Trap: Why Middle-Class Mothers and Fathers Are Going Broke.* New York: Basic Books, 2003.

Watkins-Hayes, Celeste. "Race-ing the Bootstrap Climb: Black and Latino Bureaucrats in Post-Reform Welfare Offices." *Social Problems* 56, no. 2 (2009): 285–310. https://doi.org/10.1525/sp.2009.56.2.285.

Weber, Brenda R. *Makeover TV: Selfhood, Citizenship, and Celebrity.* Durham, NC: Duke University Press, 2009.

Weeks, Kathi. *The Problem with Work: Feminism, Marxism, Antiwork Politics, and Postwork Imaginaries.* Durham, NC: Duke University Press, 2011.

White, Dana K. "Clutter Threshold: How Much Stuff Can I Handle?" *A Slob Comes Clean.* Podcast audio, February 11, 2016. https://www.aslobcomesclean.com/2016/02/083-clutter-threshold-how-much-stuff-can-i-handle-podcast/.

White, Jean M. "Sinking under the Clutter? The Organizer Can Get You Out of It." *Washington Post*, February 22, 1978, B1.

Whyte, William H. *The Organization Man.* New York: Simon & Schuster, 1956.

Wielenga, Dave. "Organizer Gets Your Act Together." *Orlando Sentinel*, September 7, 1988, E3.

Wiles, Will. "Unhappy? Clean House." *New York Times*, March 13, 2013, 10.

Wilkinson, Alec. "Let's Get Small: The Rise of the Tiny-House Movement." *The New Yorker*, July 25, 2011, 28–34.

Williams, Christine. *Still a Man's World: Men Who Do "Women's Work."* Berkeley: University of California Press, 1995.

Wilson, Julie Ann, and Emily Chivers Yochim. "Mothering through Precarity: Becoming Mamapreneurial." *Cultural Studies* 29, nos. 5–6 (2015): 669–86. https://doi.org/10.1080/09502386.2015.1017139.

Wingfield, Adia Harvey. "Racializing the Glass Escalator: Reconsidering Men's Experiences with Women's Work." *Gender & Society* 23, no. 1 (2009): 5–26.

Wingfield, Adai Harvey. *Flatlining: Race, Work, and Health Care in the New Economy.* Berkeley: University of California Press, 2019.

Wirtschafter, Valerie. "How George Floyd Changed the Online Conversation around

BLM." *Tech Stream*, June 17, 2021. https://www.brookings.edu/techstream/how
-george-floyd-changed-the-online-conversation-around-black-lives-matter/.

Woloson, Wendy. *Crap: A History of Cheap Stuff in America*. Chicago: University of Chicago Press, 2020.

Wong, Kristin. "What I Learned from Tracking My Spending for One Month." *New York Times*, November 28, 2018.

Wood, Alex. *Despotism on Demand: How Power Operates in the Flexible Workplace*. Ithaca, NY: Cornell University Press, 2020.

Wood, Martin, dir. *Christmas in the Air*. Hallmark Channel, 2017. https://www
.hallmarkmoviesandmysteries.com/christmas-in-the-air/about-christmas-in-the-air.

Woodards, Shante. "'Less Is More': Local Organizer Shreds Document Overloads." *The Capital* (Hometown Annapolis: Business section), January 29, 2012, B4.

York, Joanna. "Why It's So Hard for US Workers to Ask for Time Off." *BBC*, December 13, 2021. https://www.bbc.com/worklife/article/20211209-why-its-so-hard-for-some
-workers-to-ask-for-time-off.

Young, Molly. "Domestic Purging with Tidying Guru Marie Kondo." *New York Magazine*, February 10, 2015. https://www.thecut.com/2015/02/marie-kondo-room-purge.html.

Yourgrau, Barry. *Mess: One Man's Struggle to Clean Up His House and His Act*. New York: W. W. Norton, 2016.

Yourgrau, Barry. "The Origin Story of Marie Kondo's Decluttering Empire." *The New Yorker*, December 8, 2015. https://www.newyorker.com/books/page-turner/the
-origin-story-of-marie-kondos-decluttering-empire.

Zelizer, Viviana. *The Purchase of Intimacy*. Princeton, NJ: Princeton University Press, 2005.

Index

Page numbers in italics refer to figures.

14